Collected Poems

Phoenix ° Poets

A series edited by Robert von Hallberg

Donald Davie

Collected Poems

The University of Chicago Press

The University of Chicago Press, Chicago 60637
Carcanet Press, Ltd., Manchester

© 1990 by Donald Davie
All rights reserved. Published 1991
Printed in the United States of America

00 99 98 97 96 95 94 93 92 91   5 4 3 2 1

Library of Congress Cataloging-in-Publication Data

Davie, Donald.
  [Poems. Selections]
  Collected poems
    p.   cm.
  ISBN 0-226-13760-0 (cloth). — ISBN 0-226-13761-9 (pbk.)
PR600.A667A17   1991
821'.914—dc20   90-23046
                                                            CIP

♾ The paper used in this publication meets the minimum
requirements of the American National Standard for Information
Sciences—Permanence of Paper for Printed Library Materials,
ANSI Z39.48-1984.

Contents

I. *Poems of the 1950s*

Homage to William Cowper   17
At Knaresborough   17
The Bride of Reason   18

Brides of Reason (1955)

Among Artisans' Houses   19
Three Moral Discoveries   20
Twilight on the Waste Lands   21
Demi-Exile, Howth   22
Hypochondriac Logic   22
Creon's Mouse   23
Poem as Abstract   24
Mamertinus on Rhetoric, A.D. 291   25
Evening on the Boyne   26
Thyestes   26
Belfast on a Sunday Afternoon   27
Zip!   28
On Bertrand Russell's 'Portraits from Memory'   28
The Garden Party   29
The Owl Minerva   29
Heart Beats   30
Machineries of Shame   30
Pushkin. A Didactic Poem   31
At the Synod in St Patrick's   33
Remembering the 'Thirties   34
The Evangelist   35
An English Revenant   36
Hawkshead and Dachau in a Christmas Glass   38
Eight Years After   42
Selina, Countess of Huntingdon   42
Method. For Ronald Gaskell   43
Woodpigeons at Raheny   44
Love-Poems: for Mairi MacInnes   44
Jacob's Ladder   45

A Winter Talent and Other Poems (1957)

Time Passing, Beloved	46
Dream Forest	46
Obiter Dicta	47
Mens Sana in Corpore Sano	49
At the Cradle of Genius	49
The Mushroom Gatherers	51
The Wind at Penistone	52
Under St Paul's	53
Derbyshire Turf	55
Dissentient Voice	56
The Priory of St Saviour, Glendalough	60
Samuel Beckett's Dublin	61
North Dublin	61
Corrib. An Emblem	62
The Wearing of the Green	62
Going to Italy	63
Tuscan Morning	64
Mr Sharp in Florence	64
Via Portello	65
The Tuscan Brutus	65
The Pacer in the Fresco. John the Baptist	66
The Fountain	68
Chrysanthemums	68
Cherry Ripe	69
Hearing Russian Spoken	70
Limited Achievement	70
A Winter Talent	71
Under a Skylight	72
Gardens no Emblems	72
The Nonconformist	73
Rejoinder to a Critic	73
Heigh-ho on a Winter Afternoon	74
On Sutton Strand	75
Aubade	75
Dudwood	76
Dublin Georgian	76
Dublin Georgian (2)	77
Eden	78
The Waterfall at Powerscourt	78

from *New and Selected Poems* (1961)

Against Confidences	80
Nineteen-Seventeen	81
To a Brother in the Mystery	81
Killala	83
With the Grain	84
Red Rock of Utah	86
Reflections on Deafness	87
For an Age of Plastics	88
The Life of Service	89
The 'Sculpture' of Rhyme	90

II.   *Poems of the 1960s*

A Sequence for Francis Parkman (1961)

The Jesuits in North America	91
Lasalle	92
Frontenac	93
Montcalm	95
Pontiac	96
Bougainville	97
A Letter to Curtis Bradford	98
For Doreen. A Voice from the Garden	99

Events and Wisdoms (1964)

Two Dedications	101
1 Wide France	101
2 Barnsley Cricket Club	101
Resolutions	102
Life Encompassed	103
Hornet	103
Housekeeping	104
Low Lands	104
Green River	105
House-martin	106
Treviso, the Pescheria	106
The Prolific Spell	107
A Battlefield	108
The Cypress Avenue	108
Humanly Speaking	109
The Hill Field	110
The Feeders	111
A Lily at Noon	112

Love and the Times   113
Across the Bay   113
A Christening   114
Agave in the West   115
In California   115
New York in August   116
Viper-Man   117
In Chopin's Garden   118
Poreč   118
Barnsley and District   119
Right Wing Sympathies   120
Hyphens   122
A Meeting of Cultures   123
Metals   124
Homage to John L. Stephens   125
The Vindication of Jovan Babič   126
Bolyai, the Geometer   126
After an Accident   128
The Hardness of Light   131

Poems of 1962-1963

On Not Deserving   132
Autumn Imagined   132
Hot Hands   133
Where Depths are Surfaces   133
Vying   134

Essex Poems (1969)

Rodez   135
The North Sea   136
July, 1964   136
The Blank of the Wall   137
Out of East Anglia   138
January   138
Pietà   139
Sunburst   140
The God of Details   141
Ezra Pound in Pisa   142
Tunstall Forest   143
Orford   143
Thanks to Industrial Essex   144
Expecting Silence   145
A Winter Landscape near Ely   145

8

A Death in the West 146
From the New World 147
Stratford on Avon 149
Barnsley, 1966 150
A Conditioned Air 150
Sylvae 151
Amazonian 152
Intervals in a Busy Life 152
Iowa 153
Back of Affluence 154
Or, Solitude 155

More Essex Poems (1964-1968)

My Father's Honour 156
Rain on South-East England 156
Pentecost 157
Winter Landscapes 158
Behind the North Wind 158
Revulsion 159
Oak Openings 160
New Year Wishes for the English 160
Preoccupation's Gift 161
The North Sea, in a Snowstorm 162
To Certain English Poets 162
Democrats 163
Epistle. To Enrique Caracciolo Trejo 163
Cold Spring in Essex 165

Los Angeles Poems (1968-1969)

To Helen Keller 166
Christmas Syllabics for a Wife 167
Idyll 168
Brantôme 168
Looking out from Ferrara 169
An Oriental Visitor 170
'Abbeyforde' 171
England 172
Emigrant, to the Receding Shore 186
The Break 187
Pilate 190
Trevenen 191
Vancouver 200
Commodore Barry 203
Lady Cochrane 205

Six Epistles to Eva Hesse (1970)

I	209
II	215
III	223
IV	230
V	235
VI	241

III.   *Poems of the 1970s*

The Shires (1974)

Bedfordshire	247
Berkshire	247
Buckinghamshire	248
Cambridgeshire	248
Cheshire	249
Cornwall	250
Cumberland	251
Derbyshire	251
Devonshire	252
Dorset	252
County Durham	253
Essex	254
Gloucestershire	254
Hampshire	255
Herefordshire	256
Hertfordshire	256
Huntingdonshire	257
Kent	258
Lancashire	258
Leicestershire	259
Lincolnshire	260
Middlesex	261
Monmouthshire	261
Norfolk	262
Northamptonshire	262
Northumberland	263
Nottinghamshire	263
Oxfordshire	264
Rutland	265
Shropshire	265
Somerset	266
Staffordshire	267

Suffolk   267
Surrey   268
Sussex   268
Warwickshire   269
Westmorland   269
Wiltshire   270
Worcestershire   270
Yorkshire   271

In the Stopping Train and other poems (1977)

Father, the Cavalier   273
The Harrow   273
The Departed   274
Rousseau in his Day   275
After the Calamitous Convoy (July 1947)   275
Depravity: Two Sermons   277
Seeing Her Leave   278
Mandelstam, on Dante   279
Death of a Painter   282
Portland   282
Orpheus   283
Ars Poetica   284
In the Stopping Train   285
His Themes   292
To Thom Gunn in Los Altos, California   294
Seur, near Blois   295
Gemona-del-Friuli, 1961-1976   295
An Apparition   296
Horae Canonicae   297
Morning   299
To a Teacher of French   300
Widowers   301
Some Shires Revisited   301
Grudging Respect   303
A Spring Song   304
Townend, 1976   305

Three for Water-Music (1981)

The Fountain of Cyanë   308
Wild Boar Clough   312
The Fountain of Arethusa   315

11

The Battered Wife and other poems (1982)

The Battered Wife	320
G.M.B.	321
Short Run to Camborne	321
Livingshayes	322
The Admiral to his Lady	323
Screech-owl	324
Fare Thee Well	325
Grace in the Fore Street	326
Some Future Moon	327
Ox-bow	329
A Late Anniversary	329
No Epitaph	330
Utterings	331
Skelpick	332
Strathnaver	333
Winter's Talents	334
To Londoners	335
A Liverpool Epistle	336
Well-found Poem	340
Artifex in Extremis	342
The Bent	345
Catullus on Friendship	345
Two from Ireland	347
Penelope	348
Devil on Ice	350
Advent	351
Having No Ear	352
Siloam	353
A Christian Hero	354
An Anglican Lady	355
Mandelstam's Hope for the Best	356
Three Beyond	360
A Garland for Ronsard	361
'Pastor Errante'	367
Summer Lightning	372
Death of a Voice	377
Mandelstam's Octets	378

IV. *Poems of the 1980s*

To Scorch or Freeze (1988)

The Thirty-ninth Psalm, Adapted	382
Benedictus	383
Poet Redeemed & Dead	384
Attar of Roses	384
Sing Unto The Lord a New Song	385
'So make them melt as the dishousèd snail'	385
God Saves the King	386
Meteorologist, September	387
Vengeance Is Mine, Saith The Lord	388
Standings	388
Church Militant	389
Curtains!	390
'And Our Eternal Home'	390
Zion	391
Felicity's Fourth Order	393
Put Not Your Trust in Princes	393
Their Rectitude Their Beauty	394
Except The Lord Build The House	395
Inditing A Good Matter	396
The Creature David	397
Saw I Never The Righteous Forsaken	398
The Elect	398
The Zodiac	400
'Just You Wait!'	401
Bowing the Head	401
Widower	402
Master & Man	403
Levity	404
Witness	404
Our Lady	405
The Ironist	406
'Thou Art Near At Hand, O Lord'	407
The Nosegay	407
Gripping Serial	409
I Have Said, Ye Are Gods	409
David Dancing	410
Dancing Measures	410
Being Angry With God	411
The Comforter	412
Cannibals	413

Woe Unto Thee! 414
Kingship 415
Ordinary God 416
Nashville Mornings 417
Brilliance 419
If I Take The Wings Of The Morning 421

Uncollected Poems (1990)

North & South 422
They, to Me 423
By the Road to Upper Midhope 425
Dule of a Dewsbury Matron 426
Black Hoyden 426
The Right Lads 427
Grazia Deledda, young 428
Hermes and Mr Shaw 430
Articulacy. Hints from the Koran 431
Reminded of Bougainville 433
A Measured Tread 435
Northern Metres 436
Church of Ireland 437
The Scythian Charioteers 438
Mother 439
At the Café Parnasse 440
Though dry, not dry 441
To a Bad Poet 443
On a Proposed Celebration of Ezra Pound 443
Revenge for Love 444
A Garland for Ivor Gurney 445
Wombwell on Strike 447
After the Match 448
Mustered into the Avant-Garde 449
Sculptures in Hungary 450
Sounds of a Devon Village 451
On Generous Lines 453
Equestrian Sestina 454
Homage to George Whitefield 455
Two Widows in Tashkent 456
Helena Morley 456
Sorting the Personae 458
'1945' 460

Goodbye to the USA

Sunday Morning   462
The University of the South   464
Savannah   465
To an American Classicist   466
H.D.   467
The Trip to Huntsville   467
Alzheimer's Disease   470
Recollections of George Oppen in a letter to an   471
    English friend
West Virginia's Auburn   473
Through Bifocals   474

Homage to William Cowper

Mrs Throckmorton's bull-finch sang a song.
(Domesticate that comfortable bird!)
But still the deer has wandered from the herd,
The bard was not articulate for long.

A pasticheur of late-Augustan styles,
I too have sung the sofa and the hare,
Made nightmare ride upon a private air
And hearths, extinguished, send a chill for miles.

This costive plan, this dense upholstery,
These mice and kittens, this constrictive rhyme,
These small Infernos of another time –
What's all this modish Hecuba to me?

Most poets let the morbid fancy roam.
The squalid rat broke through the finch's fence,
Which was a cage, and still was no defence:
For Horror starts, like Charity, at home.

At Knaresborough

'Broad acres, sir.' You hear them in my talk.
As tell-tale as a pigment in the skin,
Vowels as broad as all the plain of York
Proclaim me of this country and your kin.

And, gratified to have your guess endorsed,
You warm to me. I thaw, and am approved.
But, to be frank, the sentiment is forced,
When I pretend, for your sake, to be moved.

To feel so little, when his sympathies
Would be so much engaged (he would have said),
Surprised the poet too. But there it is,
The heart is not to be solicited.

Believe me, sir, I only ply my trade,
Which is to know when I am played upon.
You might have moved, you never shall persuade.
You grow too warm. I must be moving on.

The Bride of Reason

Pragmatical old Capulet, the head,
So long has ruled, or seemed to rule, the heart,
That Juliet muse, to County Paris wed,
Lets his good sense determine all her art.

Charmed with his manners towards alternatives,
The unacceptable Romeos she has kissed,
The heart with this judicious husband lives,
And, wed to Reason, seems a moralist.

Some who have loved the lady are dismayed;
Some who have loved her first love, Romeo,
Think that impulsive gallant is betrayed,
Now Juliet's voice is so demure and low.

Only her father thinks the wench is sly,
And sees in her docility her treason;
She loves the truth he thought she must deny,
Her lyric to the music of his reason.

Among Artisans' Houses

High above Plymouth, not so high
But that the roof-tops seem to sweat
In the damp sea-mist, the damp sea-sky
Lowers on terraced houses, set
Like citadels, so blank and high;
Clothes-lines run to a handy cleat,
And plots are furiously neat.

There are not many notice this
Resourcefulness of citizens,
And few esteem it. But it is
An outcome of the civil sense,
Its small and mean utilities;
A civilization, in its way,
Its rudiments or its decay.

And if civility is gone,
As we assume it is, the moulds
Of commonwealth all broken down,
Then how explain that this still holds,
The strong though cramped and cramping tone
Of mutual respect, that cries
Out of these small civilities?

It could occur, perhaps, only here,
On these hills over Plymouth Sound,
Where continuity is clear
From Drake to now, where life is bound
Still, though obscurely, to the gear
Traditionally maritime,
And sanctioned by the use of time.

There is no moral to the scene,
Curious relic from the past.
What has and not what might have been
It serves to show now. And at last,
Shortly, nothing will be seen
By which historians may fix
The moral shape of politics.

Three Moral Discoveries

1.

Oh I can praise a cloistered virtue, such
As knows it cannot fear itself too much;
That though innate corruption breaks the laws,
Woman, for instance, is the efficient cause.
The genuine prayer, when all is said and done,
Is 'Lead us not into temptation'.

2.

As Will and I went down the hill
Who should we meet, dressed up to kill,
    But a sexual misdemeanour.

When Will and I got into the train,
There was a loose-limbed wench again,
    An inconsiderate action.

As I left the station, I missed my pipe,
And I turned on Will. He began to weep.

It wasn't until I was nearly thirty,
I noticed the will resents being dirty.

3.

I dared occasion, and came off intact,
Unharmed, not therefore ashamed. The act
Is unimportant; and the times I fell
In fact, in thought, in wish, in all but will,
Reflect how little credit falls to me,
At fault just there, in will's obduracy.

Twilight on the Waste Lands

Some quickly-weathering rock, perhaps,
Eroded by a sandy wind,
Conceals a carving, in the lapse
Of centuries so often skinned

That more than patinas escape,
And from the crag the chiselled shape
Disperses on the desert wind.

The traveller, at dusk or dawn,
Adverted by a trick of light,
Starts at a meaning, hints a form
So fugitive, the doubtful sight
Suspects no hand of man at all,
An artefact so natural
It seems the work of air and light.

Conceive of such a poem, planned
With such a nicety of touch
It quite conceals the maker's hand
And seems a votive fragment, such
As patient scholars make unclear
And, hazarding their guesses, fear
They have read into it too much.

Strung to the dominant, the voice
Guys all the intervals of speech.
Time-honoured forms present a choice
Of parody or else pastiche.
In all but what seems inchoate
We quiz the past. To see it straight
Requires a form just out of reach:

Such form as, see, the setting sun
Behind the shoulder of the bluff
Brings out there! But the beam is gone;
Old Rocky-face there in the rough,
Asleep again, has wiped the slate,
A God, a shape, that must await
A light that's sensitive enough.

Sand-blast the friable. Concede
Skin after skin, but frayed not flayed,
Not chipped to chastened bone, but freed
From every play but light and shade,
Invertebrate. The marble chills;
Be no more shapely than the hills.
See, there again, the sense betrayed!

Demi-Exile. Howth

Daisy and dandelion, speedwell, daffodil,
Lean from the parks on this sea-ward hill,
In Queen Victoria's Anglo-Ireland,
Lean from the lawns to my English hand
In Anglo-India, Anglo-Ireland,
Cities drowning in drifted sand.

Division of loyalties, dolour of exile,
Do you command a quizzical smile
Here, at the roof that once defended
Jonathan Swift's demented head?
Here, in the suburb that Hopkins visited,
Strangled in sand of its famous dead?

Flowers of England, flowers of Ireland,
Lean from earth to my empty hand.
Hands acknowledging no allegiance,
Gloved for good against brutal chance,
Pluck the shadow and not the substance,
Grasp no nettle of circumstance.

Hypochondriac Logic

Appendicitis is his worst
Obsession, mordant from the first
And unannounced. For who but he,
By curious failing schooled to see
The tiniest pain, can hope to be
Fore-warned of appendectomy?
So thinking, he thinks pain to be
More real as more illusory.

So argue all men who have thought
A truth more true as more remote,
Or in poetic worlds confide
The more their air is rarefied.
This the Shelleyan failing is,
Who feared elephantiasis,

Whose poems infect his readers too,
Who, since they're vague, suppose them true.

But lagging down a crippled street
Like fugitives from their own feet,
Some who are whole can yet observe
Disease is what we all deserve,
Or else disdain a painless life
While any squeal beneath the knife.
So, if you trace the impulse back,
The best are hypochondriac.

So poets may astonish you
With what is not, but should be, true,
And shackle on a moral shape
You only thought you could escape;
And if their scenery is queer,
Its prototype may not be here,
Unless inside a frightened mind,
Which may be dazzled, but not blind.

Creon's Mouse

Creon, I think, could never kill a mouse
When once that dangerous girl was put away,
Shut up unbridled in her rocky house,
Colossal nerve denied the light of day.

Now Europe's hero, the humaner King
Who hates himself, is humanized by shame,
Is he a curbed or a corroded spring?
A will that's bent, or buckled? Tense, or tame?

If too much daring brought (he thought) the war,
When that was over nothing else would serve
But no one must be daring any more,
A self-induced and stubborn loss of nerve.

In itching wainscot having met his match,
He waits unnerved, and hears his caverned doom,
The nausea that struggles to dispatch
Pink-handed horror in a craggy room.

The absolute endeavour was the catch;
To clean the means and never mind the end
Meant he had not to chasten but to scotch
The will he might have managed to amend.

You that may think yourselves not proud at all,
Learn this at least from humble Creon's fall:
The will that is subjèct, not overthrown,
Is humbled by some power not its own.

Poem as Abstract

'To write about a tree...you must first *be* a tree.' (W.R. Rodgers)

1.

A poem is less an orange than a grid;
It hoists a charge; it does not ooze a juice.
It has no rind, being entirely hard.

All drumming yards and open, it asserts
That clouds have way upon them, and that hills
Breast into time behind a singing strut.

A sheer abstraction, apt upon the grass
Of London parks, has emulated oak
And aped the ramage that it could surpass.

That construct, ribbed with wire across a quern,
Is caging such serenity of stress
As boughs, or fruit that breaks them, cannot learn.

For gods are gathered from the styles they wear,
And do they curl, a fœtus in a fruit,
Or, like Orion, pinned upon the air?

2.

No trowelled matron but a rigger's mate,
The pile-high poet has no time to brood.
He steps the mast; it does not germinate.

Not for ingestion but to frame the air
He flies the spar that even winter's tree
In green ambition cannot grow so spare.

The orange dangles, drops, and comes again.
To make a fruit he has to be a fruit,
A globe of pulp about a pip of pain.

But tip-toe cages lofted in a day
(To make a grid he has to *make* a grid)
Have come unprecedented, and to stay.

If poems make a style, a way of walking
With enterprise, should not a poet's gait
Be counties-wide, this stride, the pylons stalking?

Mamertinus on Rhetoric, A.D. 291

Personae seek provisional assent.
Perversities of unforeseen address
Obliquely murmur, and a sentiment
Finds not expression but expressiveness.

This is the entry of the chamberlains
To Diocletian and his fictive son.
They speak through masks. The double image feigns
To share the dye too dangerous for one.

Urbanities of Danube and Milan
(Himself at Nicomedia, at York
Constantius Chlorus) baffle, if they can,
And drown the edict in a buzz of talk.

But virtue has to rule the world alone
And scorns assistance from a trick of light,
Her ceremonies rectitude, her tone
Not florid nor austere, but coming right.

A poor decorum? So it seems, my lord,
There in your palace planted like a camp.
The Roman style, however, can afford
To think seven hills an all-sufficient ramp.

Evening on the Boyne

The Boyne at Navan swam in light,
Where children headlong through the trees
Plunged down the sward, and nicked the bright
Precarious evening with unease.

Swans at the bottom of a vale,
Sailing rapidly from sight,
Made the sweet arrangements fail
And emptied all the precious light.

A moment later all was well,
The light was full, the ranks were closed;
The fields of flags, the wading mill
Withdrew again, once more composed.

But what had happened? Who had made
This mirror tremble and subside?
The evening by what eye betrayed
Winced, like a curtain drawn aside?

The shutter of some active mind,
Panicked by a glide of swans,
Closing, made all nature blind,
Then photographed itself at once.

O bleak and lunar emptiness,
How many eyes were then belied?
A god's, a man's, a swan's, and – yes,
The very flags were iris-eyed!

Thyestes

Brush of a raven's, not an eagle's wing!
No wonder older classicists could wish
For something more cathartic than this King
Who spooned his baked-meat children from a dish.

With Jung and Frazer, Tylor, Graves and Lang,
The scholiast can wash the blood away.
But what's the use? The savage poets sang
Enormities that happen every day.

No talons raven in a titan's gut
When dreadful fathers of a fortnight's date
Are drowning kittens in a water-butt.
But see, a baby's finger in the plate!

Belfast on a Sunday Afternoon

Visiting Belfast at the end of June,
We found the Orange Lodge behind a band:
Sashes and bearskins in the afternoon,
White cotton gloves upon a crippled hand.

Pastmasters pale, elaborately grim,
Marched each alone, beneath a bowler hat:
And, catapulted on a crumpled limb,
A lame man leapt the tram-lines like a bat.

And first of all we tried to laugh it off,
Acting bemusement in the grimy sun;
But stayed to worry where we came to scoff,
As loud contingents followed, one by one.

Pipe bands, flute bands, brass bands and silver bands,
Presbyter's pibroch and the deacon's serge,
Came stamping where the iron Mænad stands,
Victoria, glum upon a grassy verge.

Some brawny striplings sprawled upon the lawn;
No man is really crippled by his hates.
Yet I remembered with a sudden scorn
Those 'passionate intensities' of Yeats.

Zip!

I'd have the silence like a heavy chock
That's kicked away as you begin to read;
And sense, responding to the tiny shock,
Roll forward, fire, and smoothly gather speed.

Lines should be hoops that, vibrantly at rest,
Devolve like cables as the switches trip,
Each syllable entailing all the rest,
And rhymes that strike, exploding like a whip.

I'd have the spark that leaps upon the gun
By one short fuse, electrically clear;
And all be done before you've well begun.
(It is reverberations that you hear.)

On Bertrand Russell's 'Portraits from Memory'

Those Cambridge generations, Russell's, Keynes' . . .
And mine? Oh mine was Wittgenstein's, no doubt:
Sweet pastoral, too, when some-one else explains,
Although my memories leave the eclogues out.

The clod's not bowed by sedentary years,
Yet, set by Thyrsis, he's a crippled man:
How singularly naked each appears,
Beside the other on this bosky plan.

Arrangements of the copse and cloister seem,
Although effective, still Utopian,
For groves find room, behind a leafy screen,
For sage and harvester, but not for man.

I wonder still which of the hemispheres
Infects the other, in this grassy globe;
The chumbling moth of Madingley, that blears
The labourer's lamp, destroys the scarlet robe.

It was the Muse that could not make her home
In that too thin and yet too sluggish air,
Too volatile to live among the loam,
Her sheaves too heavy for the talkers there.

The Garden Party

Above a stretch of still unravaged weald
In our Black Country, in a cedar-shade,
I found, shared out in tennis courts, a field
Where children of the local magnates played.

And I grew envious of their moneyed ease
In Scott Fitzgerald's unembarrassed vein.
Let prigs, I thought, fool others as they please,
I only wish I had my time again.

To crown a situation as contrived
As any in 'The Beautiful and Damned',
The phantom of my earliest love arrived;
I shook absurdly as I shook her hand.

As dusk drew in on cultivated cries,
Faces hung pearls upon a cedar-bough;
And gin could blur the glitter of her eyes,
But it's too late to learn to tango now.

My father, of a more submissive school,
Remarks the rich themselves are always sad.
There is that sort of equalizing rule;
But theirs is all the youth we might have had.

The Owl Minerva

The muse that makes pretensions to discourse,
Not sage nor sybil but a piece of both,
Astute in form, oracular in force,
Can make a proposition sound an oath.

Rapid, abrupt and violent like a blow,
An exclamation or ecstatic howl,
Still it asserts, and shows it is not so,
Articulates the hooting of an owl.

Can spells or riddles be articulate?
We take our stand, to make the music heard,
And only speech aspires to music's state.
The Owl Minerva was no singing bird.

Heart Beats

If music be the muses' paragon,
Where mostly pure relation is expressed,
The poet looks accusingly upon
This cramped performer drumming in his breast.

'Why brag,' he cries, 'of buffetings survived
To make the high-pitched harmonies of strain?
You suffered, but some colder thing contrived,
Articulated, and endorsed the pain.'

As from a cellar, unrepentant comes
The virtuoso's lunatic tattoo,
Beating to parley in a school of drums:
'I plot the passions, and endure them too.'

Machineries of Shame

Decaying teeth, before they start to ache,
Start up obscure machineries of shame,
As if the mind were fool enough to take
This, and the soul's corruption, for the same.

This is to make debility a crime;
So, too, a mere discomfiture can start
A blush as hot as, at another time,
A black place in the mouth or in the heart, –

And justly, too. Guilt, sleeping in the cell,
Sparks out upon the throwing of a switch.
If sins can do it, blunders serve as well,
And jumping nerves can make a conscience twitch.

Pushkin. A Didactic Poem

'he did not yet know well those hidden mechanisms of the person by which it achieves its isolation from others and withdraws into itself; he was entirely surrendered to his genius, disarmed by his own power; and if his pride led him to challenge God, he cancelled by that very act his own right to deny Him.'
(WLADIMIR WEIDLÉ)

What with hounds and friends and, in the winter,
Skating, he was seldom bored.
He had learned to be wary, was at pains, I think,
To remain amused?

In the matter of Pushkin, Emily Brontë
Is the best analogy in some ways
Among our poets. As in her verse,
In Pushkin's we assume the truth
That for life to be tolerable, man must
Be wary, ingenious, quick to change
Among diversions, grave or frivolous,
To keep off spleen; although for her,
As she was a woman, a narrower range
Presented itself, and so she is less
Various, flexible, fiery, though as noble
As Pushkin was, more stoical.

Pushkin's draughts-playing and his drinking,
His friends, his travelling, even some
Of his mistresses, he considered as
So many improvisations against
Boredom. But the boredom was
No vacancy nor want of occupation
Nor lack of resources. It was the spleen,

And Pushkin certainly fled before it
Or circumvented it. His poems

Record the circumventions as
Hours when the mind, turned outwards, knew
Friendships or the approach of death
As gifts. The poet exhibits here
How to be conscious in every direction
But that of the self, where deception starts.
This is nobility; not lost
Wholly perhaps, if lost to art.

Grateful tears, delicious sorrow,
Said the Russian gentleman,
Mozart will be dead tomorrow
Of this confusion.

As Byron said of Keats, 'I don't
mean he is indecent, but
viciously soliciting
his own ideas.'

(Schiller and Dostoievsky, oysters
Pearling their own disease, the saints
Full of self-help)

Long before Shakespeare wrote, or Donne,
In the modern manner, there were minds
Aware of themselves, and figuring this
In psychomachia. But the Greeks
Knew states of innocence, the will
Turned always outwards, courage the gift
Counting for virtue, and control,
As of the craven self, a notion
Lost in the social usage. Thus
Self-consciousness is not at fault
In itself. It can be kept
Other than morbid, under laws
Of disciplined sensibility, such
As the seventeenth-century Wit.
But all such disciplines depend
On disciplines of social use,
Now widely lost. Yet there are those
Few men remaining, gifted, or
Especially heroic, or,
Like Pushkin, brilliantly both.

Ask when we are diseased, and these
Will answer: When the moral will
Intervenes to sap the heart,
When the difficult feelings are
Titillated and confused
For novel combinations, or
Ransacked for virtue.

Remains the voice that moves on silence
In moral commonplace, where yet
Some thwart and stern communal sense
Whispers, before we all forget.

What need dissection of the thrust
Which motivates the skating feet,
When that can always be deduced
From the figure of eight?

What need dissection of the thrust
Which motivates the skating feet,
Skating with friends in the winter,
He foretold our defeat.

At the Synod in St Patrick's

This head meant to be massive and therefore,
Being a woman's, less than beautiful,
Is, being young and animated, more
Engaging than a less emphatic skull.

Late flowering, like a cleft-encompassed bush,
To this tradition time has left behind,
Can it be long before her fibres push
At barren rock, the backward-looking mind?

Yet, mollified not merely by their youth,
The jowl too full, the brows like heavy eaves
Bespeak, within, the climate of the truth,
Like Eden's crags with honey in their caves.

The bland and sparkling weather of the good
Extends its dry elation, and disarms
Across two pews my Lucifer that would
Learn why such light should sadden as it charms.

Remembering the 'Thirties

1.

Hearing one saga, we enact the next.
We please our elders when we sit enthralled;
But then they're puzzled; and at last they're vexed
To have their youth so avidly recalled.

It dawns upon the veterans after all
That what for them were agonies, for us
Are high-brow thrillers, though historical;
And all their feats quite strictly fabulous.

This novel written fifteen years ago,
Set in my boyhood and my boyhood home,
These poems about 'abandoned workings', show
Worlds more remote than Ithaca or Rome.

The Anschluss, Guernica – all the names
At which those poets thrilled or were afraid
For me mean schools and schoolmasters and games;
And in the process some-one is betrayed.

Ourselves perhaps. The Devil for a joke
Might carve his own initials on our desk,
And yet we'd miss the point because he spoke
An idiom too dated, Audenesque.

Ralegh's Guiana also killed his son.
A pretty pickle if we came to see
The tallest story really packed a gun,
The Telemachiad an Odyssey.

Even to them the tales were not so true
As not to be ridiculous as well;
The ironmaster met his Waterloo,
But Rider Haggard rode along the fell.

'Leave for Cape Wrath tonight!' They lounged away
On Fleming's trek or Isherwood's ascent.
England expected every man that day
To show his motives were ambivalent.

They played the fool, not to appear as fools
In time's long glass. A deprecating air
Disarmed, they thought, the jeers of later schools;
Yet irony itself is doctrinaire,

And curiously, nothing now betrays
Their type to time's derision like this coy
Insistence on the quizzical, their craze
For showing Hector was a mother's boy.

A neutral tone is nowadays preferred.
And yet it may be better, if we must,
To praise a stance impressive and absurd
Than not to see the hero for the dust.

For courage is the vegetable king,
The sprig of all ontologies, the weed
That beards the slag-heap with his hectoring,
Whose green adventure is to run to seed.

The Evangelist

'My brethren...' And a bland, elastic smile
Basks on the mobile features of Dissent.
No hypocrite, you understand. The style
Befits a church that's based on sentiment.

Solicitations of a swirling gown,
The sudden vox humana, and the pause,
The expert orchestration of a frown
Deserve, no doubt, a murmur of applause.

The tides of feeling round me rise and sink;
Bunyan, however, found a place for wit.
Yes, I am more persuaded than I think;
Which is, perhaps, why I disparage it.

You round upon me, generously keen:
The man, you say, is patently sincere.
Because he is so eloquent, you mean?
That test was never patented, my dear.

If, when he plays upon our sympathies,
I'm pleased to be fastidious, and you
To be inspired, the vice in it is this:
Each does us credit, and we know it too.

An English Revenant

1.

From easterly crepuscular arrivals
Come with me by the self-consuming north
(The North is spirit), to the loam-foot west
And opulent departures of the south.

You that went north for geysers or for grouse,
While Pullman sleepers lulled your sleeping head,
You never saw my mutilated house
Flame in the north by Sheffield as you fled.

You that went west, young man, behind the range
('Westward the course of Empire takes its way')
You never knew my west that cannot change
Its stolid dream and violent feet of clay.

And what became of Waring in the east?
He learnt what traitors generous feelings are,
And lost his nerve, and knew no Samarcand,
In Vishnu-land no hopeful Avatar.

But in the nub of war, a sullen soldier,
He saw the south, its orchards and its wine;
A rich wrap slipping from a Mayfair shoulder,
Successful chromium on his future shine.

In passing, be it understood
Most revenants are flesh and blood.

2.

My home is in the west,
But not in the far west;
And though I was born in the north,
It was not in the far north;
I am lately returned from the east,
But from the middle east;
My songs aspire to the south,
But not to the deep south.

I have cured my breast
Of its need for action;
I have taught it to rest
This side of the Western passes;
Its deeds are commendable,
Not noble.

I have laughed my mind
Out of its need for abstraction;
I have taught it not to find
Shrines in the Orient;
Its thoughts are in tune with the time;
They are not exalted.

I have cheated my will
Out of its need for command;
I have taught it not to kill
Free water into ice;
Its ways are adaptable,
Not unswerving.

Now only my singing mouth
Thirsts for the springs of the south.

3.

A craning lamb that craves an empty dug;
A murdered trunk still twitching on the ground;
A water-wheel inertly turning round
Beneath a stream that would not fill a jug.

Such mere momentum moves me still to you,
Supposed a court, a region of reward;
Cannot this wreck of compasses afford
Some south at last, deserved, and coming true?

'My country 'tis of thee...' What can I say?
'Gone in the teeth,' sang Owen and Sassoon,
Or Ezra Pound who parodied their tune.
'London, Thou art of townes A per se.'

It is, my dear, an intimate inquires
(Indigenous, with hard provincial mouth),
What news of all the olives of the south,
Since Owen's bugles blew from saddened shires?

England, we wheel and fly about you still,
The dead of that and of another war.
It is a laurel we are looking for,
Or bounty of the horn we thought to fill.

Hawkshead and Dachau in a Christmas Glass

1.

At home with my infirmities I fare
Forth to the nightfall on bald avenues,
Whose charities I shall no more refuse,
However cheaply on the blue-black air
Proffered from lighted windows, such as once,
Though more sporadic, from the mountain-road

Welcomed, where Hawkshead glowed.
Panels of domestic light!
Like labels pasted on the night,
(Pasted, opaque, rectangular,
Cut out of paper like a tinsel star –)
I see the sleigh that rocks, the bells that chime
Upon the plate-glass of suburban groceries,
Flatly announcing coming Christmas-time,
The holy time honoured in parodies.

2.

When Hawkshead's poet chose to be humane
And praise the homestead beaming from afar
His Michael's cottage was 'The Evening Star',
An elevated strain –
Oh Wordsworth! when we walked the mountain-road
So long ago, in quite another mood
We crested every contour of the fell,
Dark-blue and frost-white on the darker blue,
Our spirits swelling with the upland swell
To bulky heights and knolls we never knew.
Now these lean trees, over the parkland wall,
Delicate brush-work on a darkling ground;
That deep blue ground that, feathered by the tall
And springing brushes, seems a felted pall;
Its matt and nap as dense as if it lay
A shielding wing over the sharpest day;
I see the aspirations they invite,
I lean towards, but dare not launch in flight.

3.

As I shall not aspire
To wear the coat of fire
Which (we have proved) incinerates the heart;
Because the human mind
Cannot be far refined,
But must admit its grossness from the start;
I hope for no dark elbow-room, to win
Accommodation with the night within.

4.

Making these faces in a Christmas glass
May terrify some others as they pass;
For window-gazers, when a God is dead,
Abide no dreamed-up artefact of mind,
But by reflection from a human head
When most it lacks divinity, they find,
That is, invent, perfection in its stead.
For not by what we want is God defined,
     Only by what we lack;
By what is wanting to us; what we need,
Not what we know we need. And at our back
His eye augments our window-shopping greed.

5.

Insatiable proud buyers who could rest
     With nothing but the best,
Who pressed through to the other side
Of every flaring window, and defied
Tragedy even to reflect them right,
Still asked too little, and at best supplied
Only their aspirations. Far too bright
A light shone through the glass; their dazzled sight
Losing the lens, they put us in a fright,
Claiming it was God's face they brought to light.
     Outside the bleakest pane,
Bulging like water in a rippled glass,
My face makes such pretensions as surpass
     Insane self-deified
Projectors of a private pantheon,
Purveyors' voices from the other side
Of window-panes that heaven was pasted on.

6.

There was a time I would have scorned to think
My self-aversions so entirely eased
By neighbour windows. Such a night of ink
Required, I thought, supernal light at least.
To be believers, let us not forget
How cheaply all our petty needs are met,
All that we know of. If we blow them up

And push away the off-hand proffered cup,
        Each time we raise our price
Some unimagined need is given up,
And we are gulled, intending to be nice.
In such a time, antediluvian,
We came to Hawkshead. It was long ago,
In our own youth and in the youth of Man,
Not long ago in years, but since we know
At Dachau Man's maturity began
And that was earlier, it was long ago,
A time we could not easily outgrow.
At Dachau Yeats and Rilke died. We found,
        In those who lived before,
Our growing pains. A groaning, cracking sound,
Exploding now through each exclusive store,
Starred what we thought light of uncommon day
And damned it glass. Yet some endured the ray,
Wordsworth for one, who may have hoped for light
That never was on sea or land, but knew
The brittle thing that he was looking through,
A waving pane projected on the night.

                    7.

No wind, please God, will rise tonight. The trees
Still sprig the velvet on the pelt of night.
Still, stuck about the raw estate, one sees
The coloured labels of a Christmas light.
Still, in the stillness, only smoke aspires.
(The movement in the stillness is not ours.)

        We shut up shop, and there's
No glimmer now by which to see the wares
Banked behind glass; but in the early hours
Some mooning hobo, by inhuman fires
Of stars or moon, may, glancing in the glass,
Observe his insufficiencies, and find
A supplement there hinted, to surpass
The dearest purchase that he had in mind.

        Natural pieties,
        Unthought-of charities
Grow up about the newest housing-scheme;

Curtained or not, the light
Is tempered to our sight,
And poorest taste can dress the dearest theme,
Where cotton-wool can simulate the snow
And coloured bulbs make Bethlehem a show.

Eight Years After

If distance lends enchantment to the view,
Enormities should not be scrutinized.
What's true of white, holds of black magic too;
And, indistinct, evil is emphasized.

Gilfillan, telling how the poet Churchill
'Indulged in nameless orgies', makes us smile;
We think such large unutterables fill
Vapid lacunæ in a frowzy style.

A case however can be made for this:
The queasy Levite need not be ashamed
To have no stomach for atrocities.
We brook them better, once they have been named.

For fearsome issues, being squarely faced,
Grow fearsomely familiar. To name
Is to acknowledge. To acquire the taste
Comes on the heels of honouring the claim.

'Let nothing human be outside my range.'
Yet horrors named make exorcisms fail:
A thought once entertained is never strange,
But who forgets the face 'beyond the pale'?

Selina, Countess of Huntingdon

Your special witness, as I recollect,
Was, in your fervour, elegance; you yearned
For Grace, but only gracefully, and earned,
By sheer good taste, the title of 'elect'.

42

So perfectly well-bred that in your hands
All pieties were lavender, that scent
Lingered about your college, where you spent
Your fragrance on the burly ordinands.

In your communion, virtue was uncouth;
But now that rigour lost its cutting edge,
As charm in you drove its schismatic wedge
Between your church's beauty and its truth.

Method. For Ronald Gaskell

For such a theme (atrocities) you find
My style, you say, too neat and self-possessed.
I ought to show a more disordered mind.

But Wesley's sermons could be methodized
According to a Ramist paradigm;
Enthusiasts can never be surprised.

The method in the madness of their zeal
Discounts their laceration of the wounds
That, though so bloodied, have had time to heal.

Cassandra plays her frenzied part too well
To be convincing in hysteria.
Has discourse still its several heads, in Hell?

It has, of course; and why conceal the fact?
An even tenor's sensitive to shock,
And stains spread furthest where the floor's not cracked.

Woodpigeons at Raheny

One simple and effective rhyme
Over and over in the April light;
    And a touch of the old time
In the serving-man, stooping, aproned tight,
At the end of the dappled avenue
To the easy phrase, 'tereu-tereu',
Mulled over by the sleepy dove –
This was the poem I had to write.

White wall where the creepers climb
Year after year on the sunny side;
    And a touch of the old time
In the sandalled Capuchin's silent stride
Over the shadows and through the clear
Cushion-soft wooing of the ear
From two meadows away, by the dove –
This was the poem that was denied.

For whether it was the friar's crime,
His lean-ness suddenly out of tune;
    Or a touch of the old time
In the given phrase, with its unsought boon
Of a lax autumnal atmosphere,
Seemed quaint and out of keeping here,
I do not know. I know the dove
Outsang me down the afternoon.

Love-Poems: for Mairi MacInnes

from *Poets of the 1950s* (1955)

All these love-poems...!
Love in its place
Is simple, therefore interesting;
Inscrutable face,
Looming through leaves or water,
Unlooked-for aisle or island.

It is not the whole story,
Nor can stand for such
As 'human relations' in little;
It is not so much
A paradigm as an interruption,
Not to be looked for in a day's travel.

And all these...!
Some 'civilized,'
Some frenzied, some 'gravely moving,'
But yours surprised,
Still dazzled in the roasted glade,
Astounded after long days in the forest.

Jacob's Ladder

(Unpublished)

It was agreed we would not mount by those
Platonic ladders planted on the heart,
Minds that abide the body and its throes,
Reluctantly, and only for a start.
But Jacob's is a ladder we ascend
Without our knowing any sense of strain,
To upland air that we need not expend
One gulp of carnal breathing to attain.
So here we are upon the heights, my love,
Although in habit's level pastures still.
We want, and yet we do not want, the skill
To scale the peaks that others tell us of,
Where breathing gets so difficult, and the will
Kicks back the ground it tries to rise above.

(1955)

Time Passing, Beloved

Time passing, and the memories of love
Coming back to me, carissima, no more mockingly
Than ever before; time passing, unslackening,
Unhastening, steadily; and no more
Bitterly, beloved, the memories of love
Coming into the shore.

How will it end? Time passing and our passages of love
As ever, beloved, blind
As ever before; time binding, unbinding
About us; and yet to remember
Never less chastening, nor the flame of love
Less like an ember.

What will become of us? Time
Passing, beloved, and we in a sealed
Assurance unassailed
By memory. How can it end,
This siege of a shore that no misgivings have steeled,
No doubts defend?

Dream Forest

These have I set up,
Types of ideal virtue,
To be authenticated
By no one's Life and Times,
But by a sculptor's logic

Of whom I have commanded,
To dignify my groves,
Busts in the antique manner,
Each in the space mown down
Under its own sway:

First, or to break the circle,
Brutus, imperious, curbed
Not much by the general will,
But by a will to be curbed,
A preference for limits;

Pushkin next, protean
Who recognized no checks
Yet brooked them all – a mind
Molten and thereby fluent,
Unforced, easily strict;

The next, less fortunate,
Went honourably mad,
The angry annalist
Of hearth and marriage bed,
Strindberg – a staring head.

Classic, romantic, realist,
These have I set up.
These have I set, and a few trees.
When will a grove grow over
This mile upon mile of moor?

Obiter Dicta

Trying to understand myself, I fetch
    My father's image to me. There he is, augmenting
    The treasury of his prudence with a clutch
Of those cold eggs, Great Truths – his scrivener's hand
    Confiding apopthegms to his pocket book.
    Does mine do more than snap the elastic band
Of rhyme about them? In an age that teaches
    How pearls of wisdom only look like eggs,
    The tide, afflatus, still piles up on the beaches
Pearls that he prizes, stones that he retrieves
    Misguidedly from poetry's undertow,
    Deaf to the harsh retraction that achieves
Its scuttering backwash, ironies. And yet,
    Recalling his garrulity, I see
    There's method in it. Seeming to forget

The point at issue, the palmer tells his beads,
    Strung by connections nonchalantly weak
    Upon the thread of argument he needs
To bring them through his fingers, round and round,
    Tasting of gristle, savoury; and he hears,
    Like rubbing stones, their dry conclusive sound.

Himself an actor (He can play the clown),
    He knows the poet's a man of parts; the sage
Is one of them, buffoonery like his own,
    Means to an end. So, if he loves the page
That grows sententious with a terse distinction,
    Yet lapidary moralists are dumb
About the precepts that he acts upon,
    Brown with tobacco from his rule of thumb.

'Not bread but a stone!' – the deep-sea fishermen
    Denounce our findings, father. Pebbles, beads,
    Perspicuous dicta, gems from Emerson,
Whatever stands when all about it slides,
    Whatever in the oceanic welter
    Puts period to unpunctuated tides,
These, that we like, they hate. And after all, for you,
    To take but with a pinch of salt to take
    The maxims of the sages is the true
Great Truth of all. To keep, as you would say,
    A sense of proportion, I should portion out
    The archipelago across the bay,
One island to so much sea. Assorted
    Poetic pleasures come in bundles then,
    Strapped up by rhyme, not otherwise supported?

Turning about his various gems to take
    Each other's lustre by a temperate rule,
He walks the graveyard where I have to make
    Not centos but inscriptions, and a whole
That's moved from inward, dancing. Yet I trace
    Among his shored-up epitaphs my own:
Art, as he hints, turns on a commonplace,
    And Death is a tune to dance to, cut in stone.

Mens Sana in Corpore Sano

Certainly, Lean-shanks, you have forced the pace –
In the bath your body shows it; and you have
The right, considering your shrunken hams,
To rock on that notorious see-saw, mind
And body. But you have forced the pace,
Not forced (take heart) that alternating tempo
To an inhuman standstill – forced the flesh
To some four-minute mile, or forced the mind
To play the ruffian pandar to the blood.

Time's gradual and lenient castration
Unfilms the eye and stills the straying hand,
Unstops ear and nostril; and the tongue
Wags to expansive music, that could risk
(So loose it was till lately) only terse
And summary formulations. As for youth,
See where it throngs these garnished avenues
To deck a house under whose ageing beams
The blithe young tenant comes of age tomorrow.

You know the Stoic's one indulgence now,
The wrist that, opened, bleeds into the bath
Crimsoning Time's still water – yet with blood
(The Epicurean's boast) no violence
Has loosed upon yourself, beyond
That something less than suicidal forcing,
The acceleration of the chemistries
Of undeflected change. Prepare to open
All of the body's avenues but its veins.

At the Cradle of Genius

'Not the least enviable of your many gifts,
Being indeed (what seems unfair) implied
In that first bargain, genius, are two
Appurtenances or corollaries:
One which we hope you do not recognize
Or else it halves its value, one we hope you do
By the same token; and we mean

Charm in the first place, in the second
A narrowing of the choice of destinies.

For character may be fate, and yet vocation
(Differing from the casual gift, a flair)
Can so subsume the variants under types
That, all the issues coming clear,
The gift becomes of nothing else but freedom,
The only kind that you enjoy,
The recognition of a limitation
On idiosyncrasy, a choice
That, being narrow, can be seen as free.'

Thus your first fairy godmother, I suppose,
A learned, solemn, even a pedantic lady,
Edwardian resident of Bruges and Rome
Where she pursues her out-of-date researches
Into 'The Natural History' (save the mark)
'Of Genius'. Now I hear her sister,
The junior counsel but the cleverer,
Though in the plural, yet in other terms, address you
Not altogether to the same effect:

'The benefits that are at my discretion are
Particularizings of the general scope
This lady has endowed you with; and first,
Although a flair is of another order
Than what we give, yet as no spectacle
Is more to be pitied than of one who has
The genius, or to speak more properly
The temperament, and no aptitude, we give
Inalienable technical command.

Then, for your freedom: it is absolute.
Your law unto yourself is absolute
That you be lawless. Since you have no choice
(My colleague's paradox) you have
Absolute choice. Exceptionally fated
To break all rules, you are to find the rules
Of art and conduct waived. The moral law
Lapses before the selfless man, possessed
Of no one self, but of and by a style.'

'Not that you have,' the first impetuously
Resuming cried, 'no duty to be pure...'
'In heart', I fear she would have said; but here
The modern muse broke in on her with 'Pure,
Purged of all bearings on a human need,
The truest poem's at most a golden standish,
A tray to put your pens in.' Then a murmur
That swelled beneath the voices broke
Into a shout excluding all the muses.

It was the chorus of the acclamation lately
Accorded you as legendary hero,
Dilating on your prodigality,
Your arrogance, your abandonment, your art,
Though that seemed incidental. In the din
I caught by starts the sisters crying still,
And once the elder sounded menacing:
'Some have enjoyed what here I deny to you,
A self-betrayal not betrayed in art.'

The Mushroom Gatherers

After Mickiewicz

Strange walkers! See their processional
Perambulations under low boughs,
The birches white, and the green turf under.
These should be ghosts by moonlight wandering.

Their attitudes strange: the human tree
Slowly revolves on its bole. All around
Downcast looks; and the direct dreamer
Treads out in trance his lane, unwavering.

Strange decorum: so prodigal of bows,
Yet lost in thought and self-absorbed, they meet
Impassively, without acknowledgment.
A courteous nation, but unsociable.

Field full of folk, in their immunity
From human ills, crestfallen and serene.
Who would have thought these shades our lively friends?
Surely these acres are Elysian Fields.

The Wind at Penistone

The wind meets me at Penistone.
                              A hill
Curves empty through the township, on a slope
Not cruel, and yet steep enough to be,
Were it protracted, cruel.
                         In the street,
A plain-ness rather meagre than severe,
Affords, though quite unclassical, a vista
So bald as to be monumental.
                            Here
A lean young housewife meets me with the glance
I like to think that I can recognize
As dour, not cross.
                   And all the while the wind,
A royal catspaw, toying easily,
Flicks out of shadows from a tufted wrist,
Its mane, perhaps, this lemon-coloured sun.

The wind reserves, the hill reserves, the style
Of building houses on the hill reserves
A latent edge;
              which we can do without
In Pennine gradients and the Pennine wind,
And never miss, or, missing it, applaud
The absence of the aquiline;
                            which in her
Whose style of living in the wind reserves
An edge to meet the wind's edge, we may miss
But without prejudice.
                      And yet in art
Where all is patent, and a latency
Is manifest or nothing, even I,
Liking to think I feel these sympathies,
Can hardly praise this clenched and muffled style.

For architecture asks a cleaner edge,
Is open-handed.
                    And close-fisted people
Are mostly vulgar; only in the best,
Who draw, inflexible, upon reserves,
Is there a stern game that they play with life,
In which the rule is not to show one's hand
Until compelled.
                    And then the lion's paw!
Art that is dour and leonine in the Alps
Grows kittenish, makes curios and clocks,
Giant at play.
                    Here, nothing. So the wind
Meets me at Penistone, and, coming home,
The poet falls to special pleading, chilled
To find in Art no fellow but the wind.

Under St Paul's

Wren and Barry, Rennie and Mylne and Dance
    Under the flags, the men who stood for stone
    Lie in the stone. Carillons, pigeons once
Sluiced Ludgate's issues daily, and the dome
    Of stone-revetted crystal swung and hung
    Its wealth of waters. Wren had plugged it home
With a crypt at the nerve of London. Now the gull
    Circles the dry stone nozzles of the belfries,
    Each graceful City hydrant of the full
Eagerly brimming measure of agreement,
    Still to be tapped by any well-disposed
    Conversible man, still underneath the pavement
Purling and running, affable and in earnest,
    The conduit, Candour. Fattily urbane
    Under the great drum, pigeons foul their nest.

The whiter wing, Anger, and the gull's
Shearwater raucous over hunting hulls
Seek London's river. Rivers underground,
Under the crypt, return the sound

Of footfalls in the evening city. Out of wells,
Churchyards sunk behind Fleet Street, trickle smells
Of water where a calm conviction spoke
Now dank and standing. Leaves and our debris choke
The bell-note Candour that the pavior heard
Fluting and swelling like a crop-filled bird.

So sound the tides of love; yet man and woman
   May be my world's first movers, and the stream
   Still run no darker nowhere deeper than
Conviction's claim upon us, to deny
   Nothing that's undeniable. Light airs
   Are bent to the birds that couple as they fly
And slide and soar, yet answer to the flow
   Of this broad water under. There we ride
   Lent to the current, and convictions grow
In those they are meant for. As conviction's face
   Is darker than the speculative air,
   So and no darker is the place
For candour and love. What fowl lives underwater,
   Breeds in that dark? And hadn't a contriver
   Of alphabets, Cadmus, the gull for daughter?

Across the dark face of the waters
Flies the white bird. And the waters
Mount, mount, or should mount; we grow surer
Of what we know, if no surer
Of what we think. For on ageing
Labouring now and subsiding and nerveless wing
The gull sips the body of water, and the air
Packed at that level can hold up a minster in air.
Across the dark face of the water
Flies the white bird until nothing is left but the water.

Derbyshire Turf

That, true to the contours which round it
    Out and lie close,
The best beauty is barbarous, grounded
    On foreign bodies,
Flush to their angles, ungainly,
    Pawkily true –
Derbyshire turf, you tried vainly
    To point such a moral
When we, in our warmly remembered
    Youth, from the old
Armstrong Siddeley tourer descended
    Shouting upon you.

Then as now it was just where the boulder
    Lay scantily buried,
Or the gritstone poked up a shoulder,
    You sported your streaks
Of a specially sumptuous darkened
    Lush olive green –
Yet in those days none of us hearkened
    To this intimation
That where most intriguingly mounded
    Abrupt in its curves,
Beauty is richest and rounded
    Home on the truth.

Very well. Still we should wonder
    At farmers who loaded
Wagons with stones to lay under
    The grass of their pastures.
Much the same is the poet who prizing
    The shape of the truth
Studies to find some surprising
    Eccentric perception
To validate memory. Boys
    Are willing to guess
At the rock which lies under their joy's
    Elusiveness.

Dissentient Voice

1. *A Baptist Childhood*

When some were happy as the grass was green,
I was as happy as a glass was dark,
Chill eye beneath the chapel floor unseen
Most of the year, a mystery, the Ark.

Aboveboard rose the largely ethical
Glossy-with-graining pulpit; underground
The older Scriptures trembled for the Fall
And lapped at Adam with a sucking sound.

Grass-rooted goodness and a joy unmixed
Parch unbaptized inside a droughty head;
Arcadia's floor is not so firmly fixed
But it must tremble to a pastor's tread.

2. *Dissent. A Fable*

When Bradbury sang, 'The Roast Beef of Old England'
And Watts, 'How doth the little busy bee',
Then Doddridge blessed the pikes of Cumberland
And plunging sapphics damned eternally.

Said Watts the fox: 'Your red meat is uncouth.
We'll keep the bleeding purchase out of sight.
Arminian honey for the age's tooth!
With so much sweetness, who will ask for light?'

Wolf Bradbury mauled the synod, but the fox
Declared that men were growing more refined;
And honey greased, where blood would rust, the locks
That clicked when Calvin trapped the open mind.

The wolves threw off sheeps' clothing once or twice
(For Queen Anne dead, or the Pretender foiled).
But the fox knew that tastes were growing nice
And unction kept the hinge of dogma oiled.

Foxes however are their own worst foes;
And now their chapel door stands open wide,
Its hinge so clogged with wax it cannot close,
No fish so queer but he can swim inside.

The queerest fishes hunger for the trap
And wish the door would close on them, the rough
Jaws of Geneva and Old England snap:
They think their church not barbarous enough.

The fable seems extravagant, no doubt.
But Reynard ruled the roosts of heaven then,
And beastly pastors kept true shepherds out
While pike and barracuda fished for men.

3. *Portrait of the Artist as a Farmyard Fowl*

Pluming himself upon a sense of sin
    (Lice in his feathers' undersides)
He sported drab, the sooner Faith to win.
    Old zealots were such sobersides;
He felt their gooseflesh crawl upon his skin
    And hoped to feel their zeal besides.

Since then this would-be puritan has paced
    A cock unmatched although so spurred;
Purist who crowed at shadows, he debased
    The rate of evil and conferred
Its rights on squalor, out of sheer good taste.
    No hag would ride on such a bird.

Dark plumes, though puritanical in cut,
    Still clothe the cock of the studied walk;
A conscious carriage must become a strut;
    Fastidiousness can only stalk
And seem at last not even tasteful but
    A ruffled hen too apt to squawk.

4. *A Gathered Church*

In memoriam A.E.D. ob. 1939
Deacon, you are to recognize in this
The idlest of my avocations, fruit
Of some late casual studies and my need
(Not dire, nor much acknowledged as a claim
Upon your known munificence) for what
You as lay preacher loved and disavowed,
The mellow tang of eloquence – a food
I have some skill in rendering down from words
Suppose them choice and well matured. I heard
Such from your bee-mouth once. A tarnished sun
Swirling the motes which swarmed along its shaft
Mixed soot with spices, and with honey, dust;
And memories of that winning unction now
Must countenance this application. For
I see them tumbled in a frowzy beam,
The grains of dust or pollen from our past,
Our common stock in family and church,
Asking articulation. These affairs
Touched you no doubt more nearly; you are loath
To see them made a gaud of rhetoric. But, sir,
I will deal plainly with you. They are past,
Past hoping for as you had hoped for them
For sixty years or more the day you died,
And if I seem a fribble in this case
No matter. For I will be eloquent
And on these topics, having little choice.

You who were once an orator should know
How these things are decided, not by chance
Although to think so is our best recourse;
For we may pledge our faith that they are solved
In part by fervent feeling and in part
By strenuous intellection – so they are,
But by all these under the guise of chance,
Of happy yet exacting accident,
Out of whose bounty suddenly a word
Of no apparent pertinence or force
Will promise unaccountably to draw
The whole lax beam into a burning glass.

So here I take the husk of my research,
A form of words – the phrase, 'a gathered church',
A rallying cry of our communions once
For you perhaps still stirring, but for me
A picturesque locution, nothing more
Except for what it promises, a tang.
Here is the promise of the burning-glass;
Now turn it in the variegated light.

'A gathered church.' That posy, the elect,
Was gathered in, not into, garden-walls;
For God must out of sheer caprice resect
The jugular stalks of those He culls and calls.

Watts thought his church, though scant of privilege,
Walled in its own communion. In its walks
Some may have doubted if so sparse a hedge
Tempered the blast to blooms still on their stalks.

It was the rooted flower could be hurt:
The plucked that lived in living water felt
No more the stress of time, the tug of dirt.
Time lost for good the fragrance Heaven smelt.

When blossoms crowd into the waist of time,
Those cut and chosen for the eternal vase
Rot down to no kind humus, rather climb
And spend their charity upon the stars.

Abundant friction: not a deal of heat.
These are, you know, preliminary rites,
A form of invocation. So the glass
Is moved and dances, waterish, flashes out
Now on the wall, now on the floor... But now
Your face recalled swims up athwart the light,
The silken, heavy, iron-grey moustache
That reaffirms conciliatory smiles
Dispensing honey with a Dorset burr;
The hollow temples of a young man's brow;
The mild and beaming eye; the cheek still apple-hale.
Appealing gestures pregnantly curtailed
Conveyed impulsive courtesies, refined
The gross freak of your corpulence. That head

Was bowed beneath reproaches mostly mute
When 'Charity begins at home,' we said,
Feeling the pinch of your more public alms
Wise in our generations. And indeed
You thought so too; your home was somewhere else
And there you ran most fruitfully to seed.
Now all the churches gathered from the world
Through that most crucial bottleneck of Grace,
That more than hourglass, being waspish, waist
Where all the flutes of love are gathered in,
The girdle of Eternity, the strait
Too straitened for the sands and sons of Time,
More mean and private than the sticking-place
Of any partial loyalties – all these
In you, dear sir, are justified. Largesse,
Suppose it but of rhetoric, endears,
Disseminated quite at large to bless
The waste, superb profusion of the spheres.

The Priory of St Saviour, Glendalough

A carving on the jamb of an embrasure,
'Two birds affronted with a human head
Between their beaks' is said to be
'Uncertain in its significance but
A widely known design.' I'm not surprised.

For the guidebook cheats: the green road it advises
In fact misled; and a ring of trees
Screened in the end the level knoll on which
St Saviour's, like a ruin on a raft,
Surged through the silence.

I burst through brambles, apprehensively
Crossed an enormous meadow. I was there.
Could holy ground be such a foreign place?
I climbed the wall, and shivered. There flew out
Two birds affronted by my human face.

Samuel Beckett's Dublin

When it is cold it stinks, and not till then.
The seasonable or more rabid heats
Of love and summer in some other cities
Unseal the all too human: not in his.
When it is cold it stinks, but not before;

Smells to high heaven then most creaturely
When it is cold. It stinks, but not before
His freezing eye has done its best to maim,
To amputate limbs, livelihood and name,
Abstracting life beyond all likelihood.

When it is cold it stinks, and not till then
Can it be fragrant. On canal and street,
Colder and colder, Murphy to Molloy,
The weather hardens round the Idiot Boy,
The gleeful hero of the long retreat.

When he is cold he stinks, but not before,
This living corpse. The existential weather
Smells out in these abortive minims, men
Who barely living therefore altogether
Live till they die; and sweetly smell till then.

North Dublin

St George's, Hardwicke Street,
Is charming in the Church of Ireland fashion:
The best of Geneva, the best of Lambeth
Aesthetically speaking
In its sumptuously sober
Interior, meet.

A continuous gallery, clear glass in the windows,
An elegant conventicle
In the Ionian order –
What dissenter with taste
But would turn, on these terms
Episcopalian?

'Dissenter' and 'tasteful' are contradictions
In terms, perhaps, and my fathers
Would ride again to the Boyne
Or with scythes to Sedgemoor, or splinter
The charming fanlights in this charming slum
By their lights, rightly.

Corrib. An Emblem

Hairless and worse than leathery, the skin
Of the great ogre, Connemara, mounded
Silvery, fathoms thick. Within
The crook of tutelary arm that cradled
The Corrib's urn, the subcutaneous waters
In their still blue as bright as blood shone out,
By healed-up puckers where his pre-divinity
Was scored and trenched. To him suppose a Daphne
Pursued by art Palladian, picturesque,
Or else Hispanic through the Galway Lynches,
Merchant adventurers turning Medici,
Virtù in freight. Underneath his shoulder
Syrinx, the villa seen across the lough,
A reed now broken, flourished. In his hand
A nymph took root, and here and there a laurel.

The Wearing of the Green

Gold is not autumn's privilege;
A tawny ripening
In Meath in May burns ready in the hedge;
The yellow that will follow spring
Accentuates its wet and green array,
A sumptuous trill beneath
The shriller edge
Of Meath in May.

Green more entire must needs be evergreen,
Precluding autumn and this spring
Of Meath in May, its in-between
Of golds and yellows preluding
The liquid summer. Must the seasons stay
Their temperate career because
A flag is green
In Meath in May?

Imagination, Irish avatar,
Aches in the spring's heart and in mine, the stranger's,
In Meath in May. But to believe there are
Unchanging Springs endangers,
By that fast dye, the earth;
So blood-red green the season,
It never changes
In Meath in May.

Going to Italy

Though painters say Italian light does well
By natural features and by monuments,
Our eyes may not be fine enough to tell
Effects compounded of such elements.

And yet we trust our judgment as to fires
In their effects more subtle still, like love,
Which is a light that dwells about its squires
To tell the world what they are thinking of.

That fortunate climate is so apt for this,
As some aver, that not a thought can pass
Through spiritual natures, but it is
Seen in the air, like glitter in a glass.

If Rome should see us bathed in such a flue,
And all our even inward motions edged
Thus with the crispness of their follow-through,
I'd think not we but Rome was privileged.

Tuscan Morning

Presences are always said to brood;
And in the Boboli gardens just at noon
Toad-like Silenus squats inside a shade
While Michelangelo's giants cannot break
The curtain of their element, the haze.

But this is hardly Italy. At least
This is in Italy the hour and the place
That throw our Italy into high relief,
Which is italic cursive and alert
In early mornings and late afternoons.

High noon of the Renaissance was in Rome.
This was the Tuscan, Brunelleschi's morning,
The guidebooks say. What have renaissances
To do with noon? It is the edge of light
Goes cleaving, windless presence, like a ray.

Mr Sharp in Florence

'Mr Sharp from Sheffield, straight out of the knifebox.'

Americans are innocents abroad;
But Sharp from Sheffield is the cagey kind
And – out of the knifebox, bleeding – can't afford
To bring to Florence such an open mind.

Poor Mr Sharp! And happy transatlantic
Travellers, so ingenuous! But some
Are so alert they can finesse the trick,
So strong they know when to be overcome.

Now must he always fall between these stools?
Blind, being keen; dumb, so as not to shrill;
Grounded and ground in logic-chopping schools;
So apt in so inapposite a skill?

Beleaguered and unsleeping sentinel,
He learned the trick of it, before the end;
Saw a shape move, and could not see it well,
Yet did not challenge, but himself cried, 'Friend!'

Via Portello

'Nobody wants any more poems about . . . foreign cities.'
Mr Kingsley Amis

Rococo compositions of decay,
Each a still-life, the fruity garbage-heaps
Teem by themselves. A broad and cobbled way,
Tiepolo's and Byron's thoroughfare
Lies grand and empty in its sullied air,
And watches while the rest of Padua sleeps.

The conscious vista closed at either end,
Here by a palace, that way by a gate
At night pure Piranesi . . . Yes, my friend,
I know you have decided for your part
That poems on foreign cities and their art
Are the privileged classes' shorthand. You must wait;

Or, traversing the colonnaded mile
Of this decayed locality, extend
The warmth of your resentment to the style
Of Padua's poor. A civilization broken
Around them, theirs; and want, and no word spoken –
The conscious vista closed at either end.

The Tuscan Brutus

The Duke insists you stay; you could do worse.
You temporize, and promise him a fine
Head for his medal. As for the reverse,
That (now he jests) Lorenzo shall design.

That melancholy madman Lorenzino
De Medici, in sole attendance there,
Takes up the joke, agrees. The Duke should know
The risk he's running, but that's his affair.

There's more to this than meets your knowing eye,
Cellini, though we owe the tale to you:
You made one, but he made another die;
You were to strike the medal – he struck too.

He writes that his design is under way,
Claims that its greatness will be manifest
To later ages, and that night and day
He thinks of nothing else, and cannot rest.

A sad reverse it proved. Were you to know
Your lovely art had such a seamy side?
Amazed, you saw the spun coin fall to show
The antique motif of tyrannicide.

No end of tyrants – after Alessandro
Duke Cosimo . . . Oh you were right, of course:
For current coin his style would never do.
Yet for a medal yours was rather coarse.

The Pacer in the Fresco. John the Baptist

Already running, sprang from the womb; met,
Adored, inclined to, passed the Overtaker;
Fore-ran Him then around the course; and yet
Drew Him abreast, baptized Him into the lead
He need not challenge for – then in a stride
Took up the killing pace, and shook a bead
Of cool sweat on the Runner by his side.

Met from the first none could be waited for:
His father with a minatory gesture
Full of a blessing was fulfilled before
Much like a curse; his mother then, resigned,
Delivered still delivering – from whom

Departed running, he is first to find
The stadium packed and roaring with their doom.

Turns the last corner, round into the straight,
Into the last fierce panels of the fresco
Indomitably, the Pursuer's gait
Steady behind him and the easy breath
Fanning his cheek. He can afford to fall
Out of the running, when he sees his death,
Beating a foot, dance out along the wall;

Sees perjured judges clap the Victor in
After a lonelier circuit, and the headsman
Timekeeper plunge the stopwatch and begin
The ritual decollation of the flag
Ripe for its fall; and sees, at his command,
The pear-shaped classical canon start to sag
And sway down ripe, his ripeness come to hand.

We went to gape. But when the unflurried Athlete
Hove up behind, with high unhurried action,
Running so well within himself, His feet
Firm on the track, not flying, no one's eye
But left the lunging leader, though in profile
So aquiline, or knew him going by
Except as promise of a purer style.

The two-dimensional hero, moving fast,
Himself the movement, like the knife-edge angel
Of all annunciations, couldn't last:
He clove too cleanly ever to belong
In the close composition of the whole,
Himself too much the equilibrist for long
To tilt a saucer on the wading soul.

The Fountain

Feathers up fast, and steeples; then in clods
Thuds into its first basin; thence as surf
Smokes up and hangs; irregularly slops
Into its second, tattered like a shawl;
There, chill as rain, stipples a danker green,
Where urgent tritons lob their heavy jets.

For Berkeley this was human thought, that mounts
From bland assumptions to inquiring skies,
There glints with wit, fumes into fancies, plays
With its negations, and at last descends,
As by a law of nature, to its bowl
Of thus enlightened but still common sense.

We who have no such confidence must gaze
With all the more affection on these forms,
These spires, these plumes, these calm reflections, these
Similitudes of surf and turf and shawl,
Graceful returns upon acceptances.
We ask of fountains only that they play,

Though that was not what Berkeley meant at all.

Chrysanthemums

Chrysanthemums become a cult because
No Japanese interior is snug;
For even Fuji can be brought indoors
As lamps turn amber in an opal fog.

Here in the thick of opals, where the horn
Blurts from the seaward mountain through the pall,
Now fires are lit and the snug curtains drawn,
Shock-headed clusters warm the dripping wall.

A brazier or the perforated tin
Of watchmen huddled at a dockyard gate
Glows with such amber as the night draws in
As these bronze flowers, blossoming so late.

Chrysanthemum, cult of the Japanese,
You teach me no Penates can be lost
While men can draw together as they freeze
And make a domesticity of frost.

Yet bivouacs of Revolution throw
Threatening shadows and a scorching heat;
And embers of unequal summer glow
A hearth indeed, but in a looted street.

Cherry Ripe

On a Painting by Juan Gris

No ripening curve can be allowed to sag
On cubist's canvas or in sculptor's stone:
Informal fruit, that burgeons from the swag,
Would spoil the ripening that is art's alone.

This can be done with cherries. Other fruit
Have too much bloom of import, like the grape,
Whose opulence comes welling from a root
Struck far too deep to yield so pure a shape.

And Cherry ripe, indeed ripe, ripe, I cry.
Let orchards flourish in the poet's soul
And bear their feelings that are mastered by
Maturing rhythms, to compose a whole.

But how the shameful grapes and olives swell,
Excrescent from no cornucopia, tart,
Too near to oozing to be handled well:
Ripe, ripe, they cry, and perish in my heart.

Hearing Russian Spoken

Unsettled again and hearing Russian spoken
I think of brokenness perversely planned
By Dostoievsky's debauchees; recall
The 'visible brokenness' that is the token
Of the true believer; and connect it all
With speaking a language I cannot command.

If broken means unmusical I speak
Even in English brokenly, a man
Wretched enough, yet one who cannot borrow
Their hunger for indignity nor, weak,
Abet my weakness, drink to drown a sorrow
Or write in metres that I cannot scan.

Unsettled again at hearing Russian spoken,
'Abjure politic brokenness for good',
I tell myself. 'Recall what menaces,
What self-loathings must be re-awoken:
This girl and that, and all your promises
Your pidgin that they too well understood.'

Not just in Russian but in any tongue
Abandonment, morality's soubrette
Of lyrical surrender and excess,
Knows the weak endings equal to the strong;
She trades on broken English with success
And, disenchanted, I'm enamoured yet.

Limited Achievement

(Piranesi, *Prisons*, Plate VI)

Seeing his stale vocabulary build
The same décor – observe this 'gloomy vault' –
We tire of this good fellow, highly skilled
No doubt, but pertinacious to a fault.

The same few dismal properties, the same
Oppressive air of justified unease,
Proclaim the practised hand from which they came,
Although these show a willingness to please.

Yes, some attempt undoubtedly was made
To lift the composition, and to pierce
The bald tympana – vainly, I'm afraid;
The effect remains, as ever, gaunt and fierce.

Those were his true proclivities? Perhaps.
Successful in his single narrow track,
He branches out, but only to collapse,
Imprisoned in his own unhappy knack,

Which, when unfailing, fails him most, perhaps.

A Winter Talent

Lighting a spill late in the afternoon,
I am that coal whose heat it should unfix;
Winter is come again, and none too soon
For meditation on its raft of sticks.

Some quick bright talents can dispense with coals
And burn their boats continually, command
An unreflecting brightness that unrolls
Out of whatever firings come to hand.

What though less sunny spirits never turn
The dry detritus of an August hill
To dangerous glory? Better still to burn
Upon that gloom where all have felt a chill.

Under a Skylight

Through a wide window all Somerset might look in
At the quiet act of love, but where we lie
Under a skylight in a double bed,
I cannot ignore the scrutinizing sky
Night's Peeping Tom. Could anyone turn his head,
However coarse in fibre, to begin
(With that mild aperture so wide above)
The tumultuous quiet of the act of love?

Skylight, that's heaven's light: an easy clue
For prurient exegetes supposing shame
Brazen on earth less bold in heaven's eye.
But down the dim shaft those slanted timbers frame,
Our four eyes glitter upwards at the sky
Like pussies in a well; and we pursue
Untouched by shame a feline interest
Compulsively, at nobody's behest.

No. Let's hear nothing of those notorious twins
Identical but different, Agape
And Eros, whom the mind
Like a celibate uncle pats uncertainly;
It puzzles me the more, though, why I find
An image for the married state that wins
My uncommitted heart, in these wide-eyed
Unsleeping bodies gazing side by side.

Gardens no Emblems

Man with a scythe: the torrent of his swing
Finds its own level; and is not hauled back
But gathers fluently, like water rising
Behind the watergates that close a lock.

The gardener eased his foot into a boot;
Which action like the mower's had its mould,
Being itself a sort of taking root,
Feeling for lodgment in the leather's fold.

But forms of thought move in another plane
Whose matrices no natural forms afford
Unless subjected to prodigious strain:
Say, light proceeding edgewise, like a sword.

The Nonconformist

X, whom society's most mild command,
For instance evening dress, infuriates,
In art is seen confusingly to stand
For disciplined conformity, with Yeats.

Taxed to explain what this resentment is
He feels for small proprieties, it comes,
He likes to think, from old enormities
And keeps the faith with famous martyrdoms.

Yet it is likely, if indeed the crimes
His fathers suffered rankle in his blood,
That he finds least excusable the times
When they acceded, not when they withstood.

How else explain this bloody-minded bent
To kick against the prickings of the norm;
When to conform is easy, to dissent;
And when it is most difficult, conform?

Rejoinder to a Critic

You may be right: 'How can I dare to feel?'
May be the only question I can pose,
'And haply by abstruse research to steal
From my own nature all the natural man'
My sole resource. And I do not suppose
That others may not have a better plan.

And yet I'll quote again, and gloss it too
(You know by now my liking for collage):

Donne could be daring, but he never knew,
When he inquired, 'Who's injured by my love?'
Love's radio-active fall-out on a large
Expanse around the point it bursts above.

'Alas, alas, who's injured by my love?'
And recent history answers: Half Japan!
Not love, but hate? Well, both are versions of
The 'feeling' that you dare me to...Be dumb!
Appear concerned only to make it scan!
How dare we now be anything but numb?

Heigh-ho on a Winter Afternoon

There is a heigh-ho in these glowing coals
By which I sit wrapped in my overcoat
As if for a portrait by Whistler. And there is
A heigh-ho in the bird that noiselessly
Flew just now past my window, to alight
On winter's moulding, snow; and an alas,
A heigh-ho and a desultory chip,
Chip, chip on stone from somewhere down below.

Yes I have 'mellowed', as you said I would,
And that's a heigh-ho too for any man;
Heigh-ho that means we fall short of alas
Which sprigs the grave of higher hopes than ours.
Yet heigh-ho too has its own luxuries,
And salts with courage to be jocular
Disreputable sweets of wistfulness,
By deprecation made presentable.

What should we do to rate the long alas
But skeeter down a steeper gradient?
And then some falls are still more fortunate,
The meteors spent, the tragic heroes stunned
Who go out like a light. But here the chip,
Chip, chip will flake the stone by slow degrees,
For hour on hour the fire will gutter down,
The bird will call at longer intervals.

On Sutton Strand

I saw brown Corrib lean upon his urn,
   And shawled Andromeda by the Atlantic sea;
I thought smooth eastern provinces would turn
   To emblems of an equal suavity;
I thought that, nearer by a hundred miles
To Europe's heart, the Mediterranean styles
   And milder forms of nature would agree.

But fables worked by what was fabulous.
   It is the mildest proves intractable.
And here it is the sky that silences
   The flutes of Greece and Sicily with the full
Chime of its equability. The bright
Items of colour glitter in a light
   That makes men small and all their fables dull.

What in a seascape so entirely Dutch
   Can Orpheus do but just believe his eyes?
No more the broad brush and the master's touch;
   He has no choice now but to itemize
Bright fleck by fleck, and try by being neat
Where to command is hopeless, to compete
   With an indifference equal to the sky's.

Aubade

I wish for you that when you wake
You emulate the leaf and bird;
That like them, touched with grace, you take
Note of the wind. You have not heard
Its low-voiced billows yet, nor seen
(Lost in your less elated rest)
The empty light upon the green,
The leaves and tumbling birds that gave
The wind its due, and then redressed
That small excess, each bounding spray
A boat that dances on the wave,
A whip that tingles in the day.

Dudwood

The roads getting emptier, air in a steadily purer
Stream flowing back past the old Armstrong Siddeley tourer;
Then, the next morning, at large in the boulderstrewn woodland –
What worlds away from our nest in the chimney of England!
The turf carpets laid for us, scroll-like or star-shaped or trefoiled,
Deep pile to the tread of the spring-heel Jack Sparrows of Sheffield.

The bluff before Birchover, fronting the valley and shaded
By rowan and pine where the outcrop capped the precipitous
Comber of meadow. That way, in search of Cos lettuce
Or pony-tailed carrots, the three of us often ascended
That very first morning – all ardent and plumed, all cockaded
With springing abandonments, lost now, barely remembered.

Dublin Georgian

A room designed by Orrery receives
The Roscius of the hour.
He bows and smiles and pauses by the door
Among less battered *putti*; but perceives
Advance towards him, borne upon a sea
Of smoke and noise,
The lady of a rival company
Whose progress West, the stuccodore, convoys
With birds and flutes. Now mutually entreating
By signs, they draw together; and one sees,
As exclamations punctuate their meeting,
The crisp swags droop a little on the frieze.

Were I to move among the talkers here,
I'd soon be disabused
About this artist, hearing him traduced
Wherever laughing malice has the ear
Of Irish wit. But I avert my gaze,
Refuse to know
His marxist and his mystagogic phase,
Or the connubial scandal years ago
Retailed around me. Every Irish master

Must learn to suffer, for the nation's sake,
The national proclivity for plaster,
Mouldings that chip, and pediments that flake.

The author of the genial comedies
From which this pair plucked fruit,
The edible stucco of their shared repute,
Has made no entrance; and yet there he is,
A brow that's broader than the marble mantel
There in the wall
Which thin heads nod in front of. Broad as well
Behind the brow, the soul. Broadness of soul –
What an inelegant and Russian notion!
It's more than Orrery could cater for.
His walls distend, the cornice is in motion...
Oliver Goldsmith! Samson heaves the floor.

Dublin Georgian (2)

A thin brown orphan in his washed-out blue
Opens the door a crack
Behind its sunblind and, subdued, peers through
At the wrecked street behind us. Standing back
He lets us into elegance preserved,
As he is, from the slum;
This orphanage, number twenty, that has served
Him as asylum, harbours also some
Few sedulous fragilities refined
On wall and ceiling. As we follow him
Beneath the famous plasterwork, I find
Art too (thus orphaned) vulnerably slim.

In rapt obscenities, the instructed taste
Admires the moulding, sighs
'Ah' at the staircase, and extols the chaste
Ceilings by Stapleton; occupies
(Thin shoulders raised, a flutter of bony hands)
The pure *gestalt*
Of the double arch; expatiates, understands
How architect and plasterer had felt

The underpinning of that virile beauty
In an age's order. Later, in the street,
He held forth to me how the artist's duty
Is mutiny, evasion, and retreat.

Eden

Adam had found what was not his to seek,
Command of motives; and the world grew heated,
The self extended and the will elated.
He can, he sees, make Eve again attractive
Almost at will, using this new technique
For rousing, as for quenching, an incentive.

A sin in gardens, where the shadows' play
Makes clarity a sin. So the attendant
Shows them the door. The garden was abandoned
To twilight, seasons, and the steady tread
Of natural wants that, once met, fell away,
Chill in the evenings, gratefully exhausted.

The Waterfall at Powerscourt

Looping off feline through the leisured air
    Water, a creature not at home in water,
Takes to the air. It comes down on its forepaws, changes
    Feet on the rockface and again extended
Bounds.   For it neither
    Pours nor is poured, but only here on its quarry
Falls at last, pours. No more the amphibious otter
    Than foundered ram can walk this water thrown
Catwalk across a further element.

Water itself is not at home in water
    But fails its creatures, as a fallen nature
Swerves from its course. And, less adaptable,
    Out of an element itself thrown out
The fallen creature cannot find itself
    Nor its own level, headlong.

Or else as a sealion, heavy and limber,
    Sedately slithers its short rock chute in the zoo
(Foolish and haughty as, propped on a stock, the Prince Regent),
    And over the water it takes to
Shoots,   so the water
    Lobs itself, immerses in rock and, rebounding,
Surfaces smoothly backwards into space,
    Swimming the air as for freshwater miles offshore
The Orinoco dyes the ocean cold.

What end it answers, over the Sabine country
    Of Mrs Rafferty's Tusculum and Dublin's
Weekend hinterland, arching; or what use
    Insinuating underneath that ocean
Its chill of wit, who knows? The end it answers,
    The level it seeks, is its own.

Against Confidences

Loose lips now
Call Candour friend
Whom Candour's brow,
When clear, contemned.

Candour can live
Within no shade
That our compulsive
Needs have made

On couches where
We sleep, confess,
Couple and share
A pleased distress.

Not to dispense
With privacies,
But reticence
His practice is;

Agreeing where
Is no denial,
Not to spare
One truth from trial,

But to respect
Conviction's plight
In Intellect's
Hard equal light.

Not to permit,
To shy belief
Too bleakly lit,
The shade's relief

Clouds Candour's brow,
But to indulge
These mouths that now
Divulge, divulge.

Nineteen-Seventeen

A glass in a Liverpool drawing room cracked across.
A telegram fell out of it for Rica.
Perfidious glass that would not mirror loss,
The omen had outstripped the telegram.

A glass in Roscoe's drawing room fell apart
And handed out a telegram from France.
Rica got up from winding bandages.

The gaze of the glass was frantic and averted.
A wet and severed wrist, a hand that shook
Came from the mirror and delivered death
To Liverpool and England in a look.

She reckoned there could not be long to wait.
A wedge of wrack was hunting in from sea
As stadiums spill spectators from a gate.
The thrumming bolt approached her from the blue.
Its piercing note already shattered glass.

A world of plush and leather came to pieces,
Mahogany was shivered into glass.
She smiled farewell to all their startled faces
And steadily outstripped the telegram.

To a Brother in the Mystery

Circa 1290

The world of God has turned its two stone faces
One my way, one yours. Yet we change places
A little, slowly. After we had halved
The work between us, those grotesques I carved
There in the first bays clockwise from the door,
That was such work as I got credit for
At York and Beverley: thorn-leaves twined and bent
To frame some small and human incident

Domestic or of venery. Each time I crossed
Since then, however, underneath the vast
Span of our Mansfield limestone, to appraise
How you cut stone, my emulous hard gaze
Has got to know you as I know the stone
Where none but chisels talk for us. I have grown
Of my own way of thinking yet of yours,
Seeing your leafage burgeon there by the doors
With a light that, flickering, trenches the voussoir's line;
Learning your pre-harmonies, design
Nourished by exuberance, and fine-drawn
Severity that is tenderness, I have thought,
Looking at these last stalls that I have wrought
This side of the chapter's octagon, I find
No hand but mine at work, yet mine refined
By yours, and all the difference: my motif
Of foliate form, your godliness in leaf.
     And your last spandrel proves the debt incurred
Not all on the one side. There I see a bird
Pecks at your grapes, and after him a fowler,
A boy with a bow. Elsewhere, your leaves discover
Of late blank mask-like faces. We infect
Each other then, doubtless to good effect...
And yet, take care: this cordial knack bereaves
The mind of all its sympathy with leaves,
Even with stone. I would not take away
From your peculiar mastery, if I say
A sort of coldness is the core of it,
A sort of cruelty; that prerequisite
Perhaps I rob you of, and in exchange give
What? Vulgarity's prerogative,
Indulgence towards the frailties it indulges,
Humour called 'wryness' that acknowledges
Its own complicity. I can keep in mind
So much at all events, can always find
Fallen humanity enough, in stone,
Yes, in the medium; where we cannot own
Crispness, compactness, elegance, but the feature
Seals it and signs it work of human nature
And fallen though redeemable. You, I fear,
Will find you bought humanity too dear
At the price of some light leaves, if you begin
To find your handling of them growing thin,

Insensitive, brittle. For the common touch,
Though it warms, coarsens. Never care so much
For leaves or people, but you care for stone
A little more. The medium is its own
Thing, and not all a medium, but the stuff
Of mountains; cruel, obdurate, and rough.

Killala*

Forlorn indeed Hope on these shores,
White-breeched, under a tricorne, shouting orders
Into the wind in a European language
La gloire against the Atlantic.
                    And Enniscrone,
The unfocused village carefully grouped on absence...

Laden with Europe, toiling up out of the sea
With all the baggage of their own and Europe's
History barnacled, clammy with tawny jellies
And spotted silts, the wreck
Of unwashed hope is a more combustible flotsam
Than this more stranded,
More featureless than any conurbation.

Not memory (her lading) nor the vessel
– No, nor the vessel, for the Téméraire
Has been a dozen ships and all one venture –
But the venture persists. Such a temerity,
So bare a chance deserves a barer rock's
Less cluttered landfall. Nakedness
Is structural, asks a binnacle at sea;
By land, if not an oak, a standing stone
Hewn or unhewn in an open place, for the venture
To take a shape by. But the prudent Gael,
Disguised on the skyline as habitation tatters
A scarecrow coast, has blurred identity
By blurring shape, a flutter of rags in the wind.

* Killala: where the French landed in Ireland in 1798.

Frenchman, the beacons flare across the Midlands.
Stopping the car and hating this ugly place,
Let this be as if I had lit the first of the beacons,
Of driftwood fetched from the shore,
Announcing your identity and presence:
Not an idea, abstract notion, quality
But a being only, able for life and action,
The same it was some time ago, in France.

With the Grain

1.

Why, by an ingrained habit, deviate
    Into their own ideas
Activities like carpentry, become
    The metaphors of graining?
Gardening, the one word, tilth? Or thought,
    The idea of having ideas,
Resolved into images of tilth and graining?

An ingrained habit... This is fanciful:
    And there's the rub
Bristling, where the irritable block
    Screams underneath the blade
Of love's demand, or in crimped and gouged-out
    Shavings only, looses
Under a peeling logic its perceptions.

Language (mine, when wounding,
    Yours, back-biting) lacks
No whorl nor one-way shelving. It resists,
    Screams its remonstrance, planes
Reluctantly to a level. And the most
    Reasonable of settlements betrays
Unsmoothed resentment under the caress.

2.

The purest hue, let only the light be sufficient
    Turns colour. And I was told

If painters frequent St Ives
    It is because the light
There, under the cliff, is merciful. I dream
    Of an equable light upon words
And as painters paint in St Ives, the poets speaking.

Under that cliff we should say, my dear,
    Not what we mean, but what
The words would mean. We should speak,
    As carpenters work,
With the grain of our words. We should utter
    Unceasingly the hue of love
Safe from the battery of changeable light.

(Love, a condition of such fixed colour,
    Cornwall indeed, or Wales
Might foster. Lovers in mauve,
    Like white-robed Druids
Or the Bards in blue, would need
    A magical philtre, no less,
Like Iseult's, to change partners.)

3.

Such a fourth estate of the realm,
    Hieratic unwinking
Mauve or blue under skies steel-silver,
    Would chamfer away
A knot in the grain of a streaming light, the glitter,
    Off lances' points, that moved
A sluggish Froissart to aesthetic feeling.

And will the poet, carpenter of light,
    Work with the grain henceforward?
If glitterings won't fetch him
    Nor the refractory crystal,
Will he never again look into the source of light
    Aquiline, but fly
Always out of the sun, unseen till softly alighting?

Why, by an ingrained habit, elevate
    Into the light of ideas
The colourful trades, if not like Icarus

To climb the beam? High lights
Are always white, but this ideal sun
    Dyes only more intensely, and we find
Enough cross-graining in the most abstract nature.

Red Rock of Utah

*of golde and sylver they make commonly chaumber pottes, and
other vesselles, that serve for moste vile uses. . . .
Furthermore of the same mettalles they make greate chaines,
fetters, and gieves wherein they tie their bondmen.
Finally whosoever for anye offense be inflamed, by their eares hang
rynges of golde, upon their fyngers they weare rynges of golde,
and aboute their neckes chaines of golde, and in conclusion their
heades be tied aboute with gold.*   More's Utopia

Surely it has some virtue, having none,
Sighed to her bondman the Utopian lady
Telling the links of gold among his hair.
At wrist and ankle, fingers, head and neck
The unserviceable metal he must wear
In rings, chains, chainmail bonnets, riveted
Locked, knotted, wound on him whom her affection
Chose she conceived perversely; till she guessed
Its virtue was in helmeting that head,
A collar round the neck she hung upon.

        What colour were Utopia's rocks?
        Navajo red, the Mormon wives
        Mutter, restless in drab smocks,
        Would void the golden chamberpots
        And strike off the golden gyves
        In crimson Zion. Under the mesa's
        Coronet, taken from such base uses,
        Shall not red gold deck the wives of Utah?

        'Convicting us, convict the Lord
        Of barbarous inutilities:
        What left His hand but a very gaud,
        Red over canyon and mesa, good
        For nothing but an artifice

To adorn His favoured? Little we ask
Who wintered for Him in Nebraska:
Red gold only, a little at wrist or ankle.'

'Has it then every virtue, having none?'
Sighs to the Lord in prayer the Mormon lady
And Nephi Johnson remonstrates, 'What good
The land, if not for cotton?' But the Lord,
Dear reverend pioneers, in His red blood
Sealed more than that hard promise of a sod
To turn in Zion. Planting such dubious
Capacities in your sons as might applaud
Gauds of gratuitous ornament in your God,
Your God depraved King Utopus himself.

Reflections on Deafness

For Kenneth and Margaret Millar

1.

Making the best and most of a visitation,
The deaf can make it serve their purposes.
What else can any one use but his condition?
Is affliction turned to use the less affliction?

2.

The voice called ours, played back to us on tape,
We hate at once, disown. The nerve of selfhood
Jumps at the drill of an achieved imposture.
The deaf cannot tell the King from the Pretender.

3.

The blind have rights in that most delicate
And intimate of the senses, touch; the deaf
Lip-reader, in somnambulistic rape
On the act of sight, usurps the rights denied him.

Blindness can be rectified by reason,
Errors of calculation not in will
We tolerate; but wince to see the human,
Distinguishingly human act of speech contorted.

4.

Yes, we are deaf to their condition, hear
All that we want to hear, the blind man's stick
Redeemably tap-tapping, but the voice
That cannot hear itself we cannot hear.

For an Age of Plastics

With the effect almost of carving the hillside
        They climb in their stiff terraces, these houses
Feed the returning eye with national pride
        In the 'built to last.' Approving elegance
Where there is only decency, the eye
        Applauds the air of nothing left to chance
Or brilliantly provisional. Not the fact
        But the air of it, the illusion, we observe;
Chance in the bomb sight kept these streets intact
        And razed whole districts. Nor was the lesson lost
On the rebuilt Plymouth, how an age of chance
        Is an age of plastics. In a style pre-cast
Pre-fabricated, and as if its site
        Were the canyon's lip, it rises out of rubble
Sketchily massive, moulded in bakelite.

Annoyed to take a gloomy sort of pride
        In numbering our losses, I suppose
The ploughman ceased his carving of the hillside
        And all the coulters and the chisels broke
When he was young whom we come home to bury,
        A man like clay in the hands of his womenfolk.

A ploughman carved three harvests, each a son,
        Upon the flesh of Wales. And all were carried
Long since from those hillsides, yet this one

Comes first to threshing. Nutriment and grain
For all the mashing of the interim
    Live in the load of him. Living again
His shipwright's years, the countryman's walks in the park,
    The scrape of a mattock in a too small garden,
The marriage to the capable matriarch,
    What would he change? Perhaps a stubbornness
That bristled sometimes, for the sensible hands
    To circumvent and gentle, would be less
Amenable to their shaping. But all told,
    His edged tools still would lie in the garden shed,
Still he would flow, himself, from mould to mould.

Whatever he showed of something in the rough,
    Sluggish in flow and unadaptable,
I liked him for; affecting to be gruff,
    An awkward customer – so much was due,
He seemed to think, to what a man was, once:
    Something to build with, take a chisel to.

The Life of Service

Service, or Latin *sorbus*, European
More especially English shadbush or small tree,
Asks all the shade the fancier can find
In a walled garden. This is no plebeian
Of cottage plots, though coarse in leaf and rind.

Planted, it is persistent, of a thick
Skin, and grows strong the more it's trodden on;
Or afterwards, as an established upas,
Thrives all the better by each welcomed nick
Of aggrieved knives wielded by interlopers.

By this indeed it knows itself. Self-thwarted,
It welcomes parasites, for playing host
To what insults and saps it is its virtue
And its fulfilment. Flourishing contorted,
All its long-suffering's overbearing too.

Some cultivators hold that it repays,
By its small edible fruit (in favoured species
Of a vinous taste), its culture. It does not;
All saner growth abhors it, and the Bays
Wither, affronted, in the poisoned plot.

The 'Sculpture' of Rhyme

Potter nor iron-founder
Nor caster of bronze will he cherish,
But the monumental mason;

As if his higher stake
Than the impregnable spiders
Of self-defended music

Procured him mandibles
To chisel honey from the saxifrage,
And a mouth to graze on feldspar.

A SEQUENCE FOR FRANCIS PARKMAN

The Jesuits in North America

Récollet friars and the very Huguenots were as often as Jesuits Champlain's companions on early investigations of the seaboard of Acadia and the estuary of the St Lawrence river. It was not at his instigation, though it was with his compliance, that the Canadian mission, big with a harvest of monstrous and astonishing martyrdoms, became a monopoly of the Society of Jesus.

Curé and pastor, dead at the one time
Buried in the one grave
To see would they lie peaceable together
Who never lived so on Acadia's coast;
And the Aeneas of a destined nation
Sees uses for recalcitrance,
No matter priest or pastor,
Sectarian zeal to rib the rock, Quebec.

Only the holy fathers were
Holy and resolute enough
To live in Huron lodges;
Only the wily fathers could
Only the holy fathers
Outwit the Iroquois.

Saguenay, Ohio, Colorado
Roll gloomy waters, and the Ottawa
Plunging, boiled. Shot spray from that concussion
Smoked out of Champlain's arquebuse
In Indian wars; he knew
A demon in the cataract. Tobacco
Disbursed on foam placates the Manitou.

Only the holy fathers were
Holy and resolute enough;
Devils and devildom
Incarnate, none but they,
The incarnate God's
Adepts and ministers,
Might recognize and slay.

Savages convert the savages.

Canoe that darted out upon the still
Bay of the Trinity, dark as Acheron,
Sanctuary of solitude and silence,
The soul of Champlain, dying, took such forms
As never a Jesuit of France could tell;
More shapes than one, since all were Canada.

At Sainte-Marie the fathers' mail from France
Accumulates unread. The holy fathers
Only the holy fathers
Were resolute for martyrdom. Apache,
Last suicidal chieftain in a column
Of blowing dust, a dry soil's levity
Too late affects the Roman.
Fatuity not cowardice undid
The Huron nation, and intractable
Indolence the Iroquois. But all
Had seen too many gods, as I have seen them
Too many, and too different. There is
No God but One and He is terrible
Dwells in the Huron lodges
Outwits the Iroquois.

Lasalle

*Lasalle who, for no sordid end, pressing to the waters of the Mississippi, first
by that watery highway attained to the Gulf of Mexico, was a spirit cold and stern.*

*His followers, who shared his perplexities and endured the effects of his per-
severance, at most respected, always feared, and never loved him; a truth
sufficiently attested by the circumstances of his obscure death at their mutinous
hands in the deserts of Louisiana. In his letters written to his creditors and
friends, he has confessed that the wilderness drew him not otherwise than as a
theatre for his restless ambitions, where they would be less obstructed than in
the palaces and faubourgs of Paris by a lack of that conversibility and address
which alone, in a more civil society, can recommend and please.*

Of this aspiring burgher who disdained
(Dumb in his pride of mortified reserve)
The usufruct of half a continent,
After the dark inexorable river
Delivers him the salt breath of the sea,
Still we complain: Dark it was not, until
He made it so, inexorable, nor fatal.

He loved solitude and he loved power
And Parkman loves him for it. Better love
Profit: if no principle nor faith
Move his lids' mountains, cannot Trade unsheet
The gathered waters of five inland oceans,
A prodigal Nature's parks and pleasure grounds,
Wild swans, wild turkeys, cranes and pelicans?

He never saw it, any of it: saw
The Mississippi that was bright, as dark,
Indifferent, as inexorable; saw
(As if in those accounts he never kept)
Digits and proxies, lean alternatives
To audiences with a Monseigneur
Where he had lacked complaisance and address.

He loved solitude and he loved power
And lonely as when born of chaos, bright
Voiceless, sail-less, without sign of life
The great Gulf opened, tossing – but what for?
Not for the Faith, for glory, or for France,
Whirled on the miry vortex of his need,
The light canoes of Indian nations foundered.

Frontenac

*In what was wilderness as inviolate then as in the last century were the gorges
of the High Sierra when revealed to the astonished gaze of the intrepid John
Muir, the Marquis of Frontenac founded three hundred years ago the rude fortress
of which the all but obliterated site still, though uncertainly, preserves his name
in the city of Kingston, Ontario. There, however, a hundred will ask for Old
Fort Henry, the surviving British edifice, for the one curious traveller who
enquires after the remains of Fort Frontenac.*

*The adjacent terrain is that which the pen of Fenimore Cooper has made interesting
to all amateurs of the sublime and romantic by the adventures of the immortal
Chingachgook, in romances which, if written in a manner no less orotund, reveal
also a genius as copious and spirited as the productions of the author of 'Waverley'.
Yet however stirring and authentic the narrative, it must inevitably fail in
delineating scenes of which the impressive charm is precisely that they were for
so long untrodden, unless rarely by the moccasin of the savage and solitary
hunter, and celebrated only by the wind's pencil and the music of the cataract.*

*It was not by the force of arms, but by the framing of fraudulent contracts
and the sale of spirituous liquors, that these territories were wrested from their
original dusky citizens.*

Hearing from some how the Sierra answers
Even today, to John Muir's nails and rifle,
With human resonances,
I heard the long-tamed wilderness give back
Over the Lake and all too British Kingston
The one word, 'Frontenac.'
But after-echoes mocked: The rocky flanges
Of the Thousand Islands
Have more to do than take up challenges
From perfect strangers;
Agoraphobia among empty spaces,
The mountain ranges, the plains of corn,
Peoples the street at history's intersections
With famous faces.

Heart of Midlothian, the milky mother
(Sir Walter's Doric) of sane masterpieces
Fed at that flaccid udder, Walter Scott,
Great lax geometer, first plotted them,
Triangulations that explode
The architect's box of space, and by a torsion
As bland as violent sprain
Narrative time and the archives' single slot.

What's to be seen of old Fort Frontenac?
The British fortress, by a hundred years
More recent, but still Old
Fort Henry, draws the Buicks. Of the Frenchman
A mound remains by Kingston's waterfront
And a cadence out of Parkman: 'At Versailles
A portrait, beautiful and young, Minerva...'

Intervals in what never meets the eye
Meet the ear sooner, music's images
Not of Ontario's spaces but of spaces
Sketched by a gesture, virtual and French.

Alas for Caliban. The Thousand Islands
Were full of noises,
Landscape and history echoing back and forth
Under immense skies, till his master
Cabined his spaces in a folio
And Euclids of the tepee, leaning-to

Birch-pole isosceles in a glade of hemlocks,
Drank deafening whisky in a written treaty.

Montcalm

It is reported of General Wolfe that as he drifted by night to the secret assault of the Heights of Abraham he quoted to his companions some famous stanzas of the elegy of Grey.

The French and the British commander were alike destined to die on the morrow, and thus to illustrate the melancholy truth of the poet's reflections. Montcalm was himself a poet, and appended pious verses in French and Latin to a cross erected on his field of victory at Ticonderoga. He had the sentiments and inclinations of a country gentleman.

He died before he could learn which of his children had pre-deceased him.

In Candiac by Nîmes in Languedoc
He left a mill to grind his olives well
Who now must harvest laurels. Who had died
In Candiac? All Bougainville could tell
Was of a death. Mirète he thought had died
If it was Mirète. He never could decide
For whom the olives sighed in Languedoc.

To Candiac by Nîmes in Languedoc
A murmur reaches from the perjured wave
That floats surprise and France's great reverse:
At dawn, too late, the cliffs will answer back.
'The paths of glory lead but to the grave'
– Marmoreal verses, plumes to tuft a hearse
And scutcheons black for squires of Candiac.

From Candiac by Nîmes in Languedoc
Quoting Corneille – 'though, Christian! not Montcalm
Nor his sagacity nor up-ended trees
Nor men nor deeds checked England, but God's arm' –
Coming from this and homelier pieties
In Candiac by Nîmes in Languedoc
To earn the stucco tribute of a plaque,

Montcalm had met, if we should say his match,
We ought to mean his match in hardihood
Hardly in grace, James Wolfe, but most of all

His match in fate, his double. Did he catch
If not the low voice, still its tone, the mood?
The paths of glory led but to Quebec
From Candiac by Nîmes in Languedoc.

Both earned their stucco. Marble was reserved
To honour the intrepid, the serene
And the successful Amherst. But it served,
Pompous and frigid as it was, the phrase
'A martial glory': common ground between
The public lives, the private, Kent, Quebec,
And Candiac by Nîmes in Languedoc.

Pontiac

*Of all the savages of North America, history records none more eminent for great
abilities than Pontiac, a sachem of the Ottawas. He refused to acknowledge the
capitulation of Canada. Inflamed by him, a league of all the Western tribes
invested the ceded forts, burned many, and massacred the garrisons. At Detroit,
the most considerable of these places, he was repulsed. But not without justice
does the modern metropolis recall, by the names she accords the products of her
manufactories, not only her founder, Lamothe-Cadillac, but also him who would,
in the name of his violated nation, have razed her to the ground.*

Pontiac fires Detroit!
On Fort Duquesne afresh
The immaculate lilies! Turn,
Minavavana or
Le Grand Sauteur, and see
Behind the trader's knife
Plunging, *coureurs de bois*
Roll through the fired stockade
The unmentionable chapter –
Extermination of the Seminole,
Deportation of the Cherokee,
Transportation of the Saginaw . . .
A modern miracle of
Engineering fires
Detroit and Cadillac
Where, cast in steel
Or punched out of chrome
On a spinning wheel,

96

Freely may roam
This totem, this
Served, furbished car
With a name that's his,
Ranging so far:
Pontiac, Ottawa shade.

Bougainville

Lewis de Bougainville, lieutenant to the Marquis of Montcalm at the fall of Canada, later essayed to annex the Falkland Islands.

Baulked of this object by the more politic arrangements of His Most Christian Majesty, his next and most extraordinary venture for the glory of the French nation was a circumnavigation of the globe in the years 1766, 1767, 1768 and 1769.

See his narrative of this voyage, made into English by Mr Forster; and the later extension of this work by the celebrated Diderot, a supplement more ingenious than useful.

All the soft runs of it, the tin-white gashes
Over the muscled mesh and interaction
Of the South Seas tilt against him less unsteady
Than France had been, or a King who could destroy
Acadia sold, Montcalm betrayed by faction,
And all the meadows of the Illinois
Lost, the allies abandoned. Where the ashes
Still smoulder on the ceded Falklands, these
Islands and oceans he has failed already
Though he will navigate the seven seas.

The shame persists as scruple. The exact
Conscience of science chastens observations,
And the redaction of a log-book's soundings
Is scrupulously dry. Although the scent
Carries from Otaheite, can a nation's
Chagrin or honour weigh in the intent
Scrutiny of the sextant? Matter of fact
Dries the great deeps. And yet what tumults when
He marks the fathoms, what disorders, houndings
Of mortification, angers, drive the pen!

No accuracy there but testifies
To a concern behind it, to a feeling

In excess of its object, fact. Excesses
Of that concern (where God permits the pox
And a King is perjured) self-inflict their steeling
To this impassive dryness charting rocks,
Keys, and the set of tide-rips. Weather eyes
Whittled so blue by pains, exactitude
In the science, navigation, witnesses
To the heart's intentions answered, not eschewed.

Needing to know is always how to learn;
Needing to see brings sightings; steadiest readings
Are those that wishes father. In their ages
Of Eden's gold the archipelagos
Await his keel because he wants for Edens
Who held savannahs once and the Ohio's
Bison for France. The measure of concern
Measures the truth, and in the *philosophe*
A paradox of noble savages
Has met no need more urgent than to scoff.

A Letter to Curtis Bradford

Curtis, you've been American too long,
You don't know what it feels like. You belong,
Don't you, too entirely to divulge?
Indifferently therefore you indulge
My idle interests: Are there names perhaps
In Iowa still, to match the names on maps,
Burgundian or Picard voyageurs
Prowling the wilderness for France and furs
On the Des Moines river? And suppose there were
What would it prove? To whom would it occur
In Iowa that, suppose it so, New France
Not your New England has pre-eminence
If to belong means anything? Your smile
(Twisted) admits it doesn't. Steadily, while
You on the seaboard, they in Canada
Dribbled from floods of European war
Boiled in small pools, pressure built up behind
The dams of Europe. Dispossessed mankind,
Your destined countrymen, milled at dock-gates;

Emigrant schooners spilled aboard the States;
The dispossessed, the not to be possessed,
The alone and equal, peopled all the West.
And so what is it I am asking for,
Sipping at names? Dahcotah, Ottawa,
Horse Indian . . . Yes, but earlier (What is this
Need that I find to fill void centuries?)
Who first put up America to let?
You of the old stock paid him rent. And yet
Even so soon, crowds of another sort
Piled off the boats to take him by assault.
And a worse sort, the heroes. Who but they,
For whom the manifest was shadow-play
Of an all-absorbing inward war and plight,
Could so deny its presence and its right?
It was the given. But I only guess,
I guess at it out of my Englishness
And envy you out of England. Man with man
Is all our history; American,
You met with spirits. Neither white nor red
The melancholy, disinherited
Spirit of mid-America, but this,
The manifested copiousness, the bounties.

For Doreen. A Voice from the Garden

from *New Lines, 2* (1963)

We have a lawn of moss.
The next house is called The Beeches.
A towering squirrel-haunted
Trellis of trees, across
Our matt and trefoil, reaches
Shade where our guests have sauntered.

Cars snap by in the road.
In a famous photographed village
The High Street is our address.
Our guests write from abroad
Delighted to envisage
Rose-arbour and wilderness.

They get them, and the lilacs.
Some frenzy in us discards
Lilacs and all. It will harden,
However England stacks
Her dear discoloured cards
Against us, us to her garden.

Anglophobia rises
In Brooklyn to hysteria
At some British verses.
British, one sympathizes.
Diesel-fumes cling to wistaria.
One conceives of worse reverses.

The sough of the power brake
Makes every man an island;
But we are the island race.
We must be mad to take
Offence at our poisoned land
And the gardens that pock her face.
Trumpington

Two Dedications

1. *Wide France*

Sunlight so blurred with clouds we couldn't tell
Light from shade, driving to Vézelay
Disgusted you that Northern day. You thought
Caressing weather started at Calais,

And I had thought, in Burgundy; and still,
When we had stolen guiltily from where
Mummy lay wretched in the loud hotel,
All we found was squall-dashed street and square.

Nothing to do but go to Vézelay
That afternoon. Both worried, and the seasons
Wrong as usual, winter in our bones,
We drove the ten miles for the worst of reasons.

Let me remind you. First there was a strong
High, famous church; and where the hillside falls
Away behind it, France was spread at our feet;
And at our back old streets and gates and walls.

Poor eight-year-old, but how could you remember?
So many, before and since; and such a fuss
As we always made, as if to convince ourselves.
And now you worry about the eleven-plus.

2. *Barnsley Cricket Club*

Now the heat comes, I am demoralized.
Important letters lie unanswered, dry
Shreds of tobacco spike the typewriter,
No undertaking but is ill-advised.

Unanswerable even the shortest missive,
Replies not sealed, or sealed without conviction.
Thumb-marks dry out, leaving the paper pouchy,
Tousled with effort, desperate, inconclusive.

'A thing worth doing is worth doing well,'
Says Shaw Lane Cricket Ground
Between the showers of a July evening,
As the catch is held and staid hand-clappings swell.

This almost vertical sun, this blur of heat,
All stinging furze and snagged unravelling,
Denies the axiom which has kept
My father's summers shadowy and sweet.

Remembering many times when he has laughed
Softly, and slapped his thigh, because the trap
So suavely set was consummately sprung,
I wish, to all I love, his love of craft.

Hard to instruct myself, and then my son,
That things which would be natural are done
After a style less consummate; that an art's
More noble office is to leave half-done.

How soon the shadows fall, how soon and long!
The score-board stretches to a grandson's feet.
This layabout July in another climate
Ought not to prove firm turf, well-tended, wrong.

Resolutions

Whenever I talk of my art
You turn away like strangers,
Whereas all I mean is the chart
I keep, of my own sea-changes.

It puzzles the wisest head
How anyone's good resolution
Can securely be implemented;
Art provides a solution.

This is the assessor whose word
Can always be relied on;
It tells you when has occurred
Any change you decide on.

More preciously still, it tells
Of growth not groped towards,
In the seaway a sound of bells
From a landfall not on the cards.

Life Encompassed

How often I have said,
'This will never do,'
Of ways of feeling that now
I trust in, and pursue!

Do traverses tramped in the past,
My own, criss-crossed as I forge
Across from another quarter
Speak of a life encompassed?

Well, life is not research.
No one asks you to map the terrain,
Only to get across it
In new ways, time and again.

How many such, even now,
I dismiss out of hand
As not to my purpose, not
Unknown, just unexamined.

Hornet

In lilac trained on the colonnade's archway, what
Must be a hornet volleys lethally back
And forth in the air, on the still not hot
But blindingly white Italian stone, blue-black.

I have seldom seen them in England, although once
Years ago the foul-mouthed, obligingly bowed
Rat-catcher of Cambridge made a just pretence
To a cup of tea, for a nest cleared in the road.

Those were wasp-coloured, surely; and this blue,
Gun-metal blue, blue-black ominous ranger
Of Italy's air means an Italy stone all through,
Where every herb of holier thought's a stranger.

No call for such rage in our England of pierced shadows.
Stone's and the white sun's opposite, furious fly,
There no sun strides in a rapid creak of cicadas
And the green mould stains before the mortar is dry.

Housekeeping

From thirty years back my grandmother with us boys
Picking the ash-grimed blackberries, pint on pint, is
Housekeeping Yorkshire's thrift, and yet the noise
Is taken up from Somerset in the 'nineties.

From homestead Autumns in the vale of Chard
Translated in youth past any hope of returning,
She toiled, my father a baby, through the hard
Fellside winters, to Barnsley, soused in the Dearne.

How the sound carries! Whatever the dried-out, lank
Sticks of poor trees could say of the slow slag stealing
More berries than we did, I hear her still down the bank
Slide, knickers in evidence, laughing, modestly squealing.

And I hear not only how homestead to small home echoes
Persistence of historic habit. Berries
Ask to be plucked, and attar pleases the rose.
Contentment cries from the distance. How it carries!

Low Lands

I could not live here, though I must and do
Ungratefully inhabit the Cambridgeshire fens
And the low river delta we pass through
Is beautiful in the same uncertain sense.

Like a snake it is, its serpentine iridescence
Of slow light spilt and wheeling over calm
Inundations, and a snake's still menace
Hooding with bruised sky belfry and lonely farm.

The grasses wave on meadows fat with foison.
In granges, cellars, granaries, the rat
Runs sleek and lissom. Tedium, a poison,
Swells in the sac for the hillborn, dwelling in the flat.

How defenceless it is! How much it needs a protector
To keep its dykes! At what a price it commands
The delightful bizarre when it wears like a bus-conductor
Tickets of brown sails tucked into polders' hat-bands!

But a beauty there is, noble, dependent, unshrinking,
In being at somebody's mercy, wide and alone.
I imagine a hillborn sculptor suddenly thinking
One could live well in a country short of stone.

Green River

Green silk, or a shot silk, blue
Verging to green at the edges,
The river reflects the sky
Alas. I wish that its hue
Were the constant green of its sedges
Or the reeds it is floating by.

It reflects the entrances, dangers,
Exploits, vivid reversals
Of weather over the days.
But it learns to make these changes
By too many long rehearsals
Of overcasts and greys.

So let it take its station
Less mutably. Put it to school
Not to the sky but the land.
This endless transformation,
Because it is beautiful,
Let some of it somehow stand.

But seeing the streak of it quiver
There in the distance, my eye
Is astonished and unbelieving.
It exclaims to itself for ever:
This water is passing by!
It arrives, and it is leaving!

House-martin

I see the low black wherry
Under the alders rock,
As the ferryman strides from his ferry
And his child in its black frock

Into his powerful shadow
And out of it, skirmishing, passes
Time and again as they go
Up through the tall lush grasses.

The light of evening grieves
For the stout house of a father,
With martins under its eaves,
That cracks and sags in the weather.

Treviso, the Pescheria

Each of us has the time,
And both the times are wrong.
Our needs and likings chime
Sometimes, but not for long.

Your watch is often fast,
Mine usually slow.
And yet you cling to the past,
I laxly let it go.

You are like a ferryman's daughter,
And I the stream that blurred
Calls sent across that water,
Which loyally you have heard.

My lapsings I acknowledge.
And yet, on either hand
Combed green, the river's sedge
Sweetens the fish-wives' island.

The Prolific Spell

Day by day, such rewards,
Compassionate land!
Such things to say, and the words
And ways of saying to hand!

Bounties I cannot earn!
Nothing planned in advance!
Well, it is hard to learn,
This profiting by chance.

It is hard, learning to live
While looking the other way,
Bored and contemplative
Over a child at play.

Not everyone has a child.
All children grow away.
Sufferings drive us wild;
Not every mind can stray.

Nothing engendered, and so much
Constantly brought to birth!
This hand will lose its touch.
Profuse, illiberal earth!

Nothing could be planned
And so no credit accrues.
Ah compassionate land!
Such gain, and nothing to lose!

My utterance that turns
To always human use
Your brilliant mute concerns
Neither repays nor earns.

A Battlefield

Red mills and farms clumped soothingly here and there.
At a modest distance rose a plume of trees
On the green-bushed plain, and had from afar the air
Which poplars have in the pluck of a river breeze:

The crossing of the Piave! In what year
How many times, and by whose army, going
In which direction – none of this was clear;
With a sinking heart I felt it was not worth knowing.

A necropolis and a stand of cypress came
Predictably next, and all of it I knew
Was a peeling village with the curious name,
Victory, and fast traffic passing through.

The Cypress Avenue

My companion kept exclaiming
At fugitive aromas;
She was making a happy fuss
Of flower-naming.

And I, who had taken her there...
Not one scent could I name
In the resinous die-straight avenue's
Plume-irrigated air.

Her world was properly indexed:
The names were in my head
Familiar, double-columned, but
Hardly a page of text.

Just the swaying channel of shade;
The stippling everywhere
Of an otherwise dust-choked country;
The difference cypress made.

*

That night at the family sing-song
She had no repertoire;
Her ear was a true one, though
Her voice not very strong.

And that was an index too!
Hymns, shanties, popular numbers,
Ballads, rounds – how many
It turned out that we knew!

And what an encyclopaedia
Of smudged ill-printed feeling
They opened up, although to
Only a coarsened ear.

Humanly Speaking

After two months, already
My auspiciously begun
Adventure of blessing the world
Was turning woe-begone.

Still it might work out, I thought:
The hand-to-mouth way I live,
Not life itself, might be
What made me apprehensive.

But a truce to pieties!
I pull myself together
And get exasperated:
Damn this stupid weather!

So stupid, so uncreative...
I am rasped by a towel of wind
And boomed at by grey-green breakers
For seventy-two hours on end.

The weather invades me, throws
My every sense out of gear:
I cannot trust what I see
Or smell or taste or hear.

And because life itself
Is this one soured life I am leading,
And living it hand-to-mouth is
Natural, humanly speaking,

To swear at this barren fig-tree,
At seas uninventively breaking
In self-same pothers, becomes
A duty, humanly speaking.

But I, who had hoped no more
To have to point the finger,
Who had ventured on new feelings...
For me misgivings linger.

The Hill Field

Look there! What a wheaten
Half-loaf, halfway to bread,
A cornfield is, that is eaten
Away, and harvested:

How like a loaf, where the knife
Has cut and come again,
Jagged where the farmer's wife
Has served the farmer's men,

That steep field is, where the reaping
Has only just begun
On a wedge-shaped front, and the creeping
Steel edges glint in the sun.

See the cheese-like shape it is taking,
The sliced-off walls of the wheat
And the cheese-mite reapers making
Inroads there, in the heat?

It is Brueghel or Samuel Palmer,
Some painter, coming between
My eye and the truth of a farmer,
So massively sculpts the scene.

The sickles of poets dazzle
These eyes that were filmed from birth;
And the miller comes with an easel
To grind the fruits of earth.

The Feeders

Among the serviceable mills and
The galleries of riverside poplars,
In the holiday house, no hours
Were set aside for my writing;
It was less well-appointed than ours,
But Art found it inviting.

In that impelled present, a weight
Of water behind it, Art
And Life fed into each other:
Children who could not know
How uniquely their mother
Assisted, themselves did so,

On their long serpentine
Of that full river,
Simply by making demands.
Art liked that changeable weather.
I had only one pair of hands;
They held more, cupped together.

Now I must feed myself
On feelings fresh from their source,
Flashfloods tapped in the highlands
Under the glare of noon.
Still only one pair of hands,
And I have to hold the spoon.

In the uplands the stony beds
Chalk-white under vacant bridges...
My public has shrunk to one reader,
And that the most exacting
The hateful, insatiable feeder,
Art; and the rest, play-acting.

A Lily at Noon

Deep-sea frost, and
Lilies at noon...
Late leaves, late leaves
Toss every day.
The daymoon shines always for some.
In the marriage of a slow man
Eighteen years is soon.

Sun and moon, no
Dark between,
Foresight and hindsight
Halving the hours.
And now he collects his thoughts
Before it is too late.
But what can 'too late' mean?

Shielding with hands,
Binding to stakes...
Late leaves, late leaves
Toss every day,
The sun moves on from noon.
To freeze, to cup, to retard –
These measures terror takes.

Love and the Times

A knowledge of history fetches
Love out of its recesses,
Mapping its open stretches,
Its pits for trespassers.

Or it is staked out there,
For country airs to breathe
On seed-bed and parterre
Savour of field and heath.

Strange how we can imagine
Nothing else, although
We have no hope for the short run
That times can turn out so.

Across the Bay

A queer thing about those waters: there are no
Birds there, or hardly any.
I did not miss them, I do not remember
Missing them, or thinking it uncanny.

The beach so-called was a blinding splinter of limestone,
A quarry outraged by hulls.
We took pleasure in that: the emptiness, the hardness
Of the light, the silence, and the water's stillness.

But this was the setting for one of our murderous scenes.
This hurt, and goes on hurting:
The venomous soft jelly, the undersides.
We could stand the world if it were hard all over.

A Christening

What we do best is breed:
August Bank Holiday, whole
Populations explode

Across the wolds and in a slot
Of small cars pullulate
By couples. Millington Meadows

Flower with campstools. At
Beverley the font
Has a cover carved like a goblet.

The new baby is fed.
I stumble back to bed.
I hear the owls for a long time

Hunting. Or are they never
In the winter grey of before dawn,
Those pure long quavers,

Cries of love? I put my arms around you.
Small mice freeze among tussocks.
The baby wails in the next room.

Upstairs Mrs Ramsden
Dies, and the house
Is full of the cries of the newborn.

In red and smoky wood
A follower of Wren
Carved it at Beverley:

The generous womb that drops
Into the sanctified water immediate fruit.
What we do best is breed.

Agave in the West

I like the sidewalks of an American city,
Broad shadowed stone. I think of Agave,

Queen of the mænads, after incestuous fury
Shocked and quiescent, pleading for the cage:
Grids of a rectilinear plot, her cities.

Leaving the wilderness, she counts the loss
Of a world of signs – in algae, moss,
Guano, lichen, all the blooms of stone;
In cross-grained baulks and boles, in timber grown
Noble in groves or into monstrous shapes;
In rock-formations, cloud-formations, landscapes.
I like the sidewalks of an American city:

Sunstruck solitude of parking lots;
Taut vivid women, hair close-shaved from the armpit;
Glass walls run up, run out on the canyon's lip.
Barber my verses, pitiless vivid city.

In California

Chemicals ripen the citrus;
There are rattlesnakes in the mountains,
And on the shoreline
Hygiene, inhuman caution.

Beef in cellophane
Tall as giraffes,
The orange-rancher's daughters
Crop their own groves, mistrustful.

Perpetual summer seems
Precarious on the littoral. We drive
Inland to prove
The risk we sense. At once

Winter claps-to like a shutter
High over the Ojai valley, and discloses
A double crisis,
Winter and Drought.

Ranges on mountain-ranges,
Empty, unwatered, crumbling,
Hot colours come at the eye.
It is too cold

For picnics at the trestle-tables. Claypit
Yellow burns on the distance.
The phantom walks
Everywhere, of intolerable heat.

At Ventucopa, elevation
Two-eight-nine-six, the water hydrant frozen,
Deserted or broken settlements,
Gasoline stations closed and boarded.

By nightfall, to the snows;
And over the mile on tilted
Mile of the mountain park
The bright cars hazarded.

New York in August

(After Pasternak)

There came, for lack of sleep,
A crosspatch, drained-out look
On the old trees that keep
Scents of Schiedam and the Hook

In Flushing, as we picked out, past
Each memorized landmark,
Our route to a somnolent breakfast.
Later, to Central Park,

UNO, and the Empire State.
A haven from the heat
Was the Planetarium. We got back late,
Buffeted, dragging our feet.

Clammy, electric, torrid,
The nights bring no relief
At the latitude of Madrid.
Never the stir of a leaf.

Any night, as we went
Back, the children asleep,
To our bed in a loaned apartment,
Although I thought a deep

And savage cry from the park
Came once, as we flashed together
And the fan whirled in the dark,
For thunder, a break in the weather.

Viper-Man

Will it be one of those
Forever summers?
Will the terrace stone
Expand, unseal
Aromas, and let slip
Out of the cell of its granulations
Some mid-Victorian courtship?

Never a belle of that
Lavender century
But, though so stayed,
Basked in a settled spell;
And yet I guard
Against a change in the weather,
Snake whipped up in the yard.

In Chopin's Garden

I remember the scarlet setts
Of the little-frequented highway
From Warsaw to the West
And Chopin's house, one Sunday.

I remember outside the windows,
As the pianist plucked a ring
From her thin white finger, the rows
Of unanchored faces waiting,

And a climbing vapour, storm-wrack
Wreathing up, heavy with fruit,
Darkened the skies at their back
On the old invasion-route.

Masovia bows its birches
Resignedly. Again
A rapid army marches
Eastward over the plain,

And fast now it approaches.
Turbulence, agonies,
As the poised musician broaches
The polonaise, storm from the keys.

See them, ennobled by
The mass and passage, these
Faces stained with the sky,
Supple and fluid as trees.

Poreč

Pennies of sun's fire jazzing like silver foil,
In this off-shore pleasaunce of Croatia
Leased to the Sports Club of Munich,
Her blondeness under the swimsuit fits
That sunbrowned girl like a tunic,
And in falling light off the limestone island
Fishing boats groove water slick as oil.

Behind them is haze that is sea and sky at once.
In what was the wartime Germans'
Torpedo-boat haven in the Adriatic,
I erase the distinction between
Contemplative and athletic
As I swim, climb out, and smoke. This peacetime weather
Worries me, these seas with blurred horizons.

Stately and wide Croatia, how it shelves
To the waste of the sea, and shapes it!
The silent roadstead shimmers.
As under the narrowed eyes
Of English and German swimmers
Here in the shade, the file of the drifters passes,
We seem much pacified, seem so to ourselves.

Barnsley and District

Judy Sugden! Judy, I made you caper
With rage when I said that the British Fascist
Sheet your father sold was a jolly good paper

And you had agreed and I said, Yes, it holds
Vinegar, and everyone laughed and imagined
The feel of the fish and chips warm in its folds.

That was at Hood Green. Under our feet there shone
The modest view, its slagheaps amethyst
In distance and white walls the sunlight flashed on.

If your father's friends had succeeded, or if I
Had canvassed harder for the Peace Pledge Union,
A world of difference might have leapt to the eye

In a scene like this which shows in fact no change.
That must have been the summer of '39.
I go back sometimes, and find nothing strange –

Short-circuiting of politics engages
The Grammar School masters still. Their bright sixth-formers sport
Nuclear Disarmament badges.

And though at Stainborough no bird's-nesting boy
Nor trespasser from the town in a Sunday suit
Nor father twirling a stick can now enjoy

Meeting old Captain Wentworth, who in grey
And ancient tweeds, gun under arm, keen-eyed
And unemployable, would give a gruff Good-day,

His rhododendrons and his laurel hedge
And tussocked acres are no more unkempt
Now that the Hall is a Teachers' Training College.

The parish primary school where a mistress once
Had every little Dissenter stand on the bench
With hands on head, to make him out a dunce;

Black backs of flourmills, wafer-rusted railings
Where I ran and ran from colliers' boys in jerseys,
Wearing a blouse to show my finer feelings –

These still stand. And Bethel and Zion Baptist,
Sootblack on pavements foul with miners' spittle
And late-night spew and violence, persist.

George Arliss was on at the Star, and Janet Gaynor
Billed at the Alhambra, but the warmth
Was no more real then, nor the manners plainer.

And politics has no landscape. The Silesian
Seam crops out in prospects felt as deeply
As any of these, with as much or as little reason.

Right Wing Sympathies

France of the poujadiste!
France of the absurd
Citroëns, still on the roads
Of Marne and Doubs that summer:

Domestic and armoured,
Made out of sheets
Of corrugated iron,
They dive into the highway.

Travelling humps in the road,
Steel-snouted moles,
They gouge at each chug of their tired
Small engines a trench in the tarmac.

Walking is a perpetual
Falling down, and so is
Driving in these shovel-bills
Through the country of Jacques Tati.

Camel's head and hump
Of black rock, Briançon
Bulked not so large
But platypus must nose it

Out, and over ramp
On ramp of France
Snuffle and wheeze
Where Vauban and the Alps

Have framed the camel state,
Its ugly teeth
Yellowed at Italy,
In a geometer's heaven.

His exact nest
Of outwork polygons
Provided parking-lots
For Citroëns in bastion and embrasure

When I was there that summer,
Asking myself to explain
Myself to myself
By enrolling in a party of the Right.

In an old photograph
Dreyfus is falling down
Perpetually between
Two ranks of the backs of riflemen

For treason. But in court
The intellectual
Accuses the accusers. 'Shovel-bill!'
He tells them to their faces. 'Camel-tooth!'

So much I cannot face,
I sweat with those
Arraigned in his
Superb performances.

Hyphens

You remember Rossignano
Solvay, impossible hybrid,
Italian-Belgian? The hyphen
Was stretched to breaking.

Remember its streets, its piazzas?
The main line clove them, rammed
Through a truss of malodorous sidings
By the howling trench of the highway.

Black, smeared on the rocks
In the brilliant mornings,
Pontefract Cakes of naphtha
Stuck to the soles of swimmers.

Mazzimo, draughtsman
For Solvay chemicals,
Shrugging a bulky shoulder
At rigidity of Belgian blueprints,

Dived and hauled up
On the rocks an amphora,
Rough, plain and capacious,
Plucked from a foundered galley.

There too the hyphen stretched
In him to breaking, out of
Maremman cities where his Fiat spun
In week-end pieties

To the Ligurian polluted sea
And unpaved avenue
Which housed him, hardly less
A transient than his summer visitors.

Holding these halves together,
His Tuscan strove
For a coining of new compounds:
Firm-transient, chemical-civic.

A Meeting of Cultures

Iced with a vanilla
Of dead white stone, the Palace
Of Culture is a joke

Or better, a vast villa
In some unimaginable suburb
Of Perm or Minsk.

Ears wave and waggle
Over the poignant Vistula,
Horns of a papery stone,

Not a wedding-cake but its doily!
The Palace of Culture sacks
The centre, the dead centre

Of Europe's centre, Warsaw.
The old town,
Rebuilt, is a clockwork toy.

I walked abroad in it,
Charmed and waylaid
By a nursery joy:

Hansel's and Gretel's city!
Their house of gingerbread
That lately in

Horrific forest glooms
Of Germany
Bared its ferocity

Anew, resumes its gilt
For rocking-horse rooms
In Polish rococo.

Diseased imaginations
Extant in Warsaw's stone
Her air makes sanative.

How could a D.S.O.
Of the desert battles live,
If it were otherwise,

In his wooden cabin
In a country wood
In the heart of Warsaw

As the colonel did, who for
The sake of England took
Pains to be welcoming?

More jokes then. And the wasps humming
Into his lady's jam
That we ate with a spoon

Out in the long grass. Shades,
Russian shades out of old slow novels,
Lengthened the afternoon.

Metals

Behind the hills, from the city of an Etruscan gateway
To the city of a Sienese fortress
Through the metalliferous mountains,
If I had travelled to the age of bronze,
Of gold, the pierced axe-heads of archaic Greece,
This would have been my way.

For first we corkscrewed in a stink of borax
For climbing miles, then under the oakwoods
In unworked lodes lay poisonous zinc and copper.
With forty miles to go, the car bit gravel
Which spurted and hung in the air, and still no houses.

And I saw all stone as a weak concoction of powder,
The golden skin of the columns
Cemented as limply as a Rizla paper.
Rape may be worship. Where the sybil stands
In a pool of spent light at the heart of the mountain at Cumae,
The bowels of earth are of an unearthly weirdness.

Homage to John L. Stephens

There has to be a hero who is not
A predator but South
Of the Border down
Mexico way or wherever else she
Whispers, It's best not to linger.

Fever: bright starlight, and the sails
Flapping against the mast, the ocean
Glass, and the coastline dark,
Irregular, and portentous with volcanoes;
The Great Bear almost upon him, the North Star
Lower than ever, waning as he was waning,

And not that sort of hero, not
Conquistador Aeneas, but a tourist!
Uncoverer of the Maya, John L. Stephens,
Blest after all those beaks and prows and horses.

The Vindication of Jovan Babič

(Bosnia 1915)

Age is a pale bird, film of ice on the sea
Where I do not go, film of ice on the river
That I cross no longer after Sclavonian girls;
Cup, horse, kinsman, and the Sultan, the treasure-giver,
Gone from me now. And that old roan,
Lust, is a wryneck since my name was bandied
Among the Austrian matrons and the traders.
I pass for an old lecher since the pear-tree
Under the peeping Tom broke and betrayed us,
Me and my own house-wench. My neck is sprained
Where the boy fell on it. Now one
Of my own house can glory in collusion
With the butchers of Queen Draga, and the hysterical
Schoolboy of Sarajevo. It is a womanish time
That thinks the boudoir is historical,
Love an event. Ideal assignations
Discharge unnatural chastity in wars
Ideally total; virgins' consummations
Cannot be made except with bombs and sabres
And then are bloody. I foresee a time
When all of art and humane learning labours
To clench all history
In a child's fist at the nipple
Or straddle it with four bare legs in bed
And all in metaphor.
    My brutalities
Maimed less, for they were casual, unconsidered.
A flagging wing outsoars them, and the ice
Stiffens the pulse with a not unmanly shudder.

Bolyai, the Geometer

Arthur Allen, when he lived
In rooms beneath my rooms in Trinity,
Thought he had made a breakthrough that would turn
Mathematics inside out again,

As once geometry was spun around
Because the non-Euclidean emerged
Not out of nature, out of nothing extant
But simply as imaginable. Shade,

A flap of blackness folded back upon
Pillar and pediment that afternoon
Encroached upon the chapel portico
And there a wing whirled, flashing. So, I thought,

This turning inside-out is not so hard:
One looks across Front Square and there it is,
A wing that whirls white undersides, sustained
By what endangers it, the press of air.

And though his torque was different, not in nature,
And though my science is as pure as his,
Knowing no revolution more profound
Than that from black on white to white on black

(As though a shutter shot across the mind
One sees the lately formless as most formal,
The stanza most a unit when
Open at both ends, all transition) still

How pure is mathematics? Not enough
For Farkas Bolyai: 'Not geometry
Is altogether pure. This is a wound
Large and perpetual upon my soul.'

So with poetics: never a revolution
But has its mould. Look, in the overturning
Approaching comber, rolling inside out,
A roof of cream moves back through a mounting wall.

After an Accident

1.

Smashed, and brought up against
Last things like pines'
Steep shadows and the purple
Hole in my darling's head,

I recall as an amulet
Against my shallowness
Uncalculated kindness
So much! Death, in my dream,

Half-length as in a portrait,
Cocks his eye, leads mine
Up a toothbrush ridge of pines
With an amused complicity

At seeing what is so
Beneath us as a mountain
Tower above us when
We have run out of road.

Death is about my age,
Smiling and dark, clean-shaven.
Behind him the valley-floor
Is ledged in a purple light.

Had I not sought the shade
Of what is so
Beneath us as chagrin,
I had not been afraid

Of his mountainous purple light,
Nor should I have run out
Of the soul of gratitude
Before I ran out of death.

2. *Between Dead and Alive*

For you to be thinking how
It was no bad place to lie in,
In this there was nothing morbid;
Nor was it too composed
In me, to think of your dying
As of an emigration.

This century one in five
On that hillside has emigrated,
And this is not melancholy,
Nor the spaciousness disconcerting:
Between the dead and alive
The ratio there is a just one.

And yet I would have sworn
Such thoughts as these were tricks
Of tearful literature;
That thoughts so unresentful
As mine were could not mix
With terror and compunction.

3. *The Heartland*

And so it is clear that this
Heartland has to be painted
In unrepresentative colours;

That the forests under the mountains
Live in an orange light
Without reference to sunset.

How clear it is, and how
Incapable of being
Foreseen or offered as solace,

That remorse without regret
Is a possible state of the soul,
Like grief without resentment.

4. *Windfall*

So Death is what one day
You have run out of, like
Luck or a bank-balance.
In that case, what is
Coming into it like?

Like coming into money!
The death we run out of is
Not the life we run out of;
The death that we may
With luck come into, is.

And without money, life
Is not worth living.
How did you manage
All these years,
Living and not living?

5. *Thanks*

You never did so much
As when you nearly died;
As if you nearly died
That I might show I lived.

That was no more your motive
Than it could have been my choice.
You cannot think I live
Just to give voice!

It was no poet's need you met,
And now survive,
But the need I had as a man
To know myself alive.

You never did so much
As when you nearly died;
You had to nearly die
For me to know I lived.

The Hardness of Light

'Via Portello,' I wrote,
'The fruity garbage-heaps...'
As if someone had read my poems,
Padua eight years later
Is so hot no one sleeps.

But this is a different quarter,
Just off the *autostrada*,
Touched by that wand of transit,
Californian, hopeful...
I grow older, harder.

I wake in the night, to rain.
All the old stench released
On the risen night wind carries
Coolness across the city,
Streaming from west to east.

The equivocal breath of change,
In a clatter of sudden slats
Across the room, disturbs me
More than ever, in new
Motels and blocks of flats.

What is this abomination
When a long hot spell is breaking?
Sour smell of my own relief?
The rankness of cooling-off?
Rottenness of forsaking?

I glare. In that renowned
Hard light of burning skies
Nothing grows durable
With age. It neither solves
Nor even simplifies.

On Not Deserving

Worry hedges my days
Like a roil of thick mist at the edge of a covert
Fringing a tufted meadow. In that field
Monuments of art and sanctity
Arise in turn before
The clouded glass of my eye.
Last year the two churches of St Francis
Were piled up there, at the lowest verge of Assisi.

Autumn Imagined

The shuffle and shudder of Autumn
Are in our love.
Those last thin garments, come
Let's have them off!

Drop them about your knees.
The beech-tree rains its gold.
We are deciduous trees,
And our year grows old.

We cannot procrastinate.
Although we seem to delay
By having children late,
Our Autumn is today.

Indeed, give my body its due,
It read the signs aright
When it trembled at Autumn's hue
On our wedding night.

Hot Hands

'Warm hands, cold heart,' they say; and vice-versa.
    My hands are so hot always
That when they touch your coolness, they immerse
    Hissingly, charred and ablaze.

Folk-wisdom! For such old wives' sullen tales
    If natural law is thwarted,
If a rule of signs, not rule of law, prevails,
    Their sense is not inverted:

That hiss is the first breath I have sharply taken,
    Brought against you. Wrench
The text of the world as they will, they are mistaken.
    I am a brand you quench.

Where Depths are Surfaces

Where depths are surfaces
By the clear Tyrrhenian Sea,
I marvel at life that passes
So clearly over me.

Also I think of him,
The Englishman in me,
Whose skiffs can never skim
That deep, distrusted sea.

His trust is in the plummet.
And I seek equally.
Depths that the lead can come at,
Where all men sway with me.

But boats I would not trust
On the golden skin of the sea
Shadow those waters, thrust
Their ghostly prows at me.

For tides we need not sound through
Flow in the human sea,
Whereas the lead goes down to
Depths, depths endlessly.

Vying

Vying is our trouble;
And a devious vice it is
When we vie in abnegations,
Services, sacrifices.

Not to be devious now
(For perhaps I should not begin
Taking the blame for winning
If this were not how to win),

I assert that such is the case:
I seem to have more resources;
I thrive on enforcing the more
The less naked the force is.

Mutinies, sulks, reprisals
All play into my hand;
To be injured and forgiving
Was one of the roles I planned.

Married to me, you take
The station I command,
As if in a peopled graveyard
Deserted in an upland.

There I, the sexton, battle
Earth that will overturn
Headstones, and rifle tombs,
And spill the tilted urn.

Rodez

Northward I came, and knocked in the coated wall
At the door of a low inn scaled like a urinal
With greenish tiles. The door gave, and I came

Home to the stone north, every wynd and snicket
Known to me wherever the flattened cat
Squirmed home to a hole between housewall and paving.

Known! And in the turns of it, no welcome,
No flattery of the beckoned lighted eye
From a Rose of the rose-brick alleys of Toulouse.

Those more than tinsel garlands, more than masks,
Unfading wreaths of ancient summers, I
Sternly cast off. A stern eye is the graceless

Bulk and bruise that at the steep uphill
Confronts me with its drained-of-colour sandstone
Implacably. The Church. It is Good Friday.

Goodbye to the Middle Ages! Although some
Think that I enter them, those centuries
Of monkish superstition, here I leave them

With their true garlands, and their honest masks,
Every fresh flower cast on the porch and trodden,
Raked by the wind at the Church door on this Friday.

Goodbye to all the centuries. There is
No home in them, much as the dip and turn
Of an honest alley charmingly deceive us.

And yet not quite goodbye. Instead almost
Welcome, I said. Bleak equal centuries
Crowded the porch to be deflowered, crowned.

The North Sea

North Sea, Protestant sea,
I have come to live on your shore
In the low countries of England.
        A shallow gulf north-westward
Into the Isle of Ely
And the Soke of Peterborough
Is one long arm of the cold vexed sea of the North.

Having come to this point, I dare say
That every sea of the world
Has its own ambient meaning:
The Mediterranean, archaic, pagan;
The South Atlantic, the Roman Catholic sea.

But somewhere in mid-America
All of this grows tiresome,
The needles waver and point wildly

And then they settle and point
Somewhere on the ridge of the Andes
And the Rocky Mountains
True to the end of the world.

Pacific is the end of the world,
Pacific, peaceful.

And I do not know whether to fear
More in myself my bent to that end or
The vast polyp rising and beckoning,
Christ, grey-green, deep in the sea off Friesland.

July, 1964

I smell a smell of death.
Roethke, who died last year
with whom I drank in London,
wrote the book I am reading;

a friend, of a firm mind,
has died or is dying now,
a telegram informs me;
the wife of a neighbour died
in three quick months of cancer.

Love and art I practise;
they seem to be worth no more
and no less than they were.
The firm mind practised neither.
It practised charity
vocationally and
yet for the most part truly.
Roethke, who practised both,
was slack in his art by the end.

The practice of an art
is to convert all terms
into the terms of art.
By the end of the third stanza
death is a smell no longer;
it is a problem of style.
A man who ought to know me
wrote in a review
my emotional life was meagre.

The Blank of the Wall

after St-J. Perse

The blank of the wall is over against you; which
Is the conjuration into a circle
Of reveries. The image none the less
Emits its cry. An aftertaste of rich
Fats and sauces furs
The teeth your tongue explores
Inside the uneasy head which you have set
Upon the lived with, the familiar
Upholstery of a greasy chair; and yet
You think how clouds move purely on your island,

The green dawn growing lucid on the breast
Of the mysterious waters. And it is
The sweat of exiled juices and
There on the hearth the snapping spar,
Split from how cheap a crate, secretes
The resinous stands of all of Canada.
The need is lived with, that this answers to.

Out of East Anglia

Pacific: in Russian as
In our language
Peaceful is the word
For that last sea at the edge;
And nearer than the Americas'
Awesome, vertical falls
Into the Western Ocean
The imperceptible, tempting
Declivity, inanition!

Sometimes when all this side
Of England seems to hang
Suspenseful on that slide,
How peace might be is near.

January

Arable acres heave
Mud and a few bare trees
Behind St Michael's
Kirby le Soken, where
The pew I share
Promises the vicinity I leave.

Diatribe and
Denunciation, where
I spend my days,

Populous townships, sink
Into the haze that lowers
Over my neighbours' land.

Resignation, oh winter tree
At peace, at peace...
Read it what way you will,
A wish that fathers. In a field between
The Sokens, Thorpe and Kirby, stands
A bare Epiphany.

Pietà

Snow-white ray
coal-black earth will
swallow now.
The heaven glows
when twilight has
kissed it, but
your white face
which I kiss now does
not. Be still
acacia boughs,
I talk with my
dead one. We speak
softly. Be still.

The sky is blind
with white
cloud behind
the swooping birds. The
garden lies
round us and
birds in the dead
tree's bare
boughs shut
and open themselves. Be
still, or be
your unstill selves,
birds in the tree.

The wind is
grievous to the willow. The
underside of its
leaves as the wind
compels them is
ashen. Bow
never, nor dance
willow. How can
you bear it? My
head goes back on
my neck fighting
the pain off. Willow
in the wind, share it.

I have to learn
how time can be
passed in public
gardens. There my
dead lies idle. Much
bereaved and sitting
under a sunny wall
old women stare
through me. I
come too soon and
yet at last to
fixity, being alone and
with a crone's pastimes.
In memoriam Douglas Brown

Sunburst

The light wheels and comes in
over the seawall
and the bitten turf
that not only wind has scathed but
all this wheeling and flashing, this
sunburst comes across us.

At Holland on Sea
at an angle from here and

some miles distant
a fisherman reels back blinded,
a walker is sliced in two.
The silver disc came at them
edgewise, seconds ago.

Light that robes us, does it?
Limply, as robes do, moulded
to the frame of Nature? It
has no furious virtue?

The God of Details

after Pasternak

Come rain down words as does
The garden its dried-peel, amber,
Distractedly, profusely,
Yet sparsely, and yet sparsely.
No need to gloss the reason
Why thus punctiliously
In madder and in lemon
Leafage precipitates;

Nor who has moistened quills
And gushed across bare staves
Music on to bookshelves
Sluicing through window-slats;
Who got the rug at the door
Pencilled with small craters,
Sackcloth latticed through with
Poignant, italic tremors.

You ask, who stablishes
That August be a power?
To whom no thing is bauble,
Who goes about to staple
Light leaves to the maple,
And since Ecclesiastes
Has never left his station
Working the alabaster?

You ask, who stablishes
That asters taste, and peonies,
Agonies come September?
That the meagre leaf of the broom
From grey of caryatids
Come down upon dank flags of
Infirmaries of the fall?
You ask, who stablishes?

The omnipotent God of details,
The omnipotent God of love,
Whose sexual spark has lit
And fuelled dynasties.
I do not know the riddle
Of the pitch dark past the tomb,
But Life is, as the autumn's
Hush is, a minuteness.

Ezra Pound in Pisa

Excellence is sparse.
I am made of a Japanese mind
Concerning excellence:
However sparred or fierce
The furzy elements,
Let them be but few
And spaciously dispersed,
And excellence appears.

Not beauty. As for beauty,
That is a special thing.
Excellence is what
A man who treads a path
In a prison-yard might string
Together, day by day,
From straws blown in his path
And bits of remembering.

Sun moves, and the shadow moves,
In spare and excellent order;

I too would once repair
Most afternoons to a pierced
Shadow on gravelly ground,
Write at a flaked, green-painted
Table, and scrape my chair
As sun and shade moved round.

Tunstall Forest

Stillness! Down the dripping ride,
    The firebreak avenue
Of Tunstall Forest, at the side
    Of which we sought for you,
You did not come. The soft rain dropped,
    And quiet indeed we found:
No cars but ours, and ours was stopped,
    Rainfall the only sound.

And quiet is a lovely essence;
    Silence is of the tomb,
Austere though happy; but the tense
    Stillness did not come,
The deer did not, although they fed
    Perhaps nearby that day,
The liquid eye and elegant head
    No more than a mile away.

Orford

after Pasternak

With the actual the illusory
With the vegetable growth the granite.

As it might be in Spring on the day of the Annunciation
It is announced to us out of charity
By earth in every fissure of the stone
By a growth of grass from under every wall.

By the thrivings of life and verdure,
By the vestiges of antiquity,
By earth in every minute cranny,
By a growth of grass from under every wall;

By earth in every pockmark of the stone
By grass grown up in the warp of every floorboard;

By fragrant thick convolvulus
Through centuries twined over bushes
Twined over greatness gone
And what is to come of beauty;

By the lilac double-hued,
The purple spray and the white,
The various mixed with the steadfast,
Loose sift over the stronghold.

Where people are kin to the elements.
Elements neighbourly to people,
Earth in every hollow of the stone,
Grass growing in advance of every doorway.

Thanks to Industrial Essex

Thanks to industrial Essex,
I have spun on the greasy axis
Of business and sociometrics;
I have come to know the structures
Of public service
As well as I know the doves
Crop-full in mildewed haycocks.
I know that what they merit
Is not scorn, sometimes scorn
And hatred, but sadness really.

Italic on chalky tussocks,
The devious lovely weasel
Snakes through a privileged annex,
An enclave of directors.

Landscapes of supertax
Record a deathful failure
As clearly as the lack
Of a grand or expansively human
Scale to the buildings of Ilford.

The scale of that deprivation
Goes down in no statistics.

Expecting Silence

Whatever is said to be so
Is so, if the saying is
Of an agreeable strictness.

Unutterable until
That way uttered is
What we have lived through lately.

The confidence with which
A man goes off by himself,
Reconciled to a longish silence,

Is not for married people.
Seeds of calamity rain
On our strangulated partings.

Our forebodings say
Much about who we are,
Nothing about the future.

A Winter Landscape near Ely

It is not life being short,
Death certain, that is making
Those faintly coffee-coloured
Gridiron marks on the snow
Or that row of trees heart-breaking.

What stirs us when a curtain
Of ice-hail dashes the window?
It is the wasteness of space
That a man drives wagons into
Or plants his windbreak in.

Spaces stop time from hurting.
Over verst on verst of Russia
Are lime-tree avenues.

A Death in the West

May's, whose mouth was
Open under the gauze.
She lay like a child in her coffin.
Often in that front parlour,
Excessively peremptory,
She struggled to belie
Her timorous nature.

Her sisters found the funds
She lacked, of confidence
To train her for a trade.
Her profession was children's nurse.
Children of conspicuous parents
Grew up under her care
To figure in divorce-scandals.

She and her sister sat
Plumb on grey sands in Cornwall
One day, the two most planted
And stubborn tubs in Nature.
Vivid in pastel sweaters,
We walked along by the cliffs
Over the eye-bright shingle.

She deluded us after all.
If she could not be forceful,
Could she be stolid? She
Liked to sit on the sands,

Looking at wide wet beaches,
Scud over Cornish seas, and
Bright shirts under the cliff.

If one of her ancient charges
Had come in a beach-wrap, stalking,
His tired eyes fierce with gin
From foreign embassies,
Her eyes had been equipped
By so much seaside watching
To know him for Ulysses.

From the New World

for Paul Russell-Gebbett

Old Glory at halfmast
For Adlai Stevenson
Drooped under PepsiCola
Flashing all night on Lima.

There, smiling and contained
And lawless through
The boardrooms of New Spain
Don Felix passed;

Smiling and contained
And lawless through
The boardrooms of New Spain,
He ushered us, and was

One of us. His son
Is at Downside,
His English flawless and
His manners too.

British is what we are.
Once an imperial nation,
Our hands are clean now, empty.
Cause for congratulation.

Plaintive the airs
With sorrows when, sails set
Against miscegenation,
Our keels leaned in from Europe.

Freight of Atlantic airs
When doxies lined the rail;
Songs of the Cavaliers
Twanged on the tainted gales;

The English fever-ships,
Though hopes re-painted, fetched
Up on the Carolinas
To wailing strings.

Rubber-faced Uncle Sam!
Unhappy Adlai,
Dipping in on the clipper to
The heritable blame,

The melancholy strains
No one alive has lived with:
England's historic guilt,
France's, or Spain's.

'What', said our diplomat,
'Sort of nation is
This that I represent
In South America?' I said:

'A nation of theatre-people,
Purveyors, not creators,
Adaptable cyphers, stylists,
Educators, dandies.'

Rubber-faced Uncle Sam!
Unhappy Adlai,
A name that is of Zion...
British is what I am.

Zion, a park in Utah.
So many available styles!
Heavens, the New is New
Still, to us quizzical monsters!

Stratford on Avon

I look a long way back
To a house near Stratford.
You had come out of our black
Barnsley, a girl, to Oxford.

Beautiful, boys pursued you.
In dusk and the overgrown
Garden I, as you knew,
Watched you sitting alone

On the creosoted stair
To the girls' dormitory.
No one else was there.
You slept on the first storey.

Lanes crept by the riverside.
We had said Goodnight too soon,
Strange to that countryside
Famous under the moon.

And yet within the echo
Of our lame exchanges
No grasses ceased to grow,
No apple pair turned strangers.

And that was the summer of nineteen
Forty, the war still slack.
Twentyfive summers since then.
I look a long way back.

Barnsley, 1966

Wind-claps of soot and snow
Beat on the Railway Hotel's
Tall round-headed window;
I envy loquacious Wales.

Taciturn is the toast
Hereabouts. Were this Wales,
My father had ruled this roost,
Word-spinner, teller of tales.

If he missed his niche
I am glad of it today.
I should not have liked him rich,
Post-prandial, confident, bawdy.

He was rinsed with this town's dirt
For seventy wind-whipped years,
Chapped lips smiling at hurt,
Eyes running with dirty tears.

A Conditioned Air

A wind I know blows dirt
In and out of the town that I was born in,
The same wind blowing the same dirt in and out,
Coal-dirt, grit. No odorous cloud-cleaving
Typhoon of Crusoe grew upon the West
To satisfy your hunger for afflatus,
Masters of the last
Century, attending
A plaint in the mouth of the hearth, a night of
Wind. The wind
Was a draught in the flue of England. I attend
How the electric motor
Gulps and recovers and
The image on the television screen
Contracts and distends like a reptilian eye,
As somewhere the high wind slaps at a power-line
Out in the country. In the howling quick

Of the bud the branches suffer
Retardations much as you did. I,
Before an empty hearth
In an unfocused house,
Behind me the quietly blasting
Hot-air grille, attend
The delicate movements of
Conditioned airs
I learn to love, as small
As that is, and as prompt
In its dispersed and shaking service. My
Storm-window's foggy polythene claps and billows.

Sylvae

Not deerpark, royal chase,
Forest of Dean, of Windsor,
Not Cranborne, Savernake
Nor Sherwood nor that old
Plantation we can call
New, nor be, it is
So old, misunderstood;
But the primordial oak-wood.

This it is our hedgerows
Preserve from the pre-Saxon:
Not the perennial pastures;
Not Hanoverian georgics;
But a prodigious dapple
Of once uninterrupted
Cover we at best
Subvert by calling 'forest'.

Sprung of this cultured landscape
The fiction-makers of
My race have so completely
Made over it escapes
Nowhere from that old love,
Conniving at reversion
I think of Robin Hood,
The flecked man in my blood.

I think how the tractable Nature
Of the cultivator has
Before now, at the hand
Of many a bookish writer,
Burgeoned in garden-crops
By seasons, and he has
Made homage of them for
Patron or paramour.

But I have kept no gardens,
Am of that vanquished sort,
The gatherers, the most
Primitive of woodland cultures;
I have to offer her
To whom I most would make
Offer, no more than nuts,
Berries, and dubious roots.

Amazonian

Riparian origins... did you know
The hammock was an invention
Of Amazonian Indians? Ours
Hangs from a cricket-bat willow
To the hedgerow stump where a wasps' nest sang
Last summer. Out of hands
That could not afford to be feckless it has passed
To us who are
Improvident as primitives. Retted cordage
Rots beaded in
Green light on our overcast garden,
As it might be in Hemingford Abbotts
Beside the sliding Ouse.

Intervals in a Busy Life

'Room for manœuvre,' I say,
'I ask for an undertaking.'
Manœuvring, king-making...

Only when death happens
Do I see the tops of the trees
Out of my attic window,

And they are always there:
They have looked on the death of my friend
And on my father's death.

They are the deathly markers;
And thereby, even when leafless,
Green; ungrudging sources

At which, as at holy springs,
One does not drink
Habitually nor lightly.

Filling the intervals
Without propriety
Itself is reverential.

Iowa

The blanched tree livid behind
The smaller conifer
Looks to be entangled with it.

Dutch elm disease is in town,
Carried by worms from the eastern seaboard
Twelve hundred miles.

Gesticulating down
And around, emaciated,
This is the many-armed,

This is the elephant-headed
Ganesh of good beginnings,
God of the Hindu, gone sick.

Tomorrow, if the night is warmer,
The snow will be gone in patches
From the clay-spoil hillock.

White on white, a white
Framehouse amid the snow
Is a peculiar beauty.

The tree is an ivory colour.
In a white world there are
So many kinds of white.

They leak into black shadows
Draining them blue. I shall be
Sorry when the world goes piebald.

Red on red was a good chequer,
The red man dead in his blood;
And black on black, the weighed bough swinging

In a night of Alabama. White on white
Is a man of my colour, sick,
Falling down in the snow.

Back of Affluence

That time of the early year
When the sun has a head of hair
Crisp but growing out,
When already the long nights have
Stirred away southward, when
The engraver frost still makes
Likenesses of his sister
Snow, but with a nib
That will not hold its point,

Then the Iowan farmer,
His fodder low, looked out
And saw the prairie white.

He threw up a heavy arm,
He stamped in the house at a loss.
His wife rose lame and stiff.
His children snarled like dogs.

Then he came back with the team;
She into her best dress
Wrinkled at waist and shoulder.
No farming, a day on the town!
Rail depot through to horsepond
And lumberyard, one street.
She with a child in arms;
No place to go from the wind.

Some one has said that it
Brutalized. It did,
That poverty. And what she
Could have seen, she had not
The ease of heart to see:
The sun like a Chinese brush
Writing in delicate shadow
'Tree' on a framehouse front;
The handsomely carpentered boards
Fanned across, splayed over
With a serene springing.

Or, Solitude

A farm boy lost in the snow
Rides his good horse, Madrone,
Through Iowan snows for ever
And is called 'alone'.

Because gone from the land
Are the boys who knew it best
Or best expressed it, gone
To Boston or Out West,

And the breed of the horse Madrone,
With its bronco strain, is strange
To the broken sod of Iowa
That used to be its range,

The metaphysicality
Of poetry, how I need it!
And yet it was for years
What I refused to credit.

My Father's Honour

Dim in the glimmering room
Over against my bed...
Astonished awake, I held
My breath to see my dead,
My green-eyed, talkative
Dead father come.

That look he has! A rare one
In a vivacious man.
I grasp at the uncommon
Identifiable look,
Reproach. The charge it levels
Is no unfair one.

Hold to that guise, reproach,
Cat's eyes! Eerily glow,
Green, prominent, liquid;
Level the charge, although
I could not have done other,
And this you know.

Hold there, green eyes! But no,
Upon the nebulous ground
His merciful nature cuts
From shot to genial shot,
Indulgent now, as if
In honour bound.

Rain on South-East England

This place is so much
Mauled, I have to think
Others besides these Dutch
And low green counties drink
The summer rains, before
I hold it in my mind
What a soft rain is for:

To ease, flush through, unbind.
Tightly starred, on the flat
Marred ground once, with a thin
Unambitious mat
I mended England's ruin.
Growth these last years works
My roots into the air;
Aspiring on long stalks,
My blooms digest no fare
Coarser than light. The strain
Of self-enhancement frees:
I take no care for the rain,
Soured soil, and shattered trees.

Pentecost

Up and down stairs of the inner ear,
Its ivory chambers, stray
The stumbling, the moving voices;
The self-communers; of whom
It seems hardly to matter
Whether we say that they are
Not at home in our language
Or they are too much at home.

What faculties we are lacking!
We have eyes to see, and we see
Not, sometimes; ears to hear and
Sometimes we hear. But they have
Faculties without organs;
They see and hear with the thorax,
They are eloquent in pidgin.

Our sons and our daughters shall
Prophesy? That gift of tongues
To the Beat and post-Beat poets,
The illiterate apostles,
Is what, if I should cherish
Much or mourn my lack of
Or ape their stammerings,
I must betray myself.

Winter Landscapes

Danger, danger of dying
Gives life in its shadow such riches.
Once I saw or I dreamed
A sunless and urbanized fenland
One Sunday, and swans flying
Among electric cables.

There are so many of us,
Men and swans, in places
Congested with new dangers.
It hurts that we are mortal
Less there, for we remember
Mortal is what the race is.

Swans in unimpeded
Flight above bare hawthorn
Ask, as a more austere
Occasion, a taste for the sparse
That likes its landscapes Northern,
Serener, and more hurtful.

Behind the North Wind

'the Arctic Ocean was open during glacial stages and its
margins would have been habitable for man'

Envisage it: the Atlantic
Cold and silent, ice-sheets
Drawn to the chin of the land-mass
Far southward, but a buzz
Round the rim of the living Arctic.

I fondled a kitten once
Where a blue lake locked in the hills
Winked like cottagers' delph
Behind a forgotten Front
Of 1942.

Empty the iron hills
And the dirt-road to Murmansk,
A cat's nine lives ago;
A rinsing wind from the west
Blew over the firth from Finland.

Will oceanographers set
The Yenisei on fire?
And though a hyperborean
Thesis is revived,
Will the Ob flow backward?

More than ever I need
Places where nothing happened,
Where history is silent,
No Tartar ponies checked, and
Endurance earns repose.

Pages of an atheist journal,
The 'AntiReligioznik',
Scurried on one bald hill-top;
Even the Front up there
Had never moved in years.

Revulsion

Angry and ashamed at
Having not to look,
I have lived constricted
Among occasions
Of nausea, like this book
That I carefully leave on the train.

My strongest feeling all
My life has been,
I recognize, revulsion
From the obscene;
That more than anything
My life-consuming passion.

That so much more reaction
Than action should have swayed
My life and rhymes
Must be the heaviest charge
That can be brought against
Me, or my times.

Oak Openings

The 'I have' poem
(Have been, seen, done)
Is followed by the 'What about it?' poem.
There is plenty new under the sun,
This poem says, but what's
So new about the new?

It is not as if the attention
Steadily encroaches
Upon the encircling dark;
The circle about the torch is
Moving, it opens new
Glades by obscuring old ones.

Twigs crack under foot, as the tread
Changes. The forge-ahead style
Of our earliest ventures flags;
It becomes, as mile follows mile
Inexhaustibly, an exhausted
Wavering trudge, the explorer's.

New Year Wishes for the English

Beware the ball-point lens:
Lord Thomson and Lord Snowden be
Far from your door.

May the girl with the questionnaire
Meet only the neighbourhood zanies;
May she calibrate obsessions.

May the humanitarian
Blackmail be paid no longer;
Instead may you work a little.

May you have, against the incessant
Rain of the new, the all-new,
Indifference as an umbrella.

May you be quiet, may you
Not be hectored by me,
But left alone for a little.

May you recognize that these
Are wishes for the inception
Of a long recuperation;

That they are not what a poet
Would wish you if he could,
But the most he dares to hope for.

(1966)

Preoccupation's Gift

When all my hours are mine,
I husband them with care;
Pre-empted hours are those
    I have to spare.
Step by step, one
Calculated stage
After another, writing
    A laboured page –
Give me my freedom back
And this is how I live,
Frugally, for lack of
    Anything to give
Short of my freedom. Thrift
Gives nothing it gives up;
But absent-minded pourings
    Brim every cup.

The provocations so
Prodigal, and the response
Parsimony? No,
    No vigilance!

The North Sea, in a Snowstorm

Dark ages, calm and merry
Beside the sea of my boyhood
Sparkled on a Whitby
Of cricketers in August.

Blockhouses of 1940
In the undercliff at Walton,
The Roman Empire dying,
A Count of the Saxon Shore
Far from the sparkling synod,
I walk by a sea that is
A concave opal.

Up from its deep, its submarine, sub-zero
Unimaginable furnace,
Rigour arises where it steams and burns
With a superior cold.

Transparencies, and shivers of running greens!

To Certain English Poets

My dears, don't I know? I esteem you more than you think
    you modest and quietly spoken, you stubborn and
        unpersuaded.
    Your civil dislikes hum over a base that others
    shudder at, as at some infernal cold.
But pits full of smoky flame are sunk in the English Gehenna,
    where suffering souls like ours are bound and planted
    now in the one hot spot, now in another.

The operator is an imagination of Dante
  that plucks us out of the one and plugs us at once in another
  with an obedient pip-pip-pip at the switchboard.
Like you I look with astonished fear and revulsion
  at the gross and bearded, articulate and good-humoured
  Franco-American torso, pinned across
  the plane of human action, twitching and roaring.
Yet a restlessness less than divine comes over us, doesn't it,
    sometimes,
  to string our whole frames, ours also, in scintillant items,
  with an unabashed crackle of intercom and static?
Or will you, contained, still burn with that surly pluck?

Democrats

Four close but several trees, each green, none equal.
They are the glory of this countryside:
Sequestered households of the field and hedge,
Not copses and not spinneys and not groves.

Green and uncertain in the early summer;
Patient endurers down the depth of winter,
Immobile dancers. In these fields the axe
Of the leveller Tarquin trembles, and advances.

Epistle. To Enrique Caracciolo Trejo

(Essex)

A shrunken world
Stares from my pages.
What a pellet the authentic is!
My world of poetry,
Enrique, is not large.
Day by day it is smaller.
These poems that you have
Given me, I might
Have made them English once.

Now they are inessential.
The English that I feel in
Fears the inauthentic
Which invades it on all sides
Mortally. The style may die of it,
Die of the fear of it,
Confounding authenticity with essence.

Death, an authentic subject,
Jaime Sabinès has
Dressed with the yew-trees of funereal trope.
It cannot be his fault
If the English that I feel in
Feels itself too poor
Spirited to plant a single cypress.
It is afraid of showing, at the grave-side,
Its incapacity to venerate
Life, or the going of it. These are deaths,
These qualms and horrors shade the ancestral ground.

Sabinès in another
Poem comes down
To the sound of pigeons on a neighbour's tiles,
A manifest of gladness.
Such a descent on clapping wings the English
Contrives to trust
No longer. My own garden
Crawls with a kind of obese
Pigeon from Belgium; they burst through cracking branches
Like frigate-birds.

Still in infested gardens
The year goes round,
A smiling landscape greets returning Spring.
To see what can be said for it, on what
Secure if shallow ground
Of feeling England stands
Unshaken for
Her measure to be taken
Has taken four bad years
Of my life here. And now
I know the ground:

Humiliation, corporate and private,
Not chastens but chastises
This English and this verse.

I cannot abide the new
Absurdities day by day,
The new adulterations.
I relish your condition,
Expatriate! though it be among
A people whose constricted idiom
Cannot embrace the poets you thought to bring them.

Cold Spring in Essex

Small boy in a black hat walks among streaky shadows
Under my window, and I am at ease this morning.
This day reminds me of Budapest. All over
Europe is the North and Protestantism has conquered.

The Roman Catholic North in the black-oak cabinet of
    Antwerp
Is an irreplaceable grace-note, as at Sawston
The manorial chapel of the Huddlestons for the pilgrims.
'Which of them will make a good death?' my friend in
    Antwerp
Wondered through the plateglass over beer and coffee
Looking to the end.
                    But I am happy this morning,
Looking into my garden, seeing the cold light standing
Oblique to the grey-green tree-trunks and the grasses,
All over my illimitable future.

LOS ANGELES POEMS

To Helen Keller

Yours was the original freak-out: Samuel Beckett's
mutilated prodigies, for whose
sake these last years we bought so many tickets
and read so many books, were hotter news
when your and Anne Sullivan Macy's iron will,
back in the 'twenties, stooped to vaudeville.

One will, two persons...yes, let campus-rebels
account for education at that level,
that give, that take. I wonder if it troubles
our modish masters of sardonic revel
that you, who seemed typecast for it, were not
conscious of Black Comedy in the plot.

You were by force of circumstance, by force
of your afflictions, I suppose, the most
literary person ever was.
No sight nor sound for you was more than a ghost;
and yet because you called each phantom's name,
tame to your paddock chords and colours came.

This too, at this, the mind of our time is appalled.
The Gutenberg era, the era of rhyme, is over.
It's an end to the word-smith now, an end to the Skald,
an end to the erudite, elated rover
threading a fiord of words. Four-letter expletives
are all of that ocean's plankton that still lives.

You, who had not foreseen it, you endured it:
a life that is stripped, stripped down to the naked,
asking what ground it has, what has ensured it.
Your answer was: the language, for whose sake it
seemed worthwhile in Tuscumbia, Alabama,
month after month to grope and croak and stammer.

Christmas Syllabics for a Wife

When I think of you
dying before or
after me, I am
ashamed how little
there is for either
one of us to look
back upon as done
wholly in concert.

We have spent our lives
arming for them. Now
we see they begin
to be over, and
now is it too late
to profit by what
seems to have been a
long preparation?

The certainty that
many have scaped scot-
free or even praised
sets the adrenalin
anger flushing up
through me as often
before, but can we
wait now for justice?

Horace says, Be wise
broach the ripe wine and
carefully decant
it. Now is the time
to measure wishes
by what life has to
give. Not much. So be
from now on greedy.

Idyll

after Giorgio Bassani

As a horn of the high moon veers in clear skies over Main Street
And inflames with a fugitive heat the sea-green pavements,
Out of the town cloaked horsemen ride across sleep
On lukewarm roads that founder halfway in hayfields.

Quiet the night, and clear, and from the moist
Low meadows comes up lightly a milk that billows
In gusts of the wind, and a sound comes of distant trains
Aimed, blindly anxious, at packed market-places.

But you, a god who smiles at the gain and the loss,
Bless your black adepts all the way with spells,
All the good way past fields whose green is here!

The woman who keeps the inn, unbar her window,
Call down to the door the maids from their odorous beds,
Shine in the wine, light rapturous eyes in the shadows!

Brantôme

J'ai eu pitié des autres.
Pas assez.
                    (The Pisan Cantos)

Burly, provincial France,
Your rarefied, severe
Renaissance is
Material and four-square
Here, in a stout arrangement
Of water, stone and grass
Where the unlettered can
Come and read in the clear
Air of a weeping April
Thus rendered, the austere
Theorems of the jurist
Or fierce geometer.

I walk your foreign turf.
My native tongue was leased
Fawningly, long ago,
To the too long appeased
Long pitied vulgar. I
Speak to myself in French,
Thinking myself in a place
Where a lettered man's remorse
For intellectual pride
And ruthlessness of the mind
May be accepted, not
Pounced on and misapplied.

Looking out from Ferrara

after Giorgio Bassani

It needs there to be no one
Left in the piazza,
Only a boy on his own,
For the thunderhead that shelves
Its far slateblue over small
Lit farms in the plain, to be dealt with
Smilingly; nor is there
Need of more than his hand
Sketching a smudged goodbye,
Before the dark tower edges
Clear of the pinkish mild
Immensity of acres,
Before there be spread abroad
About the roads the darkling
Shade of an old and humble
Townland of that locale,
With, passing across it, the long
Wind of the Spring that will make
Promises some time soon
In whispers, and the drowse
Of boyhood be borne off the meadows
Freighted as high as the evening,
Warm in the wagons the dusky
Grasses, the acrid poppies.

An Oriental Visitor

To a bell in Lincoln Cathedral
A butterfly out of the fens
Of Lindsey has ascended
Up labouring steeps of air
And there, exhausted, it sleeps
Furrily clinging. In
Lincolnshire are no
Fireflies, more's the pity!

Had one of them climbed there, what
Delirious ringing
Over the railway yards
And the level-crossing
And the factories making tractors,
And the minicars at the mini-
Intersections! What
Swing of a coppery rim
To carve off episodes!

To the thunderhead it calls
'Avanti!' – the long high narrow
Pole-pennant carried in rain-squalls.

The spearmen are gone. And for those
With tufted lances, only
The tossing pampas-grass.

The tomb of Atsumori, and
Not one cherry-tree
To stand against it!

When she bites at the acrid
Persimmons of Japan,
It is that from the oldest
Wooden building in the world
A bell begins to clang.

Cloud-treader, breather of mist...
A skylark goes up
Into its element, singing.

And as for singing, the
School of the skylark and
The school of the frog dispute.

Meanwhile the one
Pure ring in the world, the moon,
And the numberless stars dispute
The dark green of the heavens.

And the clouds pile
White canvas southward
From where we stand,

And the artery of the town is
A slow-flowing stream between alders,
Though quartering wires criss-cross it.

And though the wintry river
Receives the abandoned dog's
Stiffening cadaver,

Moon-rise at evening; and
An ancient plum-tree drops
This year's first blossom on
A foreign girl's guitar.

'Abbeyforde'

Thirty years unremembered,
Monkey-faced black-bead-silken
Great-aunt I sat across from,
Gaping and apprehensive,
The thought of you suddenly fits.
Across great distances
Clement time brings in its
Amnesties, Aunt Em.

'Abbeyforde': the name
Decyphered stood for Ford
Abbey, in Somerset. There
Your brother's sweetheart Nell,

My grandmother, drew him to her,
Whom later he pitchforked North.
Such dissolutions, Em!
Such fatal distances!

'Keep still feast for ever...'
A glow comes up off the page
In which I read of a paschal
Feast of the diaspora
In Italy, in a bad
Time for the Jews, and it is
As if in that tender and sad
Light your face were illumined.

England

1.

Eight hours between us, eight
hours by the clock between us,
eleven hours flying time.

Chill and slack as you are,
the torrid is what you affect;
the slipway of greasy Anne
at Shottery launched more keels,
you think, than cleanly Helen.
Although this has to be proved.

A staring world that Engels
never underwrote:
as, of the '45 –
'some few thousand serfs
variously bludgeoned
and misled into fighting
against a few thousand proles.'
The March of the '45...
Confound it, the theme exacted
a certain elevation!

And if there is corruption
in every detail
(notably, of language)
and bed is a display-case
(coloured lights come on:
psychedelic), how
long can the civil servant
at the Ministry of Pensions
remain, as a rule, uncorrupted?

*

Heroic fuzz has been
your unparliamentary choice
all over again, I notice.
Hotspur is playing John Ball
all over again. A neutral
tone was (Note the passive
voice) preferred by no one
really, no one at all.

Entranced, my thoughts of you
climb no mountains, enter
no bowels but their track
is outward always and over
a curve of the earth, the night's
selva oscura approaching
and fleeting away beneath me
as I fly over the flattened
Pole or by some other
Great Circle route to London.

History entrances
as on the Great North Road
at Newark for instance, those
bowels we have entered;
but it is less than
visionary, whether
we enter the Edwardian boom
in Balham or Palmer's Green
about the turn of the last
century, or contend for
where Queen Eleanor slept.

Lower to lower-middle
to middle, or else downwards...
The drift of any English
conversation or memoir
is less than continental.
I dwell, intensely dwell
on my flying shadow
over the Canadian barrens,
and come to nothing else:
land migrates, and ice,
and Eskimo, and from
his social station my
father in an early
narrative by Wells.

*

Historical time is not
the dimension of these reproaches.
Unkindness is the reproach.
An emptied rectitude
in his cockaded topee
as Governor of the Islands;
a cause of much uncertain
hilarity in 'the Loyals',
in the disloyals, of hatred.
Faithful, knowing the first,
he will not prefer the second.
Unkindness is the reproach.

Sharp? Yes, you are sharp.
The heavy footfall, each
stretch, each stoop an achievement.
Suddenly, disportings!
The younger trees encircle
the thick bole's blossoming autumn.
In the polemical light
between the grey trunks, each
mushy core upheld
still by its cortical
armature of sunlight,
curved knives are out and take it.

I know a man who knows you
so well, so inside-out,
he is appalled by the knowledge;
you must not be seen to be
dishonoured, he thinks, and so he
lowers the threshold of honour;
for your sake he will revise
the entire inheritance downwards.

You are more lovely and
more temperate than you take
any pride in supposing.

Beknighted actors, youth
in tall hats, trailing feathers,
society a congeries of roles...
Napoleon was right:
a nation of purveyors.
Now we purvey ourselves.

The amused blade: 'Talk of the gods...
you have seen them?'
                    'I have not seen them.'

                    *

                    2.

And this is a poem not about you
but FOR you, for
your delectation, lady;

and turning for now on certain
characters (not heroes,
half my friends are whelmed
in deeper gulphs) who are
dislikeable: Scots on the make
who gave their names to forts
on the Coppermine River or
headlands in Arctic seas.
Donald Smith of Forres
finished up Lord Strathcona
(strath of the coffee-machine?

Glen of Conan); and
the Bonaparte of Lachine
(Cathay in French), the bastard
able diminutive George
Simpson was later Sir George,
a small inflexible pin
on which the unwieldy engine
of the Hudson's Bay Company turned,
having eaten his words and worse
for the Proprietors' sakes.

A holy terror. What
a bastard from Loch Broom,
Ross-shire; caught up on McLoughlin
20 days start from York
at River la Biche
July the 26th,
1824
at 7 in the morning. 'Shameful
mismanagement' (forks of Spokane)...
'scene of the most wasteful
extravagance...high time...
ample Field for reform...'
'Having performed the voyage
from Hudson's Bay across
to the Northern Pacific Ocean
in 84 days, thereby
gaining 20 days
on any Craft that ever
preceded us.' What a bastard!

Fascist, we have to face it.
No, but I mean, precisely;
not the mere four-letter
objurgation but
a caribou at that
stage of the class-migration.

Nothing to pay, said his kinsman
Thomas, the explorer,
contemptuously sordid,

explaining why distance was
held of little account
'in the North American wilds',
who paid, paid with his blood
for driving his *voyageurs*
cruelly over distance.

George has been blamed for that
implausibly, but still
it gives his quality as
it was discerned. He was thought
ready at need to kill
his kindred if they should
thwart the Company's will.

Or as J.H. Lefroy described him
in 1843:
'the toughest looking old
fellow I ever saw;
on the Egyptian model,
height two diameters or
one of those short square massy
pillars in a country church.'

(Lefroy, an Army man:
Victorian rectitude.
Governor of Tasmania
later, with the cockaded
topee and full-dress blues.)

Prizeman of Aberdeen
University, Thomas
Simpson had pretensions:
'The practice of mothers casting
away their female children,
common in Madagascar,
Hindostan, China, and other
countries more blest by nature
than the Mackenzie River...';
and sends us to read in Gibbon,
being immune however
from irony. The candid

inquirer, says Thomas, will
also do well to reflect...
On what? On there being never
again enough space for our children?
Or are these deeper gulphs
than any with boats or sledges
plumbed by the Romantic
admirer of 'dear Sir Walter',
in 1838
on Great Bear Lake
reading Gibbon and Hume,
Robertson, Shakespeare, Smollett,
Plutarch and dear Sir Walter?

This is the country we fly
over, over the Pole
from Los Angeles to London
or Leningrad. This is where
the Hare Indian squaw or whatever
co-ed from Oregon in
Haight-Ashbury dumps her baby.

Yes, but the driving, the king-
pin, does it have to be Lenin
on whom the unwieldy engine
turns? Is there no arranging
for Thomas Simpson, though
young and vaporous (he
was dead at 32)
to act, but through committee?

driving his crews past Boat
Extreme, Point Turnagain,
and Franklin's farthest?

*

3.

The professor is emphatic
when we speak of 'the last eccentrics.'
Bluff stuff. 'Plenty about still!'
He's working at it.

Or there's the unco' guid with
a brutal difference. 'My
father was in the Asquith
tradition, and pro-Boer.
Which is a pity because
                    I wish they'd killed the lot'.
Scotswoman on the make
at 70 plus, where the make
now is, with the teen-age newsmen:
'The qualities she most
values are curiosity,
courage and kindness.' KINDNESS!
Tergiversations of the Left.

The bluff stuff. Double bluff when
back from the Dardanelles
with lead in your lung, Ted Hughes
runs you for a long
still running season, rats
behind the industrial arras
of Mexborough, the pasteboard
Barnsley of grime and phlegm
hawked up, thrillingly mined with
rats and stoical killers.
The bluff stuff. Double bluff.
Brutal manners, brutal
simplifications as
we drag it all down.

Twenty years ago
the gloaming Hamoaze
and the Fal above Penryn
harboured the mothball fleet.
And that seems like the best
time, the point of rest,
an entr'acte of exhaustion
before the impudent flourish
of kettledrum and cornet.
Now some one has said it at last:
Defection! The renegade rats
on a ship not sinking however

but sold downriver to Long Beach,
a floating stage off Long Beach
for What the Butler Saw.

'Display,' said Lawrence, 'of
nothingness. Still, display.
Display! Display! Display!'
Nothing is left of the play
but the character-parts, the charade.

... children's voices singing
rou-cou under the drum
of language where the dung-fed
pigeon rhymes with love...
When I read the British
contemporaries I
admire, I am abashed
by the levelness of their tone.
They are saying how all children
are, whenever they are
flustered, unkind, however
mild and soaring their voices
under the drum. I have
a reading knowledge of English.

Et ô ces voix d'enfants...
those children were as little
children like my own
as doves, doves, are like pigeons!
The words of this age are spoken
from and on a stage.
The speakers are as little
children like my own...

Curtain. *Coup de théâtre!*

The stage however is larger
than a floating pier off Long Beach.
It is larger than any one can
occupy. Language envelopes.
It forestalls us always.

Connie Chatterley lives,
or did two years ago.
She asks herself (and gives
an irritated *moue*):
In this extravagant scene
of towering Queens and Queers,
just what is a girl to do?
Or who has whom by the ears
now nothing is overheard?
And what is there left to be seen
by Tom the butler now
we couple like dogs in the yard?

Display! Display! Display!

                    *

                    4.

England: a Rosciad.
A poem about or for
a superannuated
England, sapped and distracted
by vying rhetorics and
impeccably evenly-toned
social comedies and
Swadlincote, 'so ugly
it made you laugh';
                    and for
Geoff Bond, who came from Sheffield
who died the other day
at 48 and was
ironically bewildered.

(On a Sunday morning he died,
of a pain in his chest he died
within the hour, who had
lowered the threshold of honour
'Why *shouldn't* they swing the lead?' –
to save your honour, England.)

Stromness in Orkney, no,
never; Lyness I knew
in 1942,

PQ 17 assembling,
the famous fated convoy.
And I was in the old
'Iron Duke', Beatty's flagship
bottomed in concrete, anchored
for good in Scapa Flow;
and never knew, no more
than Stripey hauled back drunk
from runs ashore, whatever
Athabascan sighs
circle like gulls about
that catchment of recruits
for the traditional routes
through the Canadian wilds:
Knee Lake, Hayes River,
                              Lost
(the historians cannot be trusted)
that long Scandinavian saga.
Sinclairs were of Stromness
or of Pomona; William
Sinclair died at York
Factory, 1818.

In 1831
'Robertson brought his bit
of Brown with him
to the Settlement this spring...'
That is to say, his squaw.
And that was Governor Simpson,
got Betsy Sinclair with child,
whose mother had been a Swampy
Cree. The permafrost
spins out a skein of wings
that sting to a sexy heat;
but not Sir Alexander
Mackenzie, whose
buffaloes were attended
by their young, whose elks
would soon exhibit the same
'enlivening circumstance',
who saw Peace River as

'this theatre of nature.'
This is what we pay for:
the language that forestalled them.

The bronze that the poet, naming
his moribund friends, lays claim to
is harder to believe in
now than the Christian heaven.

*

5.

Lay-er of the ocean-cables
from Hampshire, the Anglo-Cuban,
the Anglo-Brazilian, Anglo-
Argentine, none of us young,
in a Manxman's ship on the slant
through the South Atlantic to 'home',
Our Bonny was over the ocean
We sang, not one of us Scottish.

Henry Mackenzie's Athens
of the North... My English father's
breeks and glengarry, his
Forth and Holyrood Palace,
Castle and Prince's Street
and Portobello since
1915! Arthur's
Seat swirled in a reek
of sentiment, and along
wynds of his conversation
a Burns's turbid feeling
eddied, a Carlyle's
blurred at the edge.
                    Thom Gunn
played in the overgrown
gardens of Hampstead when
already I wrote a letter
(unpublished) to *Time & Tide*
enthusiastic for
Mihajlovič, that Serb,
Bonny already over
the edge.

Browning, Millais,
Huxley, Arnold, Spencer
on the occasion of
Victoria's jubilee had
no tickets for the Abbey;
an eminent actor had,
Thomas Hardy says,
25 tickets sent him.

Shortbread tartans, a voice
for the voiceless and lachrymose English,
our kings implausibly kilted,
we all came out of the author
of *Waverley*. 'Sir Walter
Scott is no more,' wrote George
Simpson, who had not envisaged
a teen-age culture. 'Our
universally admired,
respected fellow-
countryman is gone.'
Gone, gone as the combo
starts in digging the beat
and the girls from the nearest College
of Further Education
spread their excited thighs.

And there shall be no more cakes
nor choruses nor Drambuie
under the Southern Cross.

Envoi

The plane makes travel nothing,
Ann Stanford says, not I.
Thank God it's second nature
Nowadays to fly.
Thank God that 'aviator'
Is now a queer old word,
And every passenger watches
As calmly as a bird,
Seeing the pioneer
Has played his grease-paint role,

Los Angeles to Moscow
By Fairbanks and the Pole.
Thank God to be alive,
Now we can look and learn
Geography through the eye,
And see the cosmos turn
Or the Mackenzie's fingers
Hook out on either hand
To pluck away a mountain
And pucker the anxious land.
Thank God those devil-masks
Of goggles and flaps are gone,
Gone with Hubert Wilkins
And Amy Mollison.
Thank God the histrionic
Temperament must seek
Some other job than flying
To London twice a week.
And we? We can look down
And see, or think we see,
The eider's shank shed feathers
Over the Barents Sea,
And a bewildered freighter
Bound out of Bergen crack
Under the pressure of ice,
Ribs fast-gripped to the smoke-stack.
When in all points like the North,
Lady, unmarked I arise
Across the unwinking ice,
Swilling the seals' blind eyes
With the dome of midnight, think:
I am a rimed unbudging
Mast surveyed by winter;
A sea-mark, yours at last.

Certainly air comes near it;
The idea of air does come
Near to whatever might
Now assuage the spirit.
Air, not the conquest of air
But air, a dimension we have
Polluted of course but that was
Assured by our going there.

(We smell, and leave smells behind us
And poisons, but what do we think
We are, that we should resent
Trailing our noisome remainders?)
Air, the musical crystal . . .
Look, we are buoyed upon it!
As if the Scottish down
Should steer back to the thistle,
Or clouds of pollen come
Intently homing in on
Indigenous British Sea
Starwort or Michaelmas Daisy.

Emigrant, to the Receding Shore

for the shade of Herbert Read

The weather of living in an island
That is not an island in the ocean
Crackles in the hallway. What is salt
And ancient in us dries
To an inland heat. The Atlantic
Is a pond sunk in a garden,
A concrete mole has sealed the Aleutian vents
Browned already; only beside New Zealand
Perhaps do sobs refresh
A walled-up bind of waters.

Alfred in Athelney, Hereward in the Isle
Of Ely, learn to go mounted.

Tooling through second-growth Sherwood
In an Armstrong-Siddeley tourer,
Percheron of the 'twenties,
My grandfather unmeaning
Anything but well
Discharged his quiverful:
Aridity, and levels.

The anti-cyclone regions
Of population pressure,
Respondent to the pulse of
Asia, Arabia, Kansas,
Send out their motorized
Hordes, the freely breeding.

And the Age of Chivalry prinks
Pygmy-size to my daughter's
Gymkhana, though the Godolphin
Arabian has invaded
The forested, painfully cleared
Lands of the Clydesdale, the Suffolk
And the Shire horse, the old black English.
The great trees sail the oceans,
Spill acorns on Pitcairn Island.
And all of this is over.

The Break

after Pasternak

Break it off? Listen! we have left a jagged edge,
The whole place is infected.
Sad like this, one might as well be a leper.

Angel, my angel
Of double-talk, don't pretend:
Nobody dies of it. More like
A sort of eczema of the heart, a skin sore as
Your present at parting. What was that for? Why
Unconscionably do you
Kiss as the drops of rain do, and as time
Laughingly kills, for the lot of us, here, before us?

I am so ashamed, it is a weight upon me!
I know, I know, I tell myself, this break
(I made it too soon) it is tangled with illusory hopes.
I was man enough one day, nearly; except I was mixed
With lips and the hollows of your temples and
Eyes, cheeks, shoulders, the palms of your hands.

If I had only, then,
With the whistle of a strophe,
The sign that it makes, and the cry of it, and
That constant thing, my needing you, that young thing, had I only
Thrown in all these, they asked only to be committed,
I might have beaten you out of it there and then.
Such a disgrace to me as you are!

*

Take and block me, see if you cannot. Come
                    move in upon me, clamp
Down on this bout of my pain
            that crepitates today
                    like mercury in Torricelli's tube.
Move in, move in – warm to it, come, harder!

*

I want to weave together
This choppy welter:
Chill elbows and the magisterial, satin,
Slack palms of your hands, my lady...
Bear down on them, arranger
Of regattas! Fast, and take them!
Masts in the ancient forests
In this furious follow give voice,
Fast-gorged with hallooing echoes
In Calydon, where Atalanta
Hounded like a fallow deer
The oblivious Actaeon gladeward;
Where in the illimitable
Blues there was a loving
That whistled in the ears of horses;
A kissing, the insistent
Ululation of the hunt;
And a caress, the trolling of the horn
To the crackle of the trees, of hooves and talons!

You thought you could count on distress, with her distended
Pupils, and tears, to be invincible?
In the Mass the murals were going to flake from the vault,
Jolted by some Horatio's lips performing?

188

This is a drag.
A flagellant is wanting the whip.
Your weeping capes, they might have clawed me home.

                              *

Amiable, moderate, my own, oh just as, just as at night,
                    in mid-passage by air from Bergen to the Pole,
Drifts, lofted and soft, the down
                    from the eider's shank lapping like snow,
I swear, my temperate friend, I swear I am nothing loath
When I say to you, 'Forget and fall asleep, my lovely.'

When like the ribs, fast-gripped to the very smoke-stack
                              of a lost barque out of Norway,
Her rimed unbudging masts surveyed by winter,
I rise before your boreal eyes
With jokey talk of 'Sleep, be comforted,'
All in good time, my dear, it will scab over.
                              Be calm then, and no tears.

When in all points like the North
                              past the ultimate habitations,
Unmarked across the Arctic and unwinking ice
With the dome of midnight swilling the seals' blind eyes
I speak up,
          do not rub them. Sleep, forget:
                              It is a nonsense really.

                              *

Night falls when your head nods.
Everything lies down 'under thy sovran shoulders.'
Switch off the world's light. We have forced the isthmus,

Hand-spanned it, not in flakings! This will do:
The barque in the ice is fixed, the bright privation grips.

Pilate

The chief of the civil administration
                    of the occupying power reflects
in the forty-five minutes he allows himself each morning
over a cigarette for the world to
                    re-achieve its third dimension daily
(Saving shadows and memories
                    vine on his nerves' snapped trellis):

'Between the judicial and
                    the nervously judicious
the best of Rome bleeds
                    into the sands of Judaea.'

The best? Ho-hum. The keeping up of standards
(The right ones, Roman), how it sustained him once!

The harm it does him,
                    the practice of severity
which someone has to do, he
                    knows. He knows it. He is bad at it
in his own estimation, but
some one has to and
                    whether in good faith
is no problem:
                    You keep yourself busy,
too many cases in too little time and such
scruple as there is time for.

Aggressive-pusillanimous, the harm it
did him, and perhaps it does
                    any one is known to him, wherein
virtue perhaps. He has
nothing to show to be proud of
                    from his H.Q. years but rare
acts of intellectual
                    brutality: 'This is no good...'
'No, I will not...'
                    His
skills were not of that order
                    but being of no account
until perverted, they

            patiently were perverted:
skills to the end of inspiring
emulation, that
            ingenious artifice
called 'leadership' (and what
an orator he might have been, a
poet even) were
            perverted to other ends,
to the end of sitting in judgement.

It is the lion of Judah is all claws.
Caiaphas has the style of the officer-class.

Skills to the end of finding
out short-circuited
            in finding fault, he
knows. He knows it. He is bad at it.

But if it is all he finds with
certainty? The *pax*
Romana is worth something. His
            wish to be lenient mimes
a charity he dare not
            not respect but knows he
cannot profess.
            He does not
in any event perceive
that for these responsible scruples
            the *soi-disant* King of the Jews
has very much more forbearance
than His accusers.

Trevenen

1.

His Return (Christmas, 1780)

Winds from Cook's Strait cannot blow
Hard enough to lift the snow
Already comfortably deep
Where Roseveare and Treyarnon sleep;

Knit to the centre from the far
Fastness of their peninsula,
The Cornish dream that distance can
Deliver their young gentleman
Unaltered to his mother's arms,
To be in rectories and farms,
Assembly-rooms and markets, shown
As the great Cook's and yet their own.
     Camborne's as certain as St James
That vocabulary tames
The most outlandish latitude;
That, at a pinch, to speak of rude
Hardihood will meet the case
And teach a Bligh to know his place;
And 'gallant' and 'ingenious' will
Confine their irrepressible
Midshipman who murders sleep,
Sprung from the London coach to heap
His hero-worship of the dead
Hero on each doting head.
     It would be years before he knew
Himself what it had brought him to;
What it had meant, his profiting
By the good offices of King
And Bligh, the mote-dance in the air
Of their vacated cabins where
Sea-glitters pulsed above his head
Bent to his books. And loving dread
Of his commander's furies taught
Lessons of another sort
If he could trust to having seen
How far from rational and serene
Command might be. When, at the oar
Under Cook's marginally more
Indulgent but still beetling eye,
He clawed a cutter round the high
Northwestern overhang, it meant
The profile of a continent.
So much he knew, and knew with pride;
And yet he was not satisfied,
Not now, nor later. But for now
He chatters to his mother how
Captain King he can instate

As the dead Cook's surrogate:
King, with his connections; King
In Ireland now and finishing
The narrative of the fatal cruise
(Awaited, though no longer news);
King, and his kindness (Bligh, the spurned,
Unconnected patron, burned
With a jealousy that seared
King's account, when it appeared,
With marginalia...); King, whose eyes
Smiled on skill and enterprise
Such as young Trevenen knew
He could boast, and ardour too;
Sweet James King, whom more than one
Hawaiian wanted for a son;
King, then (and so the plaudits end)
At once a mentor and a friend,
Rare composite of gall and balm,
Skilful to command and charm.

    Thus, mixed with talk of azimuth
And quadrant, to confound Redruth,
Trevenen, merrily enough,
Talks of how it merits love,
Some men's authority; and some
Clerical auditors keep mum,
Shocked to know how near they come
To greeting (so enthralled they are)
With an impious 'huzzah'
Such a sublime condition as
They've pressed on their parishioners
As more than human. 'Well, but no,'
They tell themselves, 'the boy don't know
How near he grazes Gospel-truth.
Brave spirit of ingenuous youth!'
And so they huff and puff it home
With (to their wives) 'Come, madam, come!'
Their wives and daughters half aware
Dear Papa has an absent air.

    It troubles him, as well it might,
To see in such resplendent light
Mortal redeemers crowd upon
A stage that should be cleared for One,
That One, Divine. There was some doubt

Whether Cook had been devout;
Though as to that one could not feel
Happy with excess of zeal,
Remembering saintly Wesley whose
Vexatiousness had emptied pews
Down all the stolid Duchy, packed
Gwennap Pit, and loosed in fact
Who knew what furies in deluded
Tin-mine Messiahs? So he brooded,
The honest rector. As for that,
He thought, there's worse to wonder at:
Wrong principles inflame and spread
When they aureole a head
Rank has exalted more than those
Who merely by their talents rose.
Thus, nothing's more alarming than
That too warm Christian gentleman,
Lord George Gordon, the inspired
And loved authority that fired
Prison and church, and did not spare
Lord Mansfield's house in Bloomsbury Square . . .
'Bah!' he thought, 'what has all this
To do with young men's loyalties?'

2.

Life and Contacts (1784-7)

The poet Crabbe, with whom he shared
Burke as patron, never cared
(It appears) to throw a frame
Round the poems that made his fame.
There, as if through window-glass,
Men like James Trevenen pass
Plain and unflattered. Never mind
Asking what poetic kind
Crabbe's tales belong to; they escape
Any predetermined shape,
Comic, heroic, or whatever.
Pointing morals was, however,
Crabbe's substitute. Subtitled 'Or
Hero-worship', would a more
Rationally pleasing piece,

With less of oddity and caprice
In the conduct of it, come
Of this that we're embarked upon?
Hardly: morals underlined
Outrage our taste. Besides, my mind
Is far from made up in this case
About what moral we should trace
In a story that is more
Painful than I've prepared you for.
– First, the untimely death of King.
His malady was lingering,
And yet it did not take very long
Once it attacked the second lung.
Then, the death of brother Matt
At twenty-three, beleaguered at
Okehampton in the inn, who trolled,
'Unlike the ladies of the old
Times', his song; 'their hue unfaded
That needed no calash to shade it...'
The light young tenor 'of the old
Times, the old ancient ladies' told,
Echoing in a brother's head
Cracked gaiety, the singer dead.
        A man, thus severally bereaved,
Labours not to be deceived
By smiling seas of Life, nor Art's
Flattering pledge to furnish charts.
And no such suave commitment mars
Crabbe, the realist *sans phrase*...
Perhaps had Johnson lived, whose pen
Tinkered with *The Village*, then
Some one had upheld the claims
Of spectacles defined by frames,
Or songs like Matthew's, set to airs
Traditional at country fairs;
But Johnson died, unwept by most,
And left, to rule the sprawling roost,
Crabbe's earnest, just, unfocussed page
As prolix model to an age
Which, fed on ornament, would brook
Pindaric Odes to Captain Cook
And, stretched on Ossian, did not shirk
Orations paced by Fox and Burke:

Splendid, sublime and fervent, strong
In argument, but long, but long.
    Apart from that, it can be shown
To have been an age much like our own;
As lax, as vulgar, as confused;
Its freedoms just as much abused;
Where tattle stole a hero's thunder,
His death a thrill, and nine days' wonder;
Where personalities were made,
And makers of them plied a trade
Profitable and esteemed;
Where that which was and that which seemed
Were priced the same; where men were duped
And knew they were, and felt recouped
By being town-talk for a day,
Their Gothic follies on display;
Where (and here the parallel
Comes home, I hope, and hurts as well)
Few things met with such success
As indignant righteousness.
    Burke's the paradigm of this,
Hissing at enormities
In India, at Westminster-hall
(Holy debauch, a free-for-all);
A man of principle, not able
(Like Fox, who had the gaming-table
To share his heart with politics)
To guard against the squalid tricks
That Tender Conscience and Just Rage
Play, when on a public stage;
Not keeping, in his fevered heart,
Passion and Principle apart;
But purchasing his never too
Much honoured sense of what was due
To private merit and indeed
Domestic virtue, by a need
To compensate for his serene
Privacies by public spleen...
    To King, the friend of Irish friends,
Burke gives a bed, and Jane Burke tends
His hopeless case. And King's release
Comes in that same year, in Nice,
Whither Trevenen had, with one

196   POEMS OF THE 1960s

Other, conveyed him, to the sun.
    The Burkes had sent him; and he rode
Back to them, slowly, overshadowed
Thenceforward, always, by a sense
Of human life's inconsequence.
    No man more worthy of his trust,
It might be thought – nor, if he must
Still worship, of his worship – than
The great, good Anglo-Irishman,
Edmund Burke. Secure within
That circle, guest of Inchiquin
At Cliefden, or else entertained
At Gregories itself, he gained
Dubious information how
Iniquitous were Pitt and Howe;
How unregarded was the merit
Of Cook, of King; how to inherit
Their mantle meant he must not hope
For advancement of much scope.
At other times the conversation
Was a liberal education
In men and manners; how Lord George
Gordon, once again at large
(Though, some years before, expelled
From this circle) was impelled
By honour when for the disbanded
Mariners he had demanded,
The year before, some action such
As could have shipped them for the Dutch;
How Cowper, in *The Task*, confessed
To remaining unimpressed
By the reasons given for
Incursions on Tahiti's shore;
How fractious Barry must be borne with,
Painting lineaments of myth
For all his tantrums, the antique
Burning his style down to the Greek;
How Nollekens had little sense
Of decency, yet could dispense
With it, to mould a *busto*; how
Cagliostro made his bow;
How civil good Sir Joshua was,
And Admiral Saunders; how, across

A field from where they sat, was found
The plot of venerable ground
Where slippery Waller lay; and how
Illiberal was Pitt, was Howe...
    Small wonder if his head was turned,
If a renewed resentment burned
In him to sell his rusting sword
Wherever sovereigns could afford
Ensigns announcing to the gale
Citizens of the world in sail.
Bligh gets the *Bounty*, and not he;
He's pledged himself to Muscovy.

3.

His End (The Battle of Viborg, 21 June 1790)

Long, splendid shadows! Cornwall, lit
Bronze in the evening, levels it
Off, and pays all; the yea or nay
Of switched allegiance, as the day
Dies on the old church-tower, seems
A dilemma of our dreams
Which, however urgent once,
Awake we need not countenance.
The gilding beams that reconcile
This antique issue, can for mile
On cloud-racked mile slant on, to reach
Amber on a Baltic beach...
Apollonian, reconciling
Art, that is drenched in tears, yet smiling!
Persuading us to think all's one,
Lit by a declining sun.
    Not for George Crabbe! His it is
To give untinged veracities;
And, though it's Christian, this indeed
Our baffled heroes seem to need,
Moving to their wasteful ends,
Betrayed by principles and friends –

        Cold and pain in the breast,
        Fatigue drives him to rest.
        Rising, 'to open a new

Source of comfort to you'
(Writing to his wife
The last night of his life),
Captain Trevenen, sick,
Wears on no other tack,
Aware man's born to err,
Inclined to bear and forbear.
Pretence to more is vain.
Chastened have they been.
Hope was the tempter, hope.
Ambition has its scope
(Vast: the world's esteem);
Hope is a sickly dream.
And seeking, while they live,
Happiness positive
Is sinful. Virtue alone –
This they have always known –
Is happiness below.
Therefore, she is to know,
Whatever is, is right.
That solid, serious light
Shall reconcile her to
Candidacy below
For where his sails are furled,
Far from fame and the world.

Camborne's rector would have seen
Comfort in the ghastly scene,
There in the British burial-ground
In summery Kronstadt, had he found
His son so firm, and yet so meek.
So truly Christian, truly bleak
The sentiments a man should speak,
Meeting his Maker! In our eyes
A man we cannot recognize
As Burke's or King's accomplished friend,
Cowed mumbler from the sealed-off end
Of Celtic England, glares and points;
And this raw difference disjoints
Our and Elegy's specious frame,
Framing all our deaths the same
(Our loves, our worships, levelled in
The eyes of Art, that Jacobin).

Lord George Gordon! he was found
Worshipful, the country round,
Some years before. Now no one hears
His civilly enounced ideas
Without reserve. But when, as host,
He gives his Radicals their toast,
'Mr Burke! who has afforded
Grounds for discussion', he's applauded.
And, sure enough, we may well find
Burke and the Jacobins of one mind,
One self-same ruinous frame, unless
We recollect that Burke could bless
Those death-bed words from one whose head
He may have turned, whom he misled:
         'Though Will finds worldly scope,
           We have no earthly hope.'
Edmund Burke had cried, 'Amen!'
And James King, and most other men.

Vancouver

Nobody's hero, George Vancouver, ever;
Never a woman in his life, and never
Given a thing but money. Out of luck
Out of mind, he saw no medal struck
To celebrate a second Captain Cook
Come home, in him. The only way he gained
Some jeering notice was by being caned
Publicly, off Piccadilly. Yes,
Some mystery there...biographers suppress
The incident as best they can. All told
No, no Cook. Who loved him, who extolled,
Who even liked him? An enduring glory
For Riou, Trevenen...that's another story;
Fierce Welshman, David Samwell made that claim.
And yet Vancouver's shouldered them out of fame.
       It seems he was not likeable; he made
What friends he had by a prudential trade
Of courtesies across interpreters
With his Peruvian or Andorran betters

In Spanish-speaking California, when
He warmed to Quadra or to Lasuèn.
True, he spoke of Hergest as a friend,
Whom he had known with Cook. But Hergest's end
(One of the band, Trevenen's friend and Riou's)
Lifts the record of Vancouver's cruise
Almost to myth; it makes Vancouver look
More than ever like a ghost of Cook,
Weird revenant to North Pacific air,
A presence, and yet humanly not there.
    Oahu saw poor Hergest re-enact
A play that he had sat through once. Attacked
No one knows why, and clubbed to death, he suffered
Cook's fate in duplicate. Only the island differed,
Hawaii killed them both, as if it meant
To kill the one man twice; and then a spent
Bloodless simulacrum called Vancouver,
That went through resolute motions, was left over,
A living corpse with mortal sickness on it.
(So it proved.) The double duty done it,
Freed or placated, some one's spirit fled
The expedition and its ailing head
When Hergest died.
               What nonsense! Still, it's queer,
The way the thing repeats itself; a mere
Re-run, let's say, as if Time struck a groove,
Stuck there, and rhymed, and then began to move
Clack-clack, and jerkily.
                It's less than just,
This, to Vancouver. His persistent thrust
Was crucial, and to come; the dying man
Drove, and would drive, his boat-crews, and a plan
To its fulfilment on the charts. Moreover
The drive comes though, the ruthlessness. Vancouver
Was harsh, and human; rage, tongue-lashings...Thus,
Just thus however, Cook *redivivus*
Would run a taut ship – on his third and last,
His fatal cruise, not many weeks went past
Without Cook's raging. Thus it might be shown
Even Vancouver's faults were not his own.
    The only difference was, Cook never came
Home to be caned in Conduit Street? Ill-fame,
A savage dog called Gillray, only bayed

Meat on the hoof? Not quite. He was afraid,
He must have been, Vancouver, riding home
Goitred and stiff. He knew it had to come,
Caning, or something like it. He'd transgressed
The cardinal unwritten law of caste,
Flogged the young gentleman – it was more than Cook
Had done, or dared. And, to be brought to book
For the transgression, he'd compounded it
By flogging, of all midshipmen, a Pitt,
The dangerous puppy, Camelford! There it is:
The mystery. For these audacities
What rhyme or reason? Say he was a sadist
(Which no one says), why should that nasty twist
Have sought its objects among officers
And settled on milord? The emphasis
Is obvious, and suicidal. True,
The man had been at sea for twenty-two
Years of his forty... out of touch, and yet
Not just, it's plain, an old-style martinet
Of his own quarterdeck, but some one more
Conscious of what he gambled, and what for.

    What for, if not authority? High play,
With that at stake, was common in that day:
Camelford himself, in English Bay,
Antigua, in seventeen-ninety-eight
Shot a man dead, to vindicate
His dubious seniority; and for
Mutineers of Spithead and the Nore
Courts-martial daily, hangings. This in fact
Must have saved Vancouver, when attacked
By and over Camelford. Command,
The sanctity of it, had to seem to stand,
Where possible, that year. So, in disgrace
And made to feel it, he can save his face,
And Camelford is interceded with,
Bought off, or cowed. A shabby end to myth
And to a life: no trumpets, but the sly
Susurrus of accommodations by
Pitt and his placemen – Dundas, Wedderburn –
Makes hugger mugger of a chief's return.

    Theirs was the authority he wanted,
The white whip-hands. I venture he resented,
As certainly Trevenen did, the way

Cook and his services were filed away,
And by the Pitts, the Wedderburns. No doubt
The stolid Dutchman never worked it out
(He named a creek for Wedderburn), and yet
Cook was the model he would not forget,
He'd sworn as much. Thus, loyalty to Cook
Could have been what impelled him, when he took
The whip to Camelford, and challenged Pitt
And gauged the outcome, and raged through with it.

If this is special pleading, let's admit
Vancouver needs the benefit, and may claim it;
We put the best construction that we can
On an unfriendly and a friendless man.

Commodore Barry

When Owen Roe
O'Sullivan sang Ho
For the hearts of oak
Of broken Thomond, though
Weevils and buggery should
Have wormed the wooden walls
More than De Grasse's cannon,
The sweetest of the masters
Of Gaelic verse in his time,
Lame rhymester in English, served
And laurelled Rodney's gun.

Available as ever
Implausibly, the Stuart
Claimed from the Roman stews
His sovereignty *de jure*;
But Paddy, in the packed
Orlop, the *de facto*
Sovereignty of ordure,
King George's, had to hedge
His bet upon a press
Of white legitimist sail
Off Kinsale, some morning.

A flurry of whitecaps off
The capes of the Delaware!
Barry, the Irish stud,
Has fathered the entire
American navy! Tories
Ashore pore over the stud-book,
Looking in vain for the mare,
Sovran, whom Jolly Roger
Of Wexford or Kildare
Claims in unnatural congress
He has made big with frigates.

Loyalists rate John
Paul Jones and Barry, traitors;
One Scotch, one Irish, pirate.
In Catherine the Great's
Navy, her British captains
Years later refused to sail with
The Scot-free renegade. Jones
And Barry took the plunge
Right, when the sovereigns spun;
Plenty of Irish pluck
Called wrong, was not so lucky.

'*My* sovereign,' said saucy
Jack Barry, meaning Congress;
And yes, it's true, outside
The untried, unstable recess
Of the classroom, every one has one:
A sovereign – general issue,
Like the identity-disc,
The prophylactic, the iron
Rations. Irony fails us,
Butters no parsnips, brails
No sail on a ship of the line.

Lady Cochrane

Before the House of Lords, 24 July 1862

That honoured name!
   Hero of a hundred fights!
A man who could have ruled
the world upon the sea...
    She cannot bear
    to be sitting there
to vindicate the name
for ages and for ages
'has run the World with his deeds'.

Once too often he had fenced
With the Commons, when, incensed,
    Coldly they saw depart
    Their pocket Bonaparte.
Nor would their chiefs, though too obtuse
To recognize in him a loose
    Bold travesty upon
    Cast down Napoleon
(Their fiercer Cromwell, now immured
On St Helena, and secured
    By sloop and spyglass), grieve
    To see rash Cochrane leave.

'Hero of a hundred fights!
I have stood upon the battledeck.
I have seen men fall. I have raised them.
I have fired a gun to save a man.
For the honour of my husband, I would do it again.'

So liberated Chile bought
The impenitent class-traitor out:
    The stormy petrel planes
    Again the ocean-lanes!

'Yes, I did assent
to accompany him to Scotland.'
– What time did you leave London? –
'The evening of the sixth of August
eighteen hundred and twelve.'
– How did you travel? It is

unimportant? –

          'Yes, it is unimportant.'
– With great speed, with four horses? –
'Sometimes, sometimes with two
as we could, night and day.
He named Carlisle and several other towns.
I was tired, worn. I was young.'

Demonic syren-voices choired
From St Helena, as the hired
      Condottiere sailed
      Past impetus that failed.
O'Higgins then, and San Martìn
Await him, in the Alpine, keen
      Air they have burned through, all
      Singed by an Empire's fall.

'A sort of pet name of his own
he had for me, and he said:
"It is all right, Mouse.
Mouse, we are over the Border."
He said: "You are mine for ever."
He snapped his fingers the way
that Scotchmen do
when they are pleased. I arrived
at Annan on the evening of the eighth,
and when I arrived at the Queensberry Arms
he was very joyous; I suppose
men in love are. He said:
"It is all right, it is all right."
He sat himself down as any gentleman might:
"I came here, Dick, to be married
and this is my wife," turning to me; and he bowed.'

Look! Abashed, the Portuguese
Are scoured in one year from the seas:
      So much one man can do
      That does, and knows not how.
Brazil, a Lusitanian mouth,
Can best acclaim, and will, the South
      American Lafayette,
      And pay at last her debt;
And shall she weakly countermand,

To one grown stiffer in command,
　　　His licence to hold sway
　　　Who will, at will, obey?
Does genius not inscribe and fill
Time's empty page with eagle's quill?
　　　So, when the albatross
　　　Has fished, and sailed across
One mast and tossing ensign, will
The flag direct him where to kill
　　　Next, in the self-sought, clear
　　　Taut arc of his career?

'After the paper was signed
and the servants gone, he began
to dance the Sailor's Hornpipe.
He put his hands up, so,
and "Now you are mine," he said.
– You marry like this in Scotland? –
"Oh yes," he said, "you are mine.
I have no time to spare, I have no time to lose."
He kissed me, he did not go
into my room, and he went off as he came.'

– I understand your ladyship
to say it was in order
not to displease his Uncle,
from whom he had expectations,
he kept his marriage a secret? –
'Entirely so. By a secret
marriage he would avoid
this fortune going away.'

Still voluble, still undeterred,
Our Cochranes keep their cloudy word:
　　　The same arts that did gain
　　　Them power, their power maintain,
Though thou, the war's and Fortune's son,
Terse Napoleon, bend upon
　　　Play-acting pitched so high
　　　A veiled, sardonic eye.

LOS ANGELES POEMS

207

'The old lady there, in the house
spoke a very broad Scotch. I never
heard Scotch before. I said
(I was but young you know,
perhaps a little pert)...
I said: "What kind of place
do you call this?"
                    She said:
"The Queensberry Arms at Annan."'

'I have stood on the battledeck...
I would do it again...' the voice
defensive and defiant.

SIX EPISTLES TO EVA HESSE

First Epistle

Not, I keep being told, the Time
That gets to me in one straight line
But (I knew this had to come)
A Space-cum-Time continuum;
A field of (wouldn't you know it?) force,
Not that dumb clockwork Time of course –
This and not that I should be writing,
Every one tells me. It's exciting
Stuff, all right (this Time, I mean),
A sort of poet's plasticine;
We get a date wrong – what's the odds?
We're not historians but gods.
Yet some of it seems resistant stuff
Still, and linear enough.
Trade routes like so much knotted string
Stretch out across the charts, and bring
John Jacob Astor, La Pérouse
And Captain Cook into the news
'That stays news,' poetry; in fact
Into geography, the intact
Oregon of their future where
Now in our past they haunt the air,
Faint and limp from long ago.
But although some one says we grow,
If we are poets, like a tree
Through ring on ring of history
Back into our past, instead
Of getting sun to get ahead,
Still, string or insulated wire,
Conducting trade, conducting fire,
Has a sort of truth that brings
Electric saws to redwood rings.
Oilmen and their bankers stage
This very day in Anchorage
Alaska something that no doubt
Time to come will level out...

Another string, another knot . . .
It looks like meaning, but it's not.
Instead it's news, and it will stay,
Though not so long as poems may.
Transcending's fine, but then we might
As well get what's transcended right;
No one is going to mount a stair
Planted in what isn't there.
No, Madam, Pound's a splendid poet
But a sucker, and we know it.

Given a set of random pegs –
Five fingers, or a chair's four legs –
You can do a lot with string,
And turn it into anything:
A double helix, say (and that
We know we have to goggle at);
A Manxman's three free-wheeling legs,
Although that asks a lot of pegs;
A swastika; a hammer and
Sickle; or an ampersand.
Come, given fingers deft as Madam's,
I'll outmatch Del Mar or Brooks Adams.

No, look! Unravel it, the thing,
When all is said and done, is string.
Can it, to take an instance, be
Any help, remembering three
Incentives from the Polar North,
The Northmen's three adventures forth
(I'm paraphrasing Olson now)
In the tenth century, and how
His three legs (Manxman, take a bow)
Went West, East, South – can this, I say
Help with that best of Hudson's Bay
Arctic travellers, John Rae?
Norseman from Orkney, was his fate
To come eight centuries too late?
For sanity's sake, what can it mean,
Skipping the centuries between?
Confound it, history . . . we transcend it
Not when we agree to bend it
To this cat's cradle or that theme

But when, I take it, we redeem
This man or that one. La Pérouse
Lives when he's no longer news.

Moreover (it's an obvious point)
Strings webbed from every finger-joint
Mean hands that cannot grasp at all.
('Enslave''s the meaning of 'enthrall'.)

Thinking along these lines (You see?
We're trapped in linearity),
I'm in a bind, hung up between
The Aesthete and the Philistine.
Now, bind is what cat's-cradlers do
And cradles are suspended too,
And when the wind blows the cradle will fall
And down will come baby, bathwater and all,
And therefore it appears to me
The question has some urgency.
Mum who muttered, 'This place looks
Like Troy-town', didn't know the books
That tell what troy-towns are, nor had
She found it in the *Iliad*.
Contented in her heedlessness,
All she meant was, 'It's a mess';
And that's a sense to which we come
Sooner from 'ruined Ilium'
Than from the eighty-year-old *opus*
Die Trojaburgen Nordeuropas,
Which says the troy-town was a maze
Or labyrinthine dancing-place,
A spiralling of little fosses
Copied in Somerset from Knossos,
Where feet upon the Blackdown Hills
Practised Daedalian rites and skills...
– A pretty picture, but suppose
Woodhenge and Stonehenge framed on those,
As nowadays it's thought they may be,
Will that cat's-cradle hold our baby?
I mean, for instance, this Byronic
Writing keeps architectonic
Principles entirely other
Than those so sadly missed by Mother;

Woefully linear, not to say
Rambling. Now, is this a way
To write, from now on quite uncouth,
Not qualified to tell the truth?
Henceforward must a poem twist
Back on itself, or be dismissed?
Or has it as much to do with us,
Constructing towns and epics thus
By spirals round themselves as, say,
Eirik Bloodaxe with John Rae?

Of course it may be said, and should,
That there is no more likelihood
Of worthy characters like Mother
Reading the one poem than the other,
With not much time for either. So
Why not write for those who know
What troy-towns are, and can rehearse
How Woodhenge breathes Projective Verse?
True. And yet one might insist:
What of the biophysicist?
The Muse has better things to do,
We may suppose, than bridge the Two
Cultures, but it wouldn't hurt her
To make her Araby less Deserta.
Will Crick cry, having read Christine
Brooke-Rose, 'Why, this is where I've been!
My new-found-land! Arabia felix!
This poem is a double helix'?
Will Watson, spurning from his desk
Anything that's Audenesque,
Exclaim, 'At last I'm catered for!
I like *Piers Plowman* more and more'?

No, but seriously, though
Spirals may make the whole thing go,
The way we got so fast so far
(Boring I know, but there we are)
Must be a linear affair;
Like any track from here to there,
Evolution is a thing
We picture as a length of string.

What irks me, if I have to pin it
Down is, There are no knots in it;
Everything's news, so nothing's news,
And that's bad news for La Pérouse,
Rae, Cook, or any name you choose.
I'm saying, I suppose, that Man
Leaves me cold, though Sid and Stan,
Distinguished individuals, awe me.
(Jonathan Swift said this before me.)
Yet if we hold in one equation,
As types of human adaptation,
The *polis* of Byzantium
And the distinctly separate thumb
(Expedients both to grasp and shape
Experience, beyond the ape);
I mean, if Evolution's not
Over when Man begins to plot
His emergence from his past
(A linear scheme still, first and last);
If, too, it is not Man but some
Named men by whom the breakthroughs come –
Why, then Biology makes shift
To come to terms with me and Swift.
(News, even so, is all we've got;
It looks like meaning, but it's not.)

Teleology, an upright
Darwinian, gave the Church a fright
By saying Nature works towards ends;
'It is *as if* she did,' contends
Teleonomy, his cliff-
Hanging cousin. And 'as if'
(That smart young cousin knows the score!)
Gives us the break we'd waited for.
Thus Comedy – which is all I'm after,
I want to raise no Cain but laughter –
Has raising laughter for its aim,
But aim and end are not the same.
A laying peacefully to rest
Is how one critic has expressed
The end of comedy. (If it's true,
This should be happening to you.)
But 'end', as Aristotle saw,

Implies some things that go before;
Beginnings, middles...and those are
Inextricably linear.

Therefore (for now these laughs may tend
Towards their term, if not their end)
I give you meaning, and not news:
Jean François, Comte de la Pérouse,
A person singularly winning.
And to begin with his beginning,
It was in Albi, where a square
(I first made his acquaintance there)
Holds him in effigy. For his
Youth, see the French biographies.
Take him in 1782:
That year his sails lift into view
In Hudson's Bay at Churchill Fort,
Which place he takes – an exploit fraught
(And here see History's comic sense)
With no long-lasting consequence;
But worth remembering, none the less,
For something we may call *finesse*,
And that not least in how he treated,
Civilly, those he had defeated.
To prove the civilizing role
Of France, he next, in 'La Boussole'
With 'L'Astrolabe', sets sail from Brest
To vie with Cook in searching West.
He rounds the Horn and gets his fix
(This is in 1786)
Upon Hawaii. Thence the Count
Makes headway north as far as Mount
St Elias, Alaska; reaches
After that, by pine-fringed beaches
On French leave southwards to survey
The coast as far as Monterey.
After that, Macao and
Manila draw him out, as planned.
A strait is named for him, between
Hokkaido and Sakhalin.
Kamchatka then, Samoa, Tonga,
Botany Bay. And then no longer
The grizzled admiral stems the seas.

He's lost off the New Hebrides.

There, I propose, we let him sleep,
Rocked in the cradle of the deep
Compassionate and comic Muse
Who, smiling, makes for La Pérouse
Friendlier lullabies than sing
Round epic cradles made of string.

Second Epistle

I'm going on with this affair;
Enough of comedy and to spare
In the history of the North
Western fur-trade and so forth...
Oh, but you've got there, Olson! Wait,
Miss Hesse, I must interpolate...
Olson in a magazine
Explains what his cat's-cradles mean;
Each is, he says, a *trampoline*:
'Trampolines, nets or mattings we
Stand in...' It makes sense to me;
His knots in history he intends
That we should take as means towards ends.
The strings of Time are to be plaited
Like woven canvas, bound or matted
Into (these are Olson's glosses)
A vibrant standing-place to toss us
Into who knows what upper air?
(Thus elated, who would care?)
How he bounces! Look how high!
Olson, you're the Malachi
Stilt-jack of our times, all right,
On stilts that spring you out of sight!

Oh yes, I like that. And it's time
I used a Yankee paradigm.
Shall I, I ask myself, desert
Frenchmen and such and, to avert
Any chauvinistic odium,
Lead Charles Olson to the podium?

No. 'Hero' is, however meant,
A title too ambivalent
To give a man whom in the end
I would rather call a friend.
Brief holdings after years of hope...
Heroes come dear to those who cope
With the aftermath of crisis
Or shock that follows their demises.
Still I confess I have them, clutch
At some I recognize as such...
Moreover I'm prepared to find
Their peers in regions of the mind;
Although here too I must confess a
Preference for the adroit successor
Or stout lieutenant over such
Minds as originate too much.
And Comedy suits this predilection;
Plainly, a quizzical inflection
Is always to be heard when she
Presents 'Our hero' to your scrutiny.
So with the man I have in mind;
Protagonist of a modest kind.
And if this paladin I choose
Seems to be French, like La Pérouse,
Why, History upon my plan
Is always a comedian;
And what's more comic than a scene
Where never Frenchman might have been
To plant a fort or write a sonnet,
For all the mark he's left upon it,
Place-names the one persisting, slim
And unpronounceable sign of him?
(I speak of places further South
Than the St Lawrence or its mouth.)
Anyhow, though you'll think this man
French, he is Italian.
Let me present, my verse still jaunty,
Gallicized, Henri de Tonty;
Who earned a fate I cannot choose
But think much worse than La Pérouse
In that, true mate and faithful friend,
He made too late too mild an end
Too quietly. For, like the priest,

The Muse, the Epic Muse at least,
Hopes for an edifying death
And hangs upon our last-drawn breath.
And even Comedy, it's certain,
Likes to ring down a strong last curtain.
(Though Horace taught her she must laud
A Sabine farm, in fact she's bored
With solid worth and modest ease,
Can't see the Bloody Wood for trees;
For we must make it very plain
The Comic Muse is no Plain Jane
And, never quite at home in Boston,
She wasn't always called Jane Austen.)
Moreover – here I interpose
What, like much else, is really prose –
Tonty was, I must relate,
Peculiarly unfortunate:
Geography could not abide him,
Her memorials were denied him.
Backed as he was by the Prince de Conti,
Lake Erie should have been Lac Tonty,
And Fort Niagara was a name
Supplanting on the rolls of fame
Fort Tonty. Thus we see that maps
Fool us as History does, perhaps.
Or else, Geography is more
Sinister than we took her for,
Less the comedian than her sister.
Poets, if they're wise assist her
By calling place (*all* places) holy,
Because it seems she may be slowly
Mustering her enormous forces
To blast her own, and our, resources,
Giving pollution for pollution.
A nice twist, that, to Evolution!
(What's nice about her, to be sure, is
Just that she has such vengeful furies,
Or so a poet may think who fears,
Yet wants, a Justice that inheres.
What will you do, he wants to ask her,
About the gang-rape of Alaska?)

However, Tonty's sun was setting

Some time ago. I keep forgetting.
Turn back the clock, and take the man
Now, at his meridian:
Observe him. Getting little joy
Out of the frozen Illinois,
His vigilance does not abate; he
Winters here in 1680
For his visionary chief,
La Salle, gone East, not for relief
But for the needful to equip
There, on the stocks, the half-built ship
That Tonty in that queer dockyard,
The wilderness, is left to guard.
Comes Spring, comes no La Salle. Instead,
Of the gang that Tonty led
(In theory), most decide to skip.
Though landlocked, they abandon ship,
Abandon Tonty, writing thus:
'We're savages, each one of us.'
(A sentiment reverberated
Through Badmen not yet generated,
Who were to take odd satisfaction
In savage pleas for savage action;
A practice copied by their betters –
It has its counterpart in Letters.)
Meanwhile the loyal remnant sought
Refuge and lodging in the fort
Of the assembling Illinois
Indians, whom the Iroquois
(Bless those rhyming Indian nations!
And curst be the exterminations
Of later, more enlightened times
That killed off tribes, and with them rhymes...)
Whom, I say, the Iroquois
Decided that they must destroy,
And for good reason, inasmuch
As furs the English and the Dutch
Would pay good guilders for might all
Be sent direct to Montreal,
Should Tonty or La Salle persuade
The Western tribes to ply that trade;
After which brief genuflection
In the economists' direction,

I give you Tonty, some time later,
Trying to play the mediator
Between these rival parties and
In equal peril from each band,
From both of which, to keep his head,
Wounded by one of them, he fled;
And met, in 1681
With no companions but one
Reaching Michilimackinac,
La Salle, on one more journey back.

Now, where Fidelity is the plot,
Comedy, we know, is not
Conspicuously enthusiastic;
She likes her things a bit more drastic
So she can smooth them out at last,
Lothario's peccadilloes past.
Her view is, we are all too human
And stand in need of her *dénouements*,
As by and large we do of course.
It follows Comedy perforce,
When we tell her that we've got
A mystic bond, a true-love knot,
Because her business is untying,
Supposes that we must be lying.
The point is, though, 'Auguste, his friend'
Must get some credit in the end;
And Tragedy and Epic, sold
So totally upon the bold
Unbalanced hero, are askew,
Quite hopeless from this point of view.
So we must make the Comic Muse,
If reluctantly, infuse
The homelier, more homespun virtues
With some quality of *éclat*,
A *Je ne sais* (exactly) *quoi*.
The more so, since we see anew
How History's bits of string won't do;
La Salle's French colony in Texas
Was knotted into no cash-nexus;
Nor did Tonty long enjoy
St Louis of the Illinois,
A place that Kings and History meant

Never should be permanent.
It really seems we'll have to whistle
For a hero, this epistle.
For human virtues cannot earn
The marble plinth, the sculpted urn;
And being trusty, being true,
As Tonty was, will never do.
Like La Pérouse, he had to make
History in a hero's wake,
And drudging on the track of those
Blazers of archipelagos
Means discovering *déjà vu*
Whatever strait one ventures through;
No coral isle, no sea-girt rocks
Not disfigured by the pox.
So, in the speculative seas
That wash up into libraries,
Taint on the breezes of the mind
Points to each Pitcairn that we find.
Thus, as for love of Letters and
Of Arts, it comes, we understand,
From mere debility, a state
That it can only aggravate,
Though suffering's so severe in some
Cases that it has become
Needful, to prevent expiry,
They persist in their enquiry.
(Thus said, as I suppose you know,
The insupportable Rousseau,
In the history of thought
A hero of the direst sort.)

True, there are provinces of Letters
Where these troubles don't beset us;
Regions that Rousseau never knew,
Scrub in his time, now ploughed anew.
Olson hereabouts is found,
Bounding on archaic ground;
And Pound and David Jones are planting
Glyphs with crucial pieces wanting.
Here making a distinction is
Nearly the worst of felonies,
Only exceeded, it appears,

By entertaining clear ideas.
('Cartesian', this crime is called;
A charge at which to stand appalled.)
Here no one's fooled by talk of Hector;
Troy was unspooled, Achilles wrecked her
By running counterclockwise round
The spindle of her Sacred Mound.
Here the surreal is the true,
And hashish may be good for you.
And sure enough, this province is
The nicest of dependencies.
Only, to finance it all
Depends upon the capital
Truth, not soon accumulated:
That zanies should be tolerated.
Now, I concur with those who fear
Truths like this, not crystal-clear
(For crystals take the light, and burn
With furious colours, as they turn)
But plateglass-clear, a sort of glare
Scorching our purchase on despair;
Despair, the bight that we can never
Let Enlightenment dissever,
Considering to what we tend –
The certain term, the dubious end.
And thinking of the poet's (Olson's)
Elastic traverse of the Oceans
And Epochs, how inert appears,
Beside such feats, whatever years
Of sprightly exile taught to Bayle!
That nothing be beyond the pale,
The best enforcement we can find
Is generosity of mind,
Not Toleration's equal haze
Of *plus ça change* . . . (or some such phrase).
Plainly the human lot is bettered
When deviant thinkers go unfettered;
But no one feels exhilarated
At being merely tolerated.
And yet some lump of English clay
Grounds me, and makes me grudge the play
Of mind, the freedom of it. Lean
Limbs upon a trampoline

Of zany theories, crazy rhyme,
Crossings of syncopated Time,
Leap into language. Why I should
Need to distrust such hardihood
Is a question I can face
Best by falling back on race:
How English, trying to make peace,
Reasonably, with Caprice!
(Mercurial Byron was – I'm not
Sure that it helps – of course a Scot,
Where Knox and Calvin keep the screws on
Taut nerves to bounce the Comic Muse on
As rhyming Beppo did. If Byron's
Vulgar pungency should fire one's
Emulation in this way,
One ought to know just what's in play
– Instead of Tolerance and Reason
And all things being good in season,
Byron found, as I find, handy
Rather liberal draughts of brandy.)
And Bayle knew this much: though to diddle
Both sides is easiest from the middle,
Holding the middle ground is harder
And asks more judgment, no less ardour,
Than to espouse exclusive themes
And fly to one of two extremes.
This must be part of what we mean
By talking of a trampoline
Where, yes, no bounce would have a sequel
If tension both ends were not equal.
Therefore the place I should maintain is,
So it seems, among the zanies;
And yet, I don't know how it is,
Tonty and his fidelities...
Some more common sense position
Is needed, for their recognition.

So, to resume...But why rehearse
What Parkman has, though not in verse,
Recounted nobly? Why go on
About La Salle, son of Rouen,
Or Tonty, his most faithful creature
Whose birthplace was, they say, Gaeta?

Some narrative, and then a moral . . .
With the latter you can quarrel,
And if the former you could spare,
It only comes in here and there.
Tonty should adorn a tale;
If not, it must be I who fail.
But as for pointing morals, why,
The one he prompts is rather dry:
That, pledges being given for keeps,
Whatever just reproach one heaps
(Or might) on fast-cemented love,
Its bargain, though repented of,
Is not aborted by that token;
One's word, once given, 's not unspoken.

Third Epistle

Heroic comedy, I suggest,
Fits American history best;
A charming mode not wholly lost to
Poetry since Ariosto
But, with us, rare. Since being glum
Has failed to bring millennium
At all decypherably to
The New World (or to me and you).
Let's see what being merry can
Do for the American.
Are we downhearted? Yes, we are.
But this is not peculiar;
All of us have been more or less
Bemused by our own wretchedness
Much of the time, it seems to me,
Throughout recorded history.
To raise our moan or raise a laugh,
To blubber or resort to chaff,
Are both all right, so long as we
Can do our thing inventively.
Though gay hysteria in a nation
Seems a wrong sort of adaptation
(This cap fits England, and she'll wear it
With a grin – her 'Grin and bear it'
Is a bore and lacks invention),

Still Comedy, it's my contention,
Can be magnanimous, in the sense
Of showing proper deference
To the pathfinders of our kind,
While soft on those they leave behind.
Indeed, to pay respects while smiling
Is more than usually beguiling,
It may be thought. And now's the time
To venture a Defence of Rhyme;
Rhyme, of all the tricks that are
In the Muse's repertoire
The most irrational, a mere
Foolish indulgence of the ear.
Zaniest of phenomenons,
It makes the rhymed forms open ones –
Open enough to see at once
Tonty the doughty and the dunce,
Or, while revering common sense,
Do it with jokes at her expense.
Is it prejudice to treasure
A zaniness that I can measure
(Sixteen syllables, more or less,
Is the frequency, Miss Hesse)
To random lunacies a man
May feel, but cannot learn to scan?
Total freedom in the fiction
Is of all the worst constriction,
For every licence to surprise
Turns out, in your reader's eyes,
To constitute just one more norm
To which he asks that you conform.
Thus rules we keep and rules we flout
Change places and turn inside out.
And so with rhyme: the Hudibrastic
Form of it's the least elastic,
And what was built as Liberty Hall
Allows few liberties at all.
The licences it thought to profit
By are soon demanded of it;
Surprise! Surprise! our readers cry
And, missing it, lay the volume by.
But rhyme in less licentious mode
Ensures a wavering switchback road

Which, I aver, I trust much more
Than five-lane free-verse highways for
Egotists to roar along
In self-enclosed unmeasured song.
Theirs are the closed forms, theirs the flat
Fiat of synopsis that
Makes every goddess the Great Mother
And women types of one another,
And Hathor, Circe, Aphrodite
One pair of breasts inside one nightie.
That closed-in Kosmos served by myth
Is just what Rhyme must quarrel with.

So, Muse, abandoning these loose
And heated pantheons, peruse
More frigid histories. Tune your rhymes
To Queen Victoria's costive times
When a man could come a cropper
From being in the least improper.
Sing, moreover, in hushed tones,
That most erogenous of zones,
The Arctic, where lascivious day
Whines, summer-long, on Hudson's Bay
And the months-long winters keep
Men abed who cannot sleep.
Thence stiff James Hargrave, terrified
Of waking with a squaw for bride,
Fled, for honour and dear life,
To Bonny Scotland for a wife;
And found one neither he nor I
Would ever want to deify,
For whom I none the less will claim
A sombre record, if not fame –
Letitia, of the Clan Mactavish!
Nature wasnae unco' lavish
Endowing her; not hers the face
Launched ships for Troy or any place,
Though Orkney sailors were to bend
A hawser for her at Gravesend.
Therefore, though less than heavensent,
A suitor was convenient.
So Hargrave comes, and Hargrave woos,
Is liked, and is too good to lose.

This solid man she settles for
Is sixteen years her senior.
And what a settlement it is!
Backed up against immensities
Of muskeg barrens... Theirs henceforth
The Pontine marshes of the North,
Where the swamps and foggy air
Rack the unlucky loyal pair
Through eleven years that see
A due access of progeny;
Five births, one death – one little boy
Sent home, bewildered, to enjoy
The benefits (past computation)
Of Caledonian education.
Her letters home survive, and bore.
Never an item in them for
Revolving Time to trifle with;
Domestic news, too trite for myth,
All on one cheerful-cheerless note –
The baby's colic, her sore throat;
Never a thing that can be pried
Free of the times she lived inside,
The nineteenth century's fifth decade.
Weep, Comedy, to see displayed
The short unsimple annals of
The poor in health: his qualms, his cough,
Her constipation, her confinements,
Her headaches... and of all assignments
The Company makes, its northernmost,
Busiest, least salubrious post
Year after year. Who sings the quiet
Martyrs to inappropriate diet,
To wrong and rigid hygiene, and
Dyspepsia in Prince Rupert's Land?
Who ever does can bear to see,
Dry-eyed, the tame small tragedy:
There, on the post they'd waited for,
Snug by Lake Superior,
The cholera descends, and makes
A widower upon the Lake's
Abruptly desolated shore;
She dies in 1854.

Poor child! She comes through as a sort
Of foundling waif, an awed, untaught,
Casually adopted charge
On family estates too large
For more than transient regret
When stewards' households are upset.
Baffled at best, at worst unnerved
By the culture that she served
(The legendary 'Boz', she had
Heard it rumoured, must be mad;
And flagging interest revives
In Shakespeare's romp, 'The Merry Wives
Of Windsor', only when she can
Observe that gentlemanly man,
Prince Albert, showing much good sense
And shyness, in the audience),
How many since have I not seen,
Like her, stand quivering for the Queen
With guilelessness that is construed,
The more the argument's pursued,
As stiff-necked prejudice? Alas,
God Save the Queen from thee, my lass!
God help England, and defend us
All from such obtuse befrienders
As warm Letitia...Oh, a cool
Comedian makes her look a fool
Out of her own mouth, soon enough.
Shakespeare, Dickens and such stuff
Possessed, in her days as in these,
Nothing to instruct or please
A hemmed-in way of life like hers;
And yet that way of life recurs
Each generation, with the need
We feel, or think we feel, to breed.

Mothers of the pioneers,
Patching and mending through the years,
Might come to *Lear* or *Little Dorrit*,
Some hallowed text, conceiving for it
Gratitude, as their children had
Proved loyal, or had turned out bad.
But she, who never lived to raise
One of her children, could she praise

Sincerely either version of
The rendings of parental love?
With little meaning and less news
In the record, can the Muse
Even of Comedy maintain
Hers was a life not lived in vain?
Mythographers who can elide
Centuries are not satisfied
Such mournful limits can be placed
On the exercise of taste.
For them, we notice with a shock,
An early death's no stumbling-block;
The racial memory will see
To it, the short-lived can be
Initiate of each mystery
As surely as we others who
Are spared to see the drama through.

Believing that, we might as well
Go the whole hog to Heaven and Hell,
For if blind faith's in order, why,
A crustier pie in clearer sky
Is cooked by an established Church,
Less apt to leave one in the lurch;
As indeed Letitia knew
Who lived and died with Heaven in view.
Sorrowing for her, I begin
Thinking there's some virtue in
A place where prepossessions are
Less confidently saecular
Than where the exegetes romp through
Millennia in an hour or two;
A place where Mrs Hargrave might
Have heard debate she'd think was right
About child-care and sanitation,
Paid holidays and compensation...
My native land! secure, humane,
Where no one works (I mean, for gain),
Where, though the rule is Man the Measure,
The module man shall have no leisure
More than an ailing housewife with
Five small children. What price myth
In such a world? What price the lives

Lived there, where computation thrives
To breed the social engineers
Who have the nation by the ears?
Tickets for *Lear* are not much prized
Where all's been de-mythologized,
Nor much of merriment survives
In Windsor's bright unhappy wives
Financing, out of foreign loans,
Welfare and the Rolling Stones.

No, England, if I have to choose,
There are some myths too good to lose;
And if my choice must lie between
Barbara Castle and Christine
Brooke-Rose, I have no wish to flatter
In plumping firmly for the latter.
To be more positive; I bless
All such girls as you, Miss Hesse.
Among the men, too, I prefer
Often the mythographer;
A good companion, erudite
And witty far into the night.
And yet James Hargrave might be more
Welcome as a son-in-law,
Who surely more sincerely grieved
Than livelier men, the more bereaved
In that he was resourceless in
His stolid pain, and could not spin
Tales to himself of passionate
Divorce and death, to cushion it.
I'm glad to leave that thought alone;
It comes, and cuts, too near the bone.

So Comedy, once more our saviour,
Quash such unreserved behaviour.
Do what you can (it isn't much)
To save Letitia from the touch
Of levelling and defiling time;
Cripple the measure, wrench the rhyme!

Fourth Epistle

Sparkle sparkle, little verse,
Not poetry, nor yet discourse...
Let a nation's honour be
Billed as brittle comedy;
Waste and Oblivion stalk the scene
Of *The London Magazine*
And a sickness at the heart
Talk trenchantly of Life and Art.

So, once again... But how begin?
Hero I lack, and heroine.
Perhaps a poet... Is it time
For self-congratulating rhyme
To honour as established fact
The value of the artefact?
Stoutly to trumpet Art is all
We have, or need, to disenthrall
Any of us from the chains
History loads us with? Such strains,
Wafted on the foetid air,
Are found emollient everywhere
The poet or the painter goes
Except inside the studios
Or garrets that they work in, where,
Though too preoccupied to care,
All of them notice at least two
Sides to the dubious thing they do.
    Savage Landor – there's a poet
Spurned England, and took pains to show it.
Not his the slack, impetuous style
I improvise in all this while;
Headstrong, not headlong, was his case,
Consumed with contumely of race
And insolence of rank, whose sweet
Self-love makes Como seem effete.
    Savage, all too savage Landor,
Less England's Cato than her pandar,
Pimp to her appetite, then as now,
For thinking, 'Holier than thou'.
(Florence was insolent indeed
Not to know the bulldog breed

More than Ghibelline or Guelph
Was a law unto itself.)
No surprise, then, if he's found
In the pantheon of Pound
Who, similarly unabashed,
Was the very thing he lashed:
Ole Uncle Ez, the crustiest sort
Of Yankee at King Arthur's Court.
Both poets, relishing the state
Of mortified expatriate,
Through blunder after patent blunder,
Scrape after scrape, found face to thunder
At home-grown mischiefs, and expose
Fools or knaves, in verse and prose.
    Such doubleness is on the cards
Too plainly, for self-banished bards
Who never lack for occupation,
Each hectoring his relinquished nation
Even as they exemplify
The prepossessions they decry.

Besides, we've reached rock-bottom now;
Byronic skiff and Crabbe-like scow
And Landor's lovely craft alike,
Forced upon the shoreline, strike.
They fill before they feel the shock,
In such small print it is; the rock
Of the obituaries, on whose
Shallow ubiquity the Muse
Time and again has struck and foundered.
The insignificant! The unsounded
Reaches of the trite! We grind
The lakebed gravels of the mind.
A stilted posy on the grave
Is all that Art can do to save
Poetry's and a Nation's honour:
'Canada's soil lie light upon her...'
As upon so many others,
Sickly brides, benighted mothers,
French explorers. Only places,
Patches of earth by the good graces
Of local polymaths sometimes
Name, to make exotic rhymes,

Small successes or near-failures:
Ill-bred wives, unlucky sailors.
    Thus New Zealanders maintain
The name of Marion du Fresne
Who, Skye-ward navigating, tore a
Princely botanist from his Flora
Once upon a time; who now
Knows better than to make his bow
To a no longer Young Pretender.
Instead he dwells in modest splendour
On a colonial estate
Secured in 1768
In l'Île de France (which is to say
Mauritius, at the present day).
    And yet he rushes on his doom,
Sets all at risk, and will resume
Nautical life. He sinks behind
The south-east skyline, there to find
Some paltry islands, of which one
Commemorates him: Marion
His mark, his sea-mark. (And this matters:
Astringent comedy never flatters
The ruinous Quixotes of their day,
John Franklin or Wolfe Tone or Che,
Too virginal to wed Success,
Intact in ineffectiveness.)
Not Carthaginian Hanno nor
Odysseus, prudently inshore,
Their crude technologies unripe
For the deep waters, is his type;
The mythological parallel
As usual works out far from well
As soon as we imagine how
Things really were. Take notice now,
For instance, that the second ship,
Manœuvred with poor seamanship,
Hereabouts with some commotion
Collides with his one in mid-ocean;
The culprit turning out to be
A sprig of the nobility,
The mishap cannot help but seem
Due to the *ancien régime*,
A far from mythical condition

Through which he limps upon his mission,
Hurrying now, and making for
Tasmania's vaguely charted shore
There to recoup, refit. But no,
Van Diemen Land cannot bestow
Wood, nor water, nor much ease
Not vexed by aborigines.
    In March of 1772,
Accordingly, he ploughs the blue
Waters of the Tasman Sea
Helped by a strong south-westerly,
Makes land and, weathering new mischances,
Declares New Zealand thenceforth France's.
North Island's earth lie light upon
The breast *etcetera* of one
Whose bones, outlandish treasure-trove,
Enrich Assassination Cove.
(That is to say, his bones at least;
His meat had made a Maori feast.
Comedy goes for jokes like these;
Her humour's black, like Cruelty's.
Unamiable! None the less,
Noteworthy for straightforwardness:
If in such rites she shows us how
To be as crude as Chairman Mao,
Cruelty's what she had in mind;
She won't be cruel to be kind
Nor, anthropophagous, pretend
Doing it serves some higher end.)
    From Utopian projectors
Caustic Comedy protect us!
Under whose corrosive shield
I re-affirm we ought to yield
Firm pre-eminence of status
Among projections, to Mercator's;
Trusting the lie of lands and seas
Before such lies as History's.
    Between his stanchions I can sling
My own small lattices of string,
Slack hammocks where I can compose
Into a somnolent repose
The harrowing abbreviations
Of lives endured, inured to patience

Or insensate, flailing round
Some misappropriated ground
Of pride or Polynesia or
That atoll not worth sailing for,
National honour. Lulled upon
The loll of reverie, even one
That time was at no pains to ravish –
Letitia Hargrave, born Mactavish,
Raped in her own and History's sleep –
Is comforted and learns to keep
Good company in the Isle of Skye,
The Bay of Islands and Versailles.
The dancing clews, the bulk and sway
Of slipping shadows web the day
Between decks to the music of
Strains and chafings, suave enough
To help us orchestrate a mood
By latitude and longitude;
Parameters our captains must
Abstractedly pursue and trust,
And by their grid upon the chart
Mesh fluid Nature into Art,
But which, in truth, will barely serve
To plot our conquest of the curve
Of oceanic earth. Instead
We can weave a swinging bed
(Too lax to make a trampoline)
Of the surprising, unforeseen
Conjunctions human beings prove
The more the rule, the more they move.

Most poets sail another tack:
To the Piraeus, and then back.
Browning's anxiously despairing
Enquiry, 'What's become of Waring?'
Asked of one who took his chance
In poor Marion's Austral France,
Still touchingly pursues us where
We've emigrated to, by air.
And Landor, Pound and Browning are
All in this sense too insular
To help us much, who need to probe
A way to humanize the globe

By which (upon this point I yield)
Space and Time inscribe one field,
But (and here I give no quarter)
Space is the long side, Time the shorter.

Still, older poets had the sense
At least to run a staked-out fence
Around their fields. And those fields are
Better than rectilinear;
The curve of earth takes care of that,
Unless of course you think it's flat
As apparently those do
Whose pastures melt into the blue
Unfenced Beyond of the sublime,
The mythopoeic waste of Time.
        True, the power of myth engages
Some of the old masters' pages.
(They know things are not what they seem;
That in the Polynesian scheme
Of things it may be Marion died,
A case of ritual deicide.)
But La Pérouse's rigid page
Is icy with contempt and rage,
Telling the not dissimilar end
Of his own too trusting friend,
De Langle, butchered out of reach
Of help on a Samoan beach;
Unfair it may be, but I fear
(Miss Hesse or any other dear
Reader) those bluff sailors thought
Ill of people of our sort
Whose surveys, something less than global,
Had declared the savage, noble,
Thereby fashioning a myth
Their shipmates could be murdered with.

Fifth Epistle

A thesis, though sincerely meant
Is in the end impertinent,
Comedy says. In her sharp praxis
There's no place for grinding axes;

Thesis, antithesis, the same,
A more or less convenient frame
For weaving on. The web is tattered;
Mending it's all that ever mattered.
 All the same, an axe is ground
So gratingly, on that renowned
Marmoreal paragon, Captain Cook,
Its squeak is hard to overlook.
Was it presumption when he trod
Hawaii, an acknowledged god?
Did, when he died, the Age of Reason
Learn the irrational was in season?
There, on the black sand, hacked, dismembered
Worshipfully, he remembered,
Did he, that last instant, how
A man-god could not disavow
In Gethsemane the weight
Of divinity, and fate?
Or did he, dying blindly, still
Think that, given mind and will,
Something there was a man could do
To exorcize a myth come true?

A worse hypothesis will fit him:
That he never knew what hit him.
Navigator through and through,
Hydrographer with a job to do,
Was that James Cook? The very first
(So Coleridge was to say) that burst
Into that silent sickening sea –
Professional speciality?
– A mask, perhaps; the shy, self-made
Provincial hides behind his trade.
If so, it works: the self-respecting
Yorkshireman there's no detecting.
In the Ridings we admire
The man with expertise for hire,
Who by his code austerely sells
Fierce competence, and nothing else.
Wilfrid Rhodes and Maurice Leyland
And Hedley Verity...I stand
Dwarfed by Father as we clap,
And surly Leyland tugs his cap

And (No, this *isn't* out of books)
Black as Lucifer he looks,
Coming with a racing stride
And booted thunder, past our side
Up the pavilion steps, to gain
His private dark. Aye, Bramall Lane
Will never see his like again...
And just as well – it was a poor
Cramped nobility, to be sure,
That disdainful dourness which
Had the globe for cricket-pitch
Once – which now, if it survives
At all, informs the sullen lives
Of Yorkshire bards who take perverse
Pride in writing metred verse,
All their hopes invested in
One patent, brilliant discipline.

Well, we can hardly pick and choose:
Not much to gain, but much to lose,
We find nobility where we can,
Even in a Yorkshireman.
But that is neither here nor there;
Nobility's not comic fare.
Nor are cowards – which puts paid
To the horribly afraid
Lieutenant Williamson. Nor is
The brave and brutal Bligh, whose story's
Never been told with justice, such
A theme as Thalia's light touch
Does justice to. And so we might
Scan all whom History's brought to light
Out of the muster of Cook's two
Ships and, having conned them through,
Rule the lot of them out of court.
(Our Muse is choosier than we thought.)
Instead, as you'll have guessed, there's one
Case that I've chosen – Corporal John
Ledyard.
             He's been much maligned,
Ledyard has, by those who find
Any disrespect for Cook
A hanging matter, in their book.

(Whereas, for Cook's own sake, in fact
Blemishes is what we've lacked
All this while, and any stain
Of fallibility's sheer gain.)
And Ledyard, on the other hand,
Though seldom in his native land
Remembered, was a curious man,
Authentic and American.
In 1787 he strode
Along his own untravelled road
In winter, carrying all he had,
From Stockholm round to Petrograd,
1200 miles on foot in eight
Weeks...But I anticipate:
Some years before, with Cook, he'd been
A less accomplished peregrine;
As witness his account of it,
Where passages of exquisite
Silliness reveal a man
Whose role, not yet pedestrian,
Is never to be much surprised
When sudden gusts of bowdlerized
Laurence Sterne (from whom he's stealing)
Type him as the Man of Feeling.
(Words! Insidious avengers!
Time, that brings in its revenges,
Has too keen, too true an ear:
It's not enough to be sincere,
You have to seem so. History smiles,
Custodian of exploded styles.)
'Mystic sheer distance was in thine
Eye,' wrote Olson's friend and mine,
Ed Dorn, addressing Ledyard. And
'Mystic' is right. It was the land,
Dorn's land and his, made manifest
In him its destiny, heading West
The long way round if need be, by
Tomsk and Kachuga. 'In thine eye',
Ledyard, all America smiles
Already, ribboning through miles
Of trailers, and the pent air slaps
Whick-whick against us through the gaps
Between the parked cars, as we prove

The way to live is on the move.

To wrest from Russia the distinction
Of slaughtering into extinction
Such animals as Steller's sea-
Cow and the sea-otter, he
(So the accepted version goes)
Had the prescience to propose
America dispute the ground
The Russians had, from Nootka Sound,
And thus imperiously invade
The fortune-making peltry trade
That desolated Arctic seas
To warm the backs of Cantonese.
And there's his greatness! What a man
It took, to frame so gross a plan!
What a Napoleon of crime,
Born not before, but of, his time!
Thus the historians, lost in awe
As soon as Nature's rule of law
Is breached on a sufficient scale.
Cachalot and walrus quail.
Prayed after from Connecticut,
Dissolute grave whalers gut
Leviathan's cows, and under Cape
Brett in the Bay of Islands rape
Maori women on the sands
Mauled by Marion's dying hands.

Luckily, none of this is true:
Any nation's flag would do
To plant upon the unexplored,
Unbestowable seaboard
That beckoned Ledyard like a dream,
Unprofitable and extreme.
America and Freedom earn,
It's true, apostrophes *à la* Sterne
Still, in the desultory pages
That trace him by Siberian stages
Eastward; but after John Paul Jones
And Jefferson fail to raise the loans
He'd hoped to touch them for, occurs
No mention of the trade in furs.

SIX EPISTLES TO EVA HESSE

A pretext that had failed to raise
The wind, he might as well erase
(And did) from the aspiring mind
That thought to benefit mankind...
Travelling as sheer condition!
Exploring *that* was the commission,
Self-bestowed, on which he went
Walking through a continent.
Thus was History outwitted!
He wore the motley till it fitted;
The reach-me-down of silly phrases,
Exclamation marks, self-praises,
Points and frills, falls into shape.
Can mere farrago thus escape
The times' and Comedy's clutching hands?
Yes. When Catherine countermands
Her passe-partout, and by her order
He's dumped across the Polish border,
No one has the heart to smile
At the pretensions of his style.
Deluded, verminous, alone,
The rhetoric he'd made his own
Comes true, at last his situation
Demands the note of desperation.
His fever-pitch was queered before
The Empress pushed him out the door.
Febrile, excitable, effusive
He chose to be, and chose to live
Up to what that style demands,
Grasping his fate with shaking hands.

And so he fades from us, you see...
A figure, once, of comedy,
Now asking for some other kind
Of honorarium, gone to find
Death in Cairo in the very
Year that saw his plans miscarry
Of following a Yankee star
Through the dominions of the Czar.
(I'm sorry, by the way – and yet
It's fitting, when you think of it –
That I couldn't follow through
The life of Ledyard with the due

Observance of successive time
That Comedy exacts of rhyme;
I trust that none the less you've pieced
Together, bit by bit, at least
A general notion where he went
First and last, and in the event
With what success.) There still remains
One awkward truth: for all the pains
We take at Comedy's behest
To be poised and unimpressed
And keep our heads, we cannot guard
Against, nor take account of, hard
Gamblers of the do-or-die
Variety, who make the sky
Their limit, and provoke their fate
By being disproportionate.
Comedy just cannot brook
A Ledyard, nor perhaps a Cook...
So, dear Miss Hesse, if I were you
And you were found to be the true
Empress Eva of all Russia,
Faced with a Ledyard, I should usher
Him out across my frontier fast;
Heroes are safest in the past.

Sixth Epistle

The impetus, awesome!
The imperial momentum
Flogs still: 'Among the first
And farthest...' The unslakeable thirst
Still logs its marches. If it is
Late for these intensities,
If it's too late (or else too soon)
For landing parties on the moon,
Then ponder an alternative:
That fever, easier to forgive,
When a Ruskin's narrowed eyes
Crimp to the nicer enterprise,
'Not place, but the expression on
The face of it.' The light is gone
Over the lake and off it, while

Autumn, the amber of a style,
Dyes it his in whom his own
Time and year's time mix a tone
Mellowed for it. And for this
Meshing of uncertainties
Not too late? The space for it
Is narrowed on the face of it,
Branded with a coming doom
Wreaked or suffered. Little room
Left to articulate the fine
Crowsfoot and serif, scroll and line,
When Nature's indeterminate face
Frowns, or fawns with craven grace
On her despoiler. Still, it is
An honourable emphasis –
On the refining mutual shock
When ravisher and patient lock
Looks in one haggardness that hones
Weasel and rabbit to thin bones,
To one bleached gossamer. The tension
Of a mortal apprehension
Steadies the web to such a fine
Reticule, the debile line
Parts at the pressure of a gnat.
No cradle here, to swing a cat!

Says Romance: 'You need some rope.
Put away your microscope,
Set your manikin in motion
Across what continent or what ocean
All you need's a general notion.'
Insufferable! If it's true
There's virtue in a bird's eye view,
Some better reason must be found,
Still valid when we're on the ground.
It might be this: that there is one
Abstracted potent lexicon
Of place, which helps us understand
Where, in some ultimate sense, we stand;
That heath and strand and wood and cape
Make up a grid we can't escape,
However manifestly these
Vary with localities.

And being English helps with this.
My emblem of all barrens is
The Langsett moors, and the Great Wood
Is tiny Hugsett, where we would
Cull bluebells forty years ago:
Great Wood, Great Barrens, though we know
Better, or worse. Thus 'great' and 'far',
'Remote' and 'wild' and 'trackless' are
Nomenclature that cannot fail
To stay authentic and in scale,
Being as felt. We made our claim
To them, for instance, with the name
'North America' for the last
Ruined homestead that we passed
Breasting the moor. Domesticated
Little England is, and fated
To get much more so; none the less
This way she'll march with Lyonnesse
For us, for good. And Lyonnesse
Or Tryermaine is wilderness,
Bewildering, and not lightly entered,
Where if we travel (as demented
Aberrant Ledyard punned) we are
In error. There, the near is far,
The old home unfamiliar,
The little, great. But all the same
Great this, great that, advance a claim
By authors of an island-nation
That demands substantiation,
For instance, as to climate. Why
Should we suppose a scudding sky
And chill damp airs delineate
More truly than less temperate
Weathers do, our mortal state?
Moreover, 'manikin' may do
For hobbits or an elf or two
Or for myself when, still a child,
I took for emblem of the wild
And waste, a meadow rank with clover
And vetches, long ago built over.
But Geography's too great
And fierce a power to tolerate
Being, through a Tolkien's eyes,

Toyed with, and cut down to size.
  It may well be that any scene
On land or water, whether seen
Up close or from a long way off,
Presents us with at best a rough
Approximation to the true.
And yet the snail's, the bird's eye view
Both serve us better, we may hope,
Than turning round the telescope
Until what's insular and near
Seems crisp, definitive and clear
As in Romance. Romance, though charming.
Seeming gratuitous and disarming,
Has in fact an end in view
Not always good for me or you.

Therefore, like others we've applauded,
Our final actor's a recorded
Personage – the most renowned
Hero in fact I've so far found:
Thomas Jefferson!
                My reader,
Though he's British, shouldn't need a
Résumé of *that* career.
But every one will think it queer
If I propose him as a prime
Example, in his place and time,
Of the comic. So he seems,
However, if the several themes
I've tried to tease out in this poem
Have any rhyme or reason to 'em.
Indulgent friends, like you, Miss Hesse,
Will take my drift. Let others, less
Persuaded or amused, reflect
That Comedy is circumspect;
So statesmanlike that a Romantic
Pathos winces at each antic
She performs upon the stage
Of Jefferson's or any age.
Comedy always keeps her cool
When other Muses play the fool.

The curtain rises! There, before us,
Stands a patron of explorers:
Ledyard and Meriwether Lewis.
Difficult deciding who is
The crazier of that couple. He
Sincere in his civility,
Dispatches to their destinations
Both of them, their aberrations
Noted, allowed for. When they die,
Both violently, in his eye
Brightens a pained, regretful smile
As he, in one unruffled style
(Too humane a style to break,
Too inclusive to mistake
For mischance, logic) with entire
Justice, in the steady fire
Of rational prudence immolates
Both in one memoir. In their fates
He reads excess, and so impales
The pair of them. He never fails.
... As does, for instance (I regret
Digging a little deeper yet
Into Americana) his
One-time foil in rivalries
For President, the first John Adams.
The only rhyme to that is 'madam's'
As Yeats discovered; so it's yours,
Miss Hesse, who will recall of course
Among the Adamses, that Brooks
Whose wayward, dazzling history-books
Are monotonously found
Scriptural, by Ezra Pound.
And, reader, this is no digression:
Brooks comes of John, by due succession,
And Henry too... in all we see
Men mesmerized by History.
Set Jefferson against his peer,
Adams, and the issue's clear –
The one, successful and serene;
Behind him mountains; and between
His sanguine forehead and the rim
Of the medal struck for him,
Stretching savannahs: but behind

The other's angry head, designed
By an engraver in the pay
Of secret party, some *mêlée*
Or massacre or mob-unrest,
A tumult of crossed interest,
Crowding the middle ground inside
The milled edge of resentful pride.

Of course we know which one we like:
Betrayed, traduced, and with the strike
Against him always, Adams. Yet
It's Jefferson we can't forget
Who, though he never went there, hung
All Oregon upon a young
And urgent nation's parlour-wall.
Our hearts go out to those who fall,
Success is vulgar. None the less
A breakthrough into spaciousness,
New reaches charted for the mind,
Is solid service to mankind.

Bedfordshire

Bunyan, of course. But Potton it was, or Sandy,
Threaded on the Cambridge road, that showed
Dissenting nineteenth-century demureness
In a brick chapel. I have never known
What to do with this that I am heir to.

My daughter-in-law has studied for her thesis
The Protestant Right in France between the wars,
l'Association Sully. Bedfordshire
Might nurse an English counterpart of that:

Our swords for Calvin and the Winter Queen,
The ancient frail collaborating Marshal!

Berkshire

for Michael Hamburger

Don't care for it.
               We talked of syntax and
synecdoche, the various avant-gardes,
their potencies, their puerilities.
And, Michael, one we knew
in Reading, he approved such conversations;
crippled and dying he contrived occasions
when they could come about. And yet he
felt (we knew) not scepticism, rather...
oh certainly not scepticism, rather
an eager, a too eager warmth in him
starved for a lack of body in that talk.

In his last months I stood him up for supper.
That night I should have stayed with him I stayed
talking with Christopher Middleton in town.

So nowadays as the biscuit-factory flies
past the train-window and announces Reading,
I keep my head down.

Buckinghamshire

A thin green salient aimed at the heart of London,
The trains run in and out of Baker Street.

Chalfont St Giles, Chalfont St Peter, Fenny
And Stony Stratford breathe again. The old
A6, the clamorous ditch we edge along,
Ribbons in evening sunlight south to Bletchley.

To west and east the motorways draw off
Poisons that clogged this artery. Abandoned
Transport-cafés blink at the weedy asphalt;
An old white inn by a copse-side yawns and stretches.

Cambridgeshire

'An air that kills' – Housman

Housman came, savage recluse,
Lover of boys. 'To be sure,
That also I endure,
        yet not from there
Blows into Whewell's Court
        an air that kills.'

Came wincing Gray: 'Why that
Libertine over the way,
Smart of Pembroke, should
        have had the luck
        of running mad
Is more than I can say.'

Smart stares at William Blake:
'Mad? Mad as a refuge
        merely from Locke?
Shame on the subterfuge!
        Let the wind pluck
Your wits astray, *then* talk!'

And Blake: 'I accept the reproof.
Better be sane like Housman
Than under Bedlam's roof,
Self-soiled, wind-plucked. And yet
        I think it's not
        an airless place?'

Smart, Gray, all of them, look:
The face of Harold Monro!
'An air that kills? At all
        events an air!'
Tuneless, he growls from Caius
        in his despair.

Cheshire

A lift to the spirit, when everything fell into place!
So that was what those ruined towers remained from:
Engine-houses, mills. Our Pennine crests
Had not been always mere unfettered space.

Not quite the crests, just under them. The high
Cloughs, I learned in the history-lesson, had
Belted the earliest mills, they had connived
With history then, then history passed them by.

His savage brunt and impetus, one survives it?
Finding it all unchanged and the windowless mill
Between Wincle and Congleton silent and staring, I found
The widow's weeds restorative and fit.

And Mr Auden, whom I never knew,
Is dead in Vienna. A post-industrial landscape
He celebrated often, and expounded
How it can bleakly solace. And that's true.

Cornwall

(Treasure Island)

Cornwall, the unreality
of Cornwall:

hull down, the mobile homes
are shelling the Bristol Channel

which fights right back! Storm-lanterns
swing in the black
wind, and tomorrow
perspex and fibre-glass
will slosh about in the eddies.

Cornwall, the fabulous wreckers
of Cornwall: novelists.

A county in Bermuda,
that unreality also.
It was a literary Empire.

Black Jack Pendennis has
been out again. To a lonely
inn upon Bodmin Moor
etcetera, on a wild
October night
etcetera.

Different for the Cornish,
it must be. But for us
Lancashire and Yorkshire
interlopers who
run curio-shops on the quay
it has, as an arena
for growing old in, one
desolate advantage:
it cannot be believed in.

Black patches on both eyes...

Cumberland

I tend to suppose the part I know least
Of England is the north-west.

A honeymoon in the Lake District
Is conventional matter-of-fact;

And ours was the winter of '45!
On ghyll and yew-tree grove

And packhorse-bridge, the blowtorch air
Was singeing the nostril-hair;

Snow that had lain deep for weeks
Fantasticated our walks;

And Rydal Water to our tread
Rang, till Helvellyn heard.

Exalted by love, in wintry rigours
Unlikely Cumberland rages

Thus in my memories. North-west,
I know you least, or best?

Derbyshire

We never made it. Time and time again
Sublimity went unexamined when
We turned back home through Winster, lacking heart
For walking further. Yet the Romantic part
Of Via Gellia, where it dives through chasms
To Ashbourne, is historic; there, short spasms
Of horror once in many a heaving breast
Gave Derbyshire a dreadful interest.

And I too was Romantic when I strode
Manfully, aged 12, the upland road.

Only the name of 'Via Gellia' jarred;
It seemed to mean a classical boulevard
With belvederes at intervals. I swelled
My little chest disdainfully, I 'rebelled'!

Devonshire

Discharged upon the body of the world
  Drake, Hawkins, all that semen
  Has left no stain! Instead
  The disblitzed Plymouth: first
Violin to squeal the eunuch's part
  Well-planned, a work of art.

We run through a maze of tunnels for our meat
  As rats might; underpass,
  Walkway, crash-barrier lead
  Our willing steps, as does
The questionnaire that we shall be so kind
  As to complete (unsigned)

Between North Road and Paddington. Drake's Circus
  Proffers the hoops the trained
  Corpulent animals are
  Glad to jump through. Drake,
This is the freedom that you sailed from shore
  To save us for?

Dorset

John Fowles's book, *The French Lieutenant's Woman*:
'A grand ebullient portrait certainly'
Of Thomas Hardy's country, where however
I would not strike such sparkles. Slow and vocal
Amber of a burring baritone
My grandad's voice, not Hardy's, is what stays

Inside me as a slumbrous apogee,
Meridional altitude upon
Pastoral England's longest summer day.

O golden age! Bee-mouth, and honeyed singer!

County Durham

Driving up from Tees-side
The first and only time,
I had been there before;
I might have been in Goldthorpe.

My cousin kept a shop
For baby-linen in Goldthorpe;
Doing the same in Brighouse
An aunt went out of her mind.

But mostly, visible beauty
Intruded on a coal-field
So little, one was not
Unsettled by its absence.

Coal-field! A term like tundra,
Rain-forest, *karst*, savannah;
A humanly created
Topographical constant.

Indelible! Let rosebay
Willow herb, fiery emblem,
Push as it will, let the pits
Close, there will still be Goldthorpe.

I am told at the miners' gala
They bear green boughs and, Prince-
Bishop, a Lord of Misrule
Preaches in your cathedral.

And I am supposed to be
Delighted by that survival?
My Lord, your Lord of Misrule
Ruled, and rules, in Goldthorpe.

Essex

Names and things named don't match
Ever. This is not
A plethora of language,
But language's condition;

Sooner or later the whole
Cloth of the language peels off
As wallpaper peels from a wall,
However it 'hangs together'.

With Essex moreover the case is
Especially grievous: hope,
Disappointment, fatuous shocks
And surprises pattern the fabric.

Constable's country merits
Better than I can give it
Who have unfinished business
There, with my own failures.

Gloucestershire

for Charles and Brenda

Not architecture, not
(Good heavens!) city-planning,
But a native gift for townscape
Appears to have distinguished
The pre-industrial English.

Parochialism therefore,
Though of a Tuscan kind,
Discovers in the practice
Of this one homely art
The measure of *civiltà*.

A laudable Little England
Grounded on this conviction
Would fortify the Cotswolds,
Adopting as its tribal
Metropolis Chipping Camden.

Hampshire

'Our argute voices vied among the bracken.'
    My sixth-form prize from the North
Was Ronald Bottrall's *Festivals of Fire*,
    My own precocious choice.

A chaste young sailor (one thing I was not
    Precocious at was sex),
Abruptly, two years later, I pronounced
    This verse to a willowy Wren.

An educated girl, she recognized
    The bracken where we stood
Alone together in a woodland ride,
    And took 'argute' on trust.

Past that same wood near Wickham, that same year,
    My nineteenth autumn, I
Rode the country bus from Winchester
    To 'Collingwood' at Fareham.

Alone I'd spent my week-end's leave upon
    St Catherine's Hill, upon
Wolvesey Castle, the Cathedral Close;
    Seen the Round Table, doubtful.

All the South Country that I knew from books!
    Joining the Navy meant
My first time south to London, south from there
    Into my element:

Verses and books, 'argute' and Camelot.
I could correct that Hampshire, but shall not.

Herefordshire

At Hay, or near it, 1944
on winter leave, and walking through the moonlight
the country roads with Gavin Wright, I sealed
with a prompt fear the classical commonplace:
'As one who walks alone at night and fears
each brigand bush, each clump a nest of spears...'
I read that later, out of Juvenal.

A classical region, then? I think so, yes.
Though those were the Welsh Marches, it was not
classical Europe that we beat the bounds of;
barbarians indeed were at our doors
but not round there where, in a world at war,
with atavistic Englishness I saw
the black Black Mountains menacing our acres.

Hertfordshire

Was it, I wondered, some freak
of earth or just bad technique
    on the builder's part that made
    the pavement blocks before
    our friends' house hump and crack?
Could we, as our city shoes slipped
think Hertfordshire equipped,
    as Kent and Surrey were not,
    thus to resist the encroaching
    concrete apron of London?
No hope of that, alas!

An aspiring middle-class
       could however, we saw,
       make a humanly touching thing
       out of a suburb. It was
not wholly anonymous ground
on which they moved around,
       if it could mutiny thus
       in an Anglo-Jewish enclave
       between Finchley and Barnet.
Displacement and decay
provided for, brought into play
       by a prudent builder ensure
       that, suddenly dying, we leave
       our friends with something to say.

Huntingdonshire

Italian prisoners of war still haunted
       The Huntingdon we quartered
For flats to rent, untimely family
       A student's grant supported.

Many such families, then. The shaking frames
       Of a shared memory feature
A man from Pembroke with his Serbian bride,
       A sexless rawboned creature.

They lived, they said, in a jacked, abandoned bus.
       We wondered: Could they suckle,
Those flattened breasts? And the fingers! Labour Camps
       Had broken every knuckle.

What has become of them? Foolish to ask. But to couples
       We sometimes meet, we assign a
Not dissimilar past: our Roman host
       Has a Polish wife with *angina*.

Huntingdon's bard, androgynous William Cowper,
       Announced it to us all:
That Simoïs and Mincio, like Ouse,
       Sucked down his garden-wall.

Kent

Chatham was my depot,
Chatty Chatham, 'chatty'
Meaning squalid. So it
Was, the little town
One trundled to out of London
As to a dead-end England.

Of course I knew this was
To get things upside-down;
Still, so it proved for some
Soon after, in E-Boat Alley.

Lancashire

My father was born in Horton
In Ribblesdale – the highest
Signal-box in England
He'd say, but he was biased.

Though Horton is in Yorkshire,
The Ribble flows to the west.
I have imagined that river
With awful interest:

Dark gullies, sobbing alders
Must surely mark its course;
It rolls and rounds its boulders
With more than natural force.

For down that sombre valley
(I knew, without being told)
The famous Lancashire witches
Had long ago taken hold,

And a troop of Catholic gentry
Mustered from manors near
Rode hopelessly to Preston
To join the Chevalier.

258

Liverpool, Manchester, Salford
I've seen, and felt oppressed;
But Clitheroe's haunted river
I've never put to the test.

Should anyone taunt me with this,
The sneer's well merited.
But I pray you, remember my father –
The fault's inherited.

Leicestershire

From a view to a kill in pursuit ·
Of what can't fill the belly
May do for hunting the fox;
But I.A. Richards on Shelley
Was an obfuscating splendour.

Equally there in Leicester
I listened to the aureate
Archaic tongue of Blunden,
Who through his spell as laureate
Of Oxford smiled and was speechless.

Perhaps the Leicester Poetry
Society is still calling
Its week-end schools together;
It's my fault if I've fallen
Out of touch with its sponsors.

At Loughborough, I remember,
A man too little regarded
(Dead since), V.C. Clinton-
Baddeley afforded
Several views of Yeats.

Lincolnshire

for Kathleen Wilson

Simpering sideways under a picture-hat
Gainsborough Lady, every Odeon
Or Gaumont of the 'thirties knew her well.

Those British films she regally inclined
To sponsor were, I see now, laying claim
To suavities like Gainsborough the painter's.

Tricked by the name, though, I for years envisaged
Milady at her town in Lincolnshire;
Gainsborough, a sort of Tunbridge Wells.

Beau Nash was there, Beau Brummel took the waters.
If films were shot there (not the ones we saw
Oddly enough), they were demure and tasteful.

The place to go to see the Gainsborough Lady,
As I remember, was the Globe in New Street.
Cousin Kathleen, did you ever go there?

I think you may have done, going or coming
From grandmother's in Day Street. If you did,
Were you, like me, seduced by the genteel?

Easy to see you might be. There were rough
Diamonds all about us; Barnsley-born,
In us some mincing was forgivable.

In Louth that Tory stronghold, in the trilled
Late light on the wolds, a false refinement irks
As not in grimy Gainsborough or Scunthorpe.

Middlesex

Germans, she said, were sometimes independent;
Her countrymen were all for package-tours,

A girl from Wembley Stadium serving beers
In a Greek bar. A maxiskirt from Bristol
Hawked prints on the Acropolis; from Chepstow
Another served us in a coffee-bar.
Our age-group is dependent, but not theirs.

Temporary drop-outs or true wives
To young and struggling Greeks, they do us more
Credit than we deserve, their timid parents.

The longer loop their Odysseys, the more
Warmly exact the Ithakas they remember:
Thus, home she said was Middlesex, though Wembley
I should have named, indifferently, as 'London'.

Monmouthshire

for Doreen

The colonist's 'they' that needs no antecedent;
And as self-evident for the colonized –
Both mouths remorseless. For the Silurist
Self-styled, for Henry Vaughan, both
        Unthinking pronouns missed
The peaceful point three hundred years ago.

Anglo-Welsh: that mixture took and held
Through centuries. My dear wife, we endorsed it:
Our sons are a quarter Welsh if they care to think so.
Our brother-in-law was happy, when the Sappers'
        Reunion was in Chepstow,
To gossip with old comrades of Cawnpore.

Norfolk

An arbitrary roll-call
Of worthies: Nelson, Paine,
Vancouver, Robert Walpole.

Vancouver, stolid Dutchman
Born at Lynn, forgotten;
Too much the flogging captain.

Walpole: heaven-high smell of
Whitewash on tainted beef,
Piquant in learning's nostril.

(Unprincipled, vindictive,
All that Pope said, and worse
Confirmed, and spelt as virtue.)

But Nelson and mysterious
Tom Paine, baleful in Thetford,
Napoleonic portents...

Who answers for the double
Aspect of genius, arcing
From Corsica or Norfolk?

Northamptonshire

King's Cliffe, in the evening: that Northampton stone
As fine as Cotswold, and more masculine...

Turpin on wheels, my long-lost self that rode
Southward the Great North Road, and had

This bourne in mind, that night was disconcerted:
Youth hostel, yes; also a sort of shrine.

To William Law! Well, later on I learned
To gut that author for my purposes.

Questions remain, however. William Law,
Saint of the English Church . . . And what is sainthood?

Some leading questions must be answered soon,
Lead where they will, scared schoolboy, where they will!

Northumberland

'I hear Aneurin number the dead' – (Brigg Flatts)

Johnson's pentameters, nailed by the solid *ictus*;
'Felt percussion of the marching legions.'

Late excavations on the Wall report
The garrisons lived there in their excrement;

Centurions with their centuries, some thousands
– A decimal system drills to a count of ten –
Barked to a halt when Aneurin numbered the dead.

The laboured mole dilapidates, surmounted
By barrel-chests, Aegean or Cymric metres.

Nottinghamshire

Rosebay willow herb pushing
through patches of old slag
in the curtains of driving rain
obscured the Major Oak.

Or else (our steam was blurring
the windows of the Hillman)
it was our being hounded
out of doors that felled
the last tall stands of Sherwood.

Robin of Locksley, Guy
of Gisborne, and the Sheriff

of Nottingham had been dapples
under my mother's smiles
all down the glades of boyhood.

But now she could take no more
of us, and of our baby.

In the country of *Sons and Lovers*
we think we know all too much
about the love of mothers.

Angry and defiant,
rash on industrial waste,
the rosebay willow herb
is, of all the flowers
she taught me, one I remember.

Oxfordshire

'Start such a fire in England, Master Ridley,
As shall not be put out' – the coupled martyrs
That Oxford steers by in its Morris Minors
Fried for a quibble in Scripture or Canon Law!

Saints we remember, must we remember martyrs?
Baptists though we were, I knew from childhood
Latimer's words, and knew the fire he meant:
Godly work, the pious Reformation.

Crucifixions! Hideousness of burning,
Sizzle of fats, the hideous martyrdoms:
Palach consumed in Prague, a human torch;
A Saigon Buddhist, robe a more lambent saffron;

Dead for a country, dead for a Constitution
(Allende, in his mouth the emptied chamber
Of prompt and fluent deputies), were these
Crucifixions? They were suicides.

'Martyrs may seek their death, but may not seize it...'
Fine scruples, fine distinctions! Can there be
Any too fine for fine-toned Oxford, in
The smell of roast meat and the glare of torches?

Rutland

for George Dekker

Joke county, smallest in England.
But I remember distinctly, more than once,
Swinging the car at the bend by the railway yards
In Oakham, Rutland's county town. The last
Time was to see – I think you remember, George,
For your own reasons – paintings by my old
Friend, Bill Partridge. Dead now. Had you noticed?

How heavy that weighs, how wide the narrowest shire!

Shropshire

This has to be for my school-chum Billy Greaves
Who surfaced out of the past two years ago,
Breaking his journey to Fiji off one of his leaves;
He spoke to me by phone from San Francisco.

If we had met (we agreed upon 'next time'),
Would reminiscences have turned to Clun,
Clungunford, Clunbury, and Housman's rhyme?
('Quietest places,' he called them, 'under the sun.')

Possibly not; though once we wore out brake-blocks
Coasting from Wenlock Edge. And days gone by
Furnish a line of talk that's orthodox
For chance-met class-mates under a foreign sky.

Things change. Gone now the troublesome chores of Empire
That might earn such indulgences. We've seen,
Billy and I, our fractious nation tire
Too soon of holding Suva for the Queen.

Our parents at their tennis-club...A high
Lob in the last light hangs like Nemesis
On 1912! Deceived, my father's eye
Foresees the easy smash that he will miss.

Still, I'd quite like it, Billy, if you could
Recall for me above what gravelly flats
In what fly-haunted stream it was, we stood
In the weak light, pyjama-ed, swiping at bats.

Somerset

Antennae of the race,
'the damned and despised *literati*...'

Just how, she wanted to know
(swinging a shopping-bag
from Bridgewater), could
William Pitt have depended
for his intelligence on
a coterie in Racedown:
Coleridge and Southey, Wordsworth?

Big as a mule, a stag
through hedgerows down from Exmoor,
wall-eyed, nostrils flaring,
could not intrude more rudely
upon an *avant-garde*
seminar in the Quantocks.

Staffordshire

The jaunty style of Arnold Bennett's 'Card' . . .

From years ago I call to mind my father,
flushed and uncertain, stalling time after time
a borrowed car in Newcastle-under-Lyme,

who had sung as a young man, 'I was one of the knuts'.

Suffolk

Something gone, something gone out with Nelson,
With him or by him. Something in its place:
A Dynamo! Broke of the Shannon takes,
Crippled in his retirement, a sedate
Pride in totting up the butcher's bills
Of single-ship engagements, finds his own
(His head still singing from an American cutlass)
The bloodiest yet. Audacity of Nelson
Sired Broke and calloused him; Jane Austen's hero,
Honourable, monogamous and sober,
Gunnery-expert, servant of the State,
His small estate was somewhere here, in Suffolk.
A better image should be found for it.

My education gave me this bad habit
Of reading history for a hidden plot
And finding it; invariably the same one,
Its fraudulent title always, 'Something Gone'.

Gainsborough might have painted him, with his
Wife and children and a sleek retriever
(Thomas Gainsborough, born at Sudbury)
In a less glaring light, a truer one.

Surrey

'In yonder grave a Druid lies' – ('Ode on the Death of Thomson')

Who now reads Thomson or Collins?

'Conifer country of Surrey',
wrote Betjeman, 'approached through
remarkable wrought-iron gates.'

No missing the affection
there, nor the observation.

But on the Thames at Richmond
less tenderly, an eye for
the general more than the pungent
had lifted it to grandeur:

'Suspend the dashing oar.'

Sussex

Chiddingly, pronounced
Chiddinglye: the oast-house
Received us with warm brick,
A croquet-lawn, and squirrels.

And like the transatlantic
Visitors we were,
Our self-congratulations
And charmed response were fervent.

The most poeticized
Of English counties, and
An alien poet's eye,
Mine, there to endorse it.

We had to pinch ourselves
To know we knew the rules
Of cricket played on the green.
Our boy will never learn them.

'Brain-drain' one hears no more of,
And there's no loss. There is
Another emigration:
Draining away of love.

Warwickshire

for Roy Fisher

Eye on the object, eye on the congeries
of objects, eye on the scene
with figures of course, eye on the scene with figures,
delivers us Birmingham. Who is to say it squints?

And yet Spaghetti Junction on the M
6 is, shall we say,
a comparable alternative solution
(to a problem of traffic-flow
in several ways at once on several levels)
to the Piazza d'Aracoeli. Shall we
say that much or in
the Shakespeare country can we? If the tongue
writhes on the foreign syllables, it shows
small relish for your balder registrations,

intent, monocular, faithful.

Westmorland

Kendal...Shap Fell! Is that in Westmorland?
For one who espouses the North,
I am hazy about it, frankly. It's a chosen
North of the mind I take my bearings by,
A stripped style and a wintry;

As on Shap Fell, the only time I was there,
Wind cutting over and snowflakes beginning to sail
Slantwise across, on haulage vans clashing their gears
And me who had walked from Glasgow.

An end-of-October taste, a shade too late
For the right full ripeness. The style is decadent almost,
Emaciated, flayed. One knows such shapes,
Such minds, such people, always in need of a touch
Of frost, not to go pulpy.

Wiltshire

A brutally sheared-off cliff
Walling a cutting between
Barnsley and Doncaster is
The Railway Age in essence.

More cliffs, the hanging gardens
Of gossamer soot as the train
Creeps into Liverpool Street –
This too is in keeping.

But also consider the bugle
And stage-coach clatter silenced;
The beep and vroom of the Daimler
Unheard, and on the chalk

The human beetle rising
And falling for hours in the silence,
The distance: Jude the Obscure
Approaching, on Salisbury Plain.

Worcestershire

for Doreen

The best way in (not that I've checked the map)
Might be from West by North, as once we came
After a drive through spooky Radnor Forest
Where you had sat upon a picnic rug
And wept and wept. I laboured into verse
My sense of that, and made no sense at all.

Maria Theresa, I addressed you as,
Imperial sorrow. God knows what I meant
By that, or thought I meant. If I could not
Make you Fair Austria then, I shall not now;
But spin you down, down by whatever stages
Wise maps might tell me, into the blossoming plains.

Feed you with apples, stay you with flagons, Empress!
Acre on acre of orchards of Worcester Pearmains!

Yorkshire

Of Graces

The graces, yes – and the airs! To airs and graces
Equally the West Riding gave no houseroom
When I was young. Ballooning and mincing airs
Put on in the 'down there' of England! I was
Already out of place in the heraldic
Cities of the Midlands – Warwick, Leicester, the South...

   – And therefore it is a strain, thinking of Brough
   And Appleby gone from King John to a Frenchman
   For dirty work done on the roads of Poitou.

This helps me – not to pipe like your reed, Bunting,
Master of Northern stops – but to remember,
Never quite well enough, Kirkby Stephen
By Aisgill on to Hawes, to Aysgarth, Askrigg,
The narrow dale past a hump of broken stones.
Slant light out of Lancashire burnished the fell.

Alix, Kate, Eleanor, Anne – Angevin names –
You were not my hopscotch-mates; but Rhoda,
Thelma and Mona. Enormous their mottled
Fore-arms drove flat-irons later, strove with sheets
In old steam-laundries. There the Saxons queened it
No less – the Elfridas, Enids, many Hildas.

Ladies, ladies! Shirley or Diane or...
Which of you girls will be mine? Which of you all
In my dishonourable dreams sits smiling
Alone, at dusk, and knowledgeably sidelong,
Perched on a heap of stones, where 'Dangerous' says
The leaning board, on a green hill south of Brough?

Where is the elf-queen? Where the beldam Belle Dame?
Feyness of the North, kelpie of some small beck
In a swale of marble swirls over Durham,
Irrigates Elmet, combs the peat in Ewden.
And I have no faith in that: *le fay* thinned out
Into a pulse in the grass, St Winifred.

Eleanor rather, Alix, ladies of Latins,
I call you down. (And Mary, Mother of Heaven?)
Justice and Prudence (Prue, a name not given
North of the Trent), Courage, and Temperance were
Your erudite names, mothers of Latin earth.
What *royaume* of earth, elf-queen, did you sway ever?

Charites or *Gratiae*, the Graces,
Lemprière says, 'presided over kindness',
Each dam in her own kind fructive. Only two.
(Three came later.) Two: *Hegemone*, the Queen,
And *Auxo*, Increase. Queen of Elfland, in what
Assize did you sit, what increase ever foster?

Now every girl has this elvish admixture.
Thomas of Ercildoune, what you dreamed of once
Fogs every brae-side: lank black the hair hangs down,
The curves of the cheek are hollow and ravaged.
Their womanhood a problematic burden
To them and their castrated mates, they go past.

I have a Grace. Whether or no the Muses
Patronize me, I have a Grace in my house
And no elf-lady. Queen she is called, and Increase,
Though late-come, straitened, of a Northern Province.

Father, the Cavalier

I have a photograph here
  In California where
You never were, of yourself
  Riding a white horse. And
The horse and you are dead
  Years ago, although
  Still you are more alive
  To me than anyone living.

As for the horse: an ugly
  Wall-eyed brute, apparently
Biddable though, for I cannot
  Believe you were ever much of
A horseman. That all came late:
  Suddenly, in your forties,
Learning to ride! A surrogate
  Virility, perhaps...

For me to think so could not
  Make you any more
Alive than you have been here,
  Open-necked cricket-shirt
And narrow head, behind
  The pricked ungainly ears
Of your white steed – all these
  Years, unnoticed mostly.

The Harrow

Unimaginable beings –
Our own dead friends, the dead
Notabilities, mourned and mourning,
Hallam and Tennyson...is it
Our loss of them that harrows?

Or is it not rather
Our loss of images for them?
The continued being of Claude
Simpson can be imagined.
We cannot imagine its mode.

Us too in this He harrows. It is not
Only on Easter Saturday
That it is harrowing
To think of Mother dead,
To think, and not to imagine.

He descended into –
Not into Hell but
Into the field of the dead
Where he roughs them up like a tractor
Dragging its tray of links.

Up and down the field, a tender bruising,
A rolling rug of iron, for the dead
Them also, the Virtuous Pagans
And others, He came, He comes
On Easter Saturday and

Not only then He comes
Harrowing them – that they,
In case they doubted it, may
Quicken and in more
Than our stale memories stir.

The Departed

They see his face!

Live in the light of ...

Such shadows as they must
cast, sharp-edged;
the whole floor, said to be crystal,
barry with them. And long!

Spokes that reach even to us,
Pinned as we are to the rim.

Rousseau in his Day

So many nights the solitary lamp had burned;
So many nights his lone mind, slowing down
Deliberately, had questioned, as it turned
Mooning upon its drying stem, what arc
Over a lifetime day had moved him through.

Always he hoped he might deserve a Plutarch,
Not to be one posterity forgot.
Nor have we. He has left his mark: one tight
Inched-around circuit of the screw of light,
As glowing shadows track the life of roses
Over unchosen soil-crumbs. It was not
What he'd expected or the world supposes.

After the Calamitous Convoy (July 1942)

An island cast
its shadow across
the water. Where
they sat upon
the Arctic shore
it shadowed them.

The mainland rose
tawny before
their eyes and closed
round them in capes
the island must
have slid from, once.

Under one horn
of land not quite
naked, above
the anchorage
white masonry
massed round a square.

From there one gained
the waterfront
by, they perceived,
a wooden stair
that wound down through
workshops and godowns.

Admiringly
their eyes explored
make-do-and-mend:
arrangements that
the earth lent – stairs,
cabins on struts,

stages of raised
catwalks between
stair and railed stair,
staked angles, ramps
and landings in
the open air.

Roof of the world,
not ceiling. One
hung to it not
as flies do but
as steeplejacks
move over rungs.

Survivors off
the Russian run,
years later they
believed the one
stable terrain
that Arctic one.

Depravity: Two Sermons

1. *Americans: for their Bicentennial*

The best, who could, went back – because they nursed
A need to find depravity less dispersed,
Less, as it seemed, diluted by crass hope.
So back went Henry James to evil Europe,
Unjust, unequal, cruel. Localized,
The universal could be realized
In words and not in words; not by the Press
Nor the theatrical Pulpit. Prefaces
Delineate the exquisite pains he took
To bottle up a bad smell in a book.
Inordinate pains! For Paris, London, Rome
Were not much less disorderly than back home;
There too, already, what he sought was traced
Upon no maps, but must be found by Taste,
A nostril lifted to the tainted gale
Of words, of words – all shop-soiled, all for sale.
Each year that he survived, things fell apart
Till H.G. Wells was 'Life', and he was 'Art'.
'Life'! Is it something else than life, to live
On the scent always of that faint, pervasive
Smell that alone explains what we've become?
What ought to be, and once was, axiom?

2. *St Paul's Revisited*

'The change of Philomel, by the barbarous king,
So rudely forced'.
*[In the myth, Philomela became a nightingale, and
Tereus, her ravisher, a hoopoe.]*

Anger, a white wing? No, a hoopoe's wing,
King Tereus, Hatred. Crested ravisher,
The motley lapwing whoops and whoops it up
Greek Street and Fleet Street till the gutters run
Their serial feature. Liquid, yellow, thick,
It pools here, fed from the Antipodes,
The Antilles... For the seven seas run with bile
To the Pool of London, sink where the ordure, talent
At home in this world, gathers. And it pools

Not only there but in whatever head
Recalls with rage the choir of Christ and Wren.

Horned and self-soiling, not the barbarous king
Of Thrace and the anthologies, nor a brute,
A plain quick killer, but degenerate,
The rapist lapwings sideways through our heads
And finds no exit. There's a place it might:
The A-to-Z preserves no record of it
Though Strype or any antique gazetteer
Describes it well enough, a Thames-side borough
Decayed already, called Depravity.
If we could find it now, our hoopoes might
Hop from inside our heads, and Thames run cleaner.

Anger won't do it. Ire! Its hooked bill gouges
The chicken-livers of its young. Irate,
We are depraved, and by that token. Gulls
Cry, and they skeeter on a candid wing
Down slopes of air, but not for anger's sake.
Spite, malice, arrogance and 'Fuck you, Jack',
Birds in the gables of Depravity
Twitter and cheep, but most inside my head
And can be lived with. But the hoopoe whoops
Always inside, and rancorous. Rancour! Rancour!
Oh patriotic and indignant bird!

Seeing Her Leave

'gardens bare and Greek' – Yvor Winters

This West! this ocean! The bare
Beaches, the stony creek
That no human affair
Has soiled . . . Yes, it is Greek,

What she saw as the plane
Lifted from San Jose.
Under the shadow of Wren
She walks her ward today;

Once more my tall young woman
Has nerved herself to abandon
This Greece for the Graeco-Roman
Peristyles of London,

Where the archaic, the heated,
Dishevelled and frantic Greek
Has been planed and bevelled, fitted
To the civic, the moralistic.

And that has been noble, I think,
In her and others. Such
Centuries, sweat, and ink
Spent to achieve that much!

Lloyds of London, some
Indemnity for our daughters!
Those who trust the dome
Of St Paul's to the waters...

So much of the price is missed
In the tally of toil, ink, years;
Count, neo-classicist,
The choking back of tears.

(California)

Mandelstam, on Dante

1.

Russian Jew, for you
    To re-think Dante, dissolve
Into fluids that four-square slab
    Of Christendom, meant a resolve

(So it must seem) to taunt
    And tempt the unsteadied Gentile,
As it might be me, to act
    In nettled Stalin's style.

Dangerous, those corrosives
    You handle. First and last
Powder the graven image!
    'Jew' means 'iconoclast'.

Can we believe the impulse
    Consciously suicidal?
Or was the play of mind
    Lordly, the interest idle?

2.

About the skies, you went wrong somewhere. Let
Some nearer neighbour of theirs make the corrections.
For them it was easier, them the nine Olympic
Dantescan discuses, to clang directions!

You are not to be thought of apart from the life you lived
And what Life intends is at once to kill and caress
That thus the distress which beat in on your ears, on your eyes
And the sockets of your eyes, be Florentine.

Let us not then assign to you, no, let us not fit about your
Hollowed-out temples that bittersweet prickle, the laurel –
Better in your case if we should split your
Heart into blue and clamorous bits of ocean.

For when you died, having served out your time,
You in your time friend to all lifetime-livers,
Yes, there transpired a broader, a loftier chime
Sent from the skies in your entire chest's heavings.

3. *(Voronezh, 1937)*

'About the skies, I went wrong somewhere. Let
Some nearer neighbour of theirs make the corrections.
For you it was easier, you the nine Olympic
Dantescan discuses, to clang directions,
Be out of breath, get black and blue contusions...

But Thou, if Thou art not the heretofore's
Nothing-accomplishing hero, if Thou art bent
Standing over me now, wine-steward, to proffer the cup,

Pour me the strong wine, not the ephemeral ferment
To drink of, to pledge the vertiginous, towering, straight-up
Insane blue-azure's hand-to-hand engagement.

Dovecotes, black holes, starlings' nesting-boxes,
Blue of the bluest, case of the key at its keenest,
Ice of the heretofore, high ice! – ice of the Spring...
Clouds, look – the clouds, against soft collusions embattled...
Quiet now! Storm-clouds, see where they lead them out, bridled.'

4.

Rhyme, you once said, only
    Points it up, tags it, the blue
Cabinet-making of Heaven
    And Earth, the elegant joints
All of them flush as given!

Symmetries in this blue
    Cabinet, the small
Rooms of stanzas – in this
    No woe, you said, but the happy
Chances of mathematics.

Clouds come and go like a French
    Polisher's breath on walnut,
Protean, fluid... And you
    A lordly squandering playboy!
No bequest but you blue it!

At home in the Empyrean...
    Yes, but one joint had sprung
Long, long ago. The woe
    Came, and was Florentine?
As well say: Galilean.

Death of a Painter

in memoriam William Partridge

Behind the grid, the radiant
planes and translucent ledges
of colour,

the constructions,

feelingful but extreme
distortions, as my eye found them,

three or four trees and a Norman
church-tower in Leicestershire? Well
yes, if you say so.
You painted always from nature.
That mattered, you always said.

Hard to see why, unless

among these cobalts and
pale yellows, these
increments and crumblings,

in that or another churchyard
we are permitted to speak
to a Divine Distorter
these lines that you occasion.

Portland

after Pasternak

Portland, the Isle of Portland – how I love
Not the place, its name! It is as if
These names were your name, and the cliff, the breaking
Of waves along a reach of tumbled stone
Were a configuration of your own
Firm slopes and curves – your clavicles, your shoulder.
A glimpse of that can set the hallway shaking.
And I am a night sky that is tired of shining,
Tired of its own hard brilliance, and I sink.

Tomorrow morning, grateful, I shall seem
Keen, but be less clear-headed than I think;
A brightness more than clarity will sail
Off lips that vapour formulations, make
Clear sound, full rhyme, and rational order take
Account of a dream, a sighing cry, a moan.

Like foam on all three sides at midnight lighting
Up, far off, a seaward jut of stone.

Orpheus

named them
and they danced
they danced: the rocks, stones, trees.

What had possessed them,
or him? How did it help?

What had got into those stones,
throwing up puffs
of yellow dust as they bounced, and could he
hear them, an irregular percussion
there in the blinding sunlight
like a discotheque at a distance?

No, I'm afraid not: weightless.
For them to dance
they had to be light as air,
as the puff of air that named them.

Thistledown rocks! Who needs them?

Well but, they danced for joy,
his holy joy
in stones, in there being stones
there, that stones should be,
and boulders too, and trees...

Is that how it was? One hopes so.

Ars Poetica

in memoriam Michael Ayrton, sculptor

Walk quietly around in
A space cleared for the purpose.

Most poems, or the best,
Describe their own birth, and this
Is what they are – a space
Cleared to walk around in.

Their various symmetries are
Guarantees that the space has
Boundaries, and beyond them
The turbulence it was cleared from.

Small clearances, small poems;
Unlikely now the enormous
Louring, resonant spaces
Carved out by a Virgil.

The old man likes to sit
Here, in his black-tiled *loggia*
A patch of sun, and to muse
On Pasternak, Michael Ayrton.

Ayrton, he remembers.
Soon after reading his
Obituary, behold!
A vision of him:

The bearded, heavy-shouldered
London clubman, smiling
Against a *quattrocento*
View of the upper Arno.

This was in answer to prayer:
A pledge, a sufficient solace.
Poor rhyme, and are you there?
Bless Michael with your promise.

The old man likes to look
Out on his tiny *cortile*,
A flask of 'Yosemite Road'
Cheap Chablis at his elbow.
                              (California)

In the Stopping Train

*

I have got into the slow train
again. I made the mistake
knowing what I was doing,
knowing who had to be punished.

I know who has to be punished:
the man going mad inside me;
whether I am fleeing
from him or towards him.

This journey will punish the bastard:
he'll have his flowering gardens
to stare at through the hot window;
words like 'laurel' won't help.

He abhors his fellows,
especially children; let there
not for pity's sake
be a crying child in the carriage.

So much for pity's sake.
The rest for the sake of justice:
torment him with his hatreds
and love of fictions.

The punishing slow pace
punishes also places along the line
for having, some of them, Norman
or Hanoverian stone-work:

his old familiars, his
exclusive prophylactics.
He'll stare his fill at their
emptiness on this journey.

Jonquil is a sweet word.
Is it a flowering bush?
Let him helplessly wonder
for hours if perhaps he's seen it.

Has it a white and yellow
flower, the jonquil? Has it
a perfume? Oh his art could
always pretend it had.

He never needed to see,
not with his art to help him.
He never needed to use his
nose, except for language.

Torment him with his hatreds,
torment him with his false
loves. Torment him with time
that has disclosed their falsehood.

Time, the exquisite torment!
His future is a slow
and stopping train through places
whose names used to have virtue.

*

A stopping train, I thought,
was a train that was going to stop.
Why board it then, in the first place?

Oh no, they explained, it is stopping
and starting, stopping and starting.

How could it, they reasoned gently,
be always stopping unless
also it was always starting?

I saw the logic of that;
grown-ups were good at explaining.

Going to stop was the same
as stopping to go. What madness!
It made a sort of sense, though.

It's not, I explained, that I mind
getting to the end of the line.
Expresses have to do that.

No, they said. We see...
But do you? I said. It's not
the last stop that is bad...

No, they said, it's the last
start, the little one; yes,
the one that doesn't last.

Well, they said, you'll learn
all about that when you're older.

Of course they learned it first.
Oh naturally, yes.

*

The man in the stopping train
sees them along the highway
with a recklessness like breeding
passing and re-passing:
dormobile, Vauxhall, Volvo.

He is shrieking silently: 'Rabbits!'
He abhors his fellows.
Yet even the meagre arts
of television can
restore them to him sometimes,

when the man in uniform faces
the unrelenting camera
with a bewildered fierceness
beside the burnt-out Simca.

*

What's all this about flowers?
They have an importance he can't
explain, or else their names have.

Spring, he says, 'stirs'. It is what
he has learned to say, he can say
nothing but what he has learned.

And Spring, he knows, means flowers.
Already he observes this.
Some people claim to love them.

Love *them*? Love flowers? Love,
love...the word is hopeless:
gratitude, maybe, pity...

Pitiful, the flowers.
He turns that around in his head:
what on earth can it mean?

Flowers, it seems, are important.
And he can name them all,
identify hardly any.

*

Judith Wright, Australian

'...has become', I said, 'the voice
of her unhappy nation.'
O wistfully I said it.

Unhappier than it knows,
her nation. And though she will tell it,
it cannot understand:

with its terrible future before it,
glaring at its terrible past;

its disequilibrium, its
cancers in bud and growing;

288   POEMS OF THE 1970s

all its enormous sadness
still taking off, still arcing

over the unhistoried
Pacific, humming to Chile.

Stone heads of Easter Island!
Spoiled archipelagos!

How they have suffered already
on Australia's account

and England's. They will suffer
no more on England's.

Judith Wright, Australian,
'has become', I said,

'the voice of her unhappy,
still-to-be-guilty nation.'

Wistfully I said it,
there in the stopping train.

                    *

The things he has been spared . . .
'Gross egotist!' Why don't
his wife, his daughter, shrill
that in his face?

Love and pity seem
the likeliest explanations;
another occurs to him –
despair too would be quiet.

                    *

Time and again he gave battle,
furious, mostly effective;
nobody counts the wear
and tear of rebuttal.

Time and again he rose
to the flagrantly offered occasion;
nobody's hanged for a slow
murder by provocation.

Time and again he applauded
the stand he had taken; how much
it mattered, or to what
assize, is not recorded.

Time and again he hardened
his heart and his perceptions;
nobody knows just how
truths turn into deceptions.

Time and again, oh time and
that stopping train!
Who knows when it comes to a stand,
and will not start again?

* *(Son et Lumière)*

I have travelled with him many times
now. Already we nod,
we are almost on speaking terms.

Once I thought that he sketched
an apologetic gesture
at what we turned away from.

Apologies won't help him:
his spectacles flared like paired
lamps as he turned his head.

I knew they had been ranging,
paired eyes like mine,
igniting and occluding

coppice and crisp chateau,
thatched corner, spray of leaf,
curved street, a swell of furrows,

where still the irrelevant vales
were flowering, and the still
silver rivers slid west.

*

The dance of words
is a circling prison, thought
the passenger staring through
the hot unmoving pane
of boredom. It is not
thank God a dancing pain,
he thought, though it starts to jig
now. (The train is moving.) 'This',
he thought in rising panic
(Sit down! Sit down!)
'this much I can command,
exclude. Dulled words, keep still!
Be the inadequate, cloddish
despair of me!' No good:
they danced, as the smiling land
fled past the pane, the pun's
galvanized *tarantelle*.

*

'A shared humanity...' He
pummels his temples. 'Surely,
surely that means something.'

He knew too few in love,
too few in love.

That sort of foolish beard
masks an uncertain mouth.
And so it proved: he took
some weird girl off to a weird
commune, clutching at youth.

Dear reader, this is not
our chap, but another.
Catch our clean-shaven hero
tied up in such a knot?
A cause of so much bother?

He knew too few in love.

His Themes

(after reading Edmond Jabès)

His themes? Ah yes he had themes.
It was what we all liked about him.
Especially I liked it.
One knew, nearly always one knew
what he was talking about, and he talked
in such a ringing voice.

What did he talk about? What,
just what were his themes?
Oh, of the most important!

Loss was one of his themes;
he told us, as any bard should,
    the story of our people
    (tribe), he had memorized
    chronologies, genealogies,
    the names and deeds of heroes,
    the succession of our kings,
    our priests, the sept of our pipers,
    the mediations...and this
    while, young and old,
    we extolled the immediate, meaning
    the unremembering. *Yes,*
    and what was his theme? His theme, you said, was...?
Loss. Loss was his theme.

And duty. He taught us our duty;
he taught us, as any
legislator should,
    the rules of hygiene, the clean
    and the unclean meats, the times and
    the means of fumigation,
    the strewing and spreading, of fires,
    and what to do with the old
    and how to dispose of the dead
    and how to live with our losses
    uncomplaining...and this
    while, young and old,
    we did our best to be free,
    meaning unruly. *Yes,*
    and what was his theme? What did you say his theme was?

Duty. His theme was duty.

Fear also. Fear was a theme;
he taught us, as all seers must,
continual apprehension:
>of one another, of
>our womenfolk and our
>male children, of
>the next clan over the mountains
>and of the mountains, also
>the waters, the heavenly bodies
>wheeling and colliding,
>of the wild beasts both large
>and infinitesimal, of
>revenants and of the future,
>and of the structure of matter
>and of the unknown...and all this
>while, young and old,
>we tried to keep our nerve,
>meaning, to be heedless. *Yes,*
>*and what was the theme, did you say, of this voice both hollow and*
>>>>*ringing?*

Fear. Fear was the theme.

We like to be told these things.
We need to be reminded.

He sounds like a sort of priest.
What was your priesthood doing?

Nonsensical things, like spinning
a shallow great bowl of words
poised on the stick of a question,
pointing it this way and that
for an answering flash, as the bend
of a river may come in a flash
over miles and miles
from a fold in the hills, over miles.

We paid them no attention.

To Thom Gunn in Los Altos, California

Conquistador! Live dangerously, my Byron,
In this metropolis
Of Finistère. Drop off
The edge repeatedly, and come
Back to tell us! Dogs and cherry-trees
Are not your element, although
You like them well enough when, cast
Ashore and briefly beached, our Commodore,
You take a turn among them, your cigar
Fragrant along a sunny garden wall,
Home between voyages, with your aunts in Kent.

Home...Is that home? Is even Land's End 'home'?
You shrug and say we are mid-Atlantic people,
You and I. I'd say for you
The mid-Pacific rather: somewhere out
On the International Dateline, so far out
Midsummer Oregon and midwinter Chile
Are equidistant, and 'the slow
Pacific swell' you generate lifts and crunches
Under the opalescent high fog with as much
Patience in one hemisphere as the other,
An exhalation from the depths you sound to.

The plesiosaur! Your lead-line has gone down to
The Age of Reptiles, even as
Over your head the flying lizard
Sprung from its Lompoc silo, Vandenberg Airforce Base,
Tracks high across mid-ocean to its target.
Ignore it, though a tidal wave will rage
From where it plunges, flood Japan
And poison Asia. This is the pacific
Ocean, the peacemaker. Nothing rhymes with this
Lethal indifference that you plumbed to even
Once in a bath-house in Sonoma County.

This is the end of the world. At the end, at the edge
We live among those for whom
As is natural enough
The edge is the navel of earth, and the end, the beginning.
Hope springs not eternal nor everywhere – does it

Spring in Kent? For these our friends, however,
It springs, it springs. Have we a share in it?
This is the Garden of Eden, the serpent coiled
Inside it is sleepy, reposeful. It need not flex
A muscle to take us. What are we doing here?
What am I doing, I who am scared of edges?

Seur, near Blois

That a toss of wheat-ears lapping
Church-walls should placate us
Is easy to understand
In the abstract. That in fact
The instance of seeing also
A well with its wrought-iron stanchion,
Of feeling a balmy coolness,
Of hearing a Sunday noon silence,
Of smelling the six ragged lime-trees,
A church-door avenue, should
Placate, compose, is as much
As to say that the eye and the nose,
Also the ear and the very
Surface of one's skin is
An ethical organ; and further,
If indeed it is further
Or even other, a learned
Historian of man's culture.

Gemona-del-Friuli, 1961-1976

We have written to Giulia, saying
'Are you still alive?'
And no reply comes.
This is a bad look out.

What sort of a life this is
I thought I knew, or I learned,
Some 15 years ago
Precisely in Giulia's country:

Gemona, the heartland, the forests
Living in an orange light
After calamity. That one!
That was the place;

Where a calamity, not
In any case undeserved,
Chastened, I thought, and instructed
Gravely, biddable me

As to the proper proportions
Of the dead to the living, of death
To life, and out of all
Proportion, love...Now this!

Earthquake! And the entire
Small city of Gemona
Flat in one enormous
Stir of that rock-ribbed earth

Which had not in 700
Years – for some of Gemona
Had stood that long – not stirred
Like that in 700 years.

What colour of justification,
What nice, austere proportion
Now can be put on the mountains?
At whose hand this chastisement?

An Apparition

Gina, I saw you walk
Suddenly, in white
Brassiere and panties under
A fish-net wrap; your sallow skin,

Firm and sullen to fire,
Inflamed the Panamanian
Day to exceptional ardours
In Tehuantepec Bay

As our Edwardian prow
Ploughed southward, and decrepit
Bodies basked in renewed
Delusory bronze and vigour.

The posh ships, P. & O.,
Trace in phosphorescent
Peppermint-fire on the oceans
An after-image of Empire.

The sun stooped down to take you,
Stiff on your bed in Boulder,
Colorado, Gina;
You will never grow older,

Nor will your empire ever,
Italo-American girl,
Crumble in Eritrea,
Dear wraith, raped by Apollo.

Horae Canonicae

Prime

New every morning is the love
Our wakening and uprising prove,
Bond it in warranty a hundred proof.
Giving his thanks for roof, for bed and board,
Mr Saint Keble, meek and lowly,
White with rite, and clean with holy,
Wordplays to the morning's Lord.

Terce

New every morning is the power
That activates us, active though we are . . .
At 9 o'clock, the scriptural 3rd hour,
Mr Saint William Law is eating his
Sweet humble pie: 'We have no more
Power of our own to move a hand or stir
A foot, than to stop clouds, or move the sun.'

Sext

'Filling us with such bowels of
Compassion as when' (Come, Mr Law, we are furnished
With bowels, and they are full, or they are not;
What room for other organs?), glimpsing her
Appallingly in Cambridge Circus, tracing
The faceless angel who mounted her once and vanished,
'We see the miseries of an hospital.'

Nones

At 3 o'clock in the afternoon,
Loggy with gin, with wine, with Mexican beer,
Resignation to the will of God
Comes easy. That it should be 'hardly worth
Living in a world so full of changes
And revolutions' – ah, how wrong! Yet dozing,
Fanned in a garden-chair, is hardly 'prayer'.

Vespers

This one for the telling of sins. And for
The original horror, the victimization, no problem.
But for our own, our particular own, in the sorry
Unrollings, where was the harm? Not nowhere, but
Where? In prayer, no place for 'all-over-the-place',
It comes to seem... My instructors' awful calm
Tell-tales the stink: half spunk, half frightened sweat.

Compline

Now I lay me down to sleep
Perhaps not to wake, and I am alone in the house!
How much alone in whatever house of bone,
Suddenly I love my fellow creatures
So much, though for that hour was Sext, was noon.
I tell you over feverishly, my loved ones.
You are my own, you are? My own! My own?

Morning

Rose late: the jarring and whining
Of the parked cars under my windows, their batteries drained,
Somehow was spared. When I let out our schoolboy
Into the street, it was light: the place was alive and scented.

Spared too, for the most part, the puzzling tremulousness
That afflicts me often, these mornings. (I think
Either I need, so early, the day's first drink or
This is what a sense of sin amounts to:
Aghast incredulity at the continued success
Of an impersonation, the front put on to the world,
The responsibilities . . .)
                          Let all that go:
Better things throng these nondescript, barged-through streets
(The sun! The February sun, so happily far and hazy . . .)
Than a mill of ideas.
                     Sin, I will say, comes awake
With all the other energies, even at last the spark
Leaps on the sluggard battery, and one should have
Prosopopoeia everywhere: Stout Labour
Gets up with his pipe in his mouth or lighting
The day's first *Gauloise-filtre*; then stout
Caffein like a fierce masseur
Rams him abreast of the day; stout Sin
Is properly a-tremble; stout
Vociferous Electricity chokes and chokes,
Stumbles at last into coughings, and will soon
Come to the door with a telegram – 'Operation
Some Day This Week'; and stout
Love gets up out of rumpled sheets and goes singing
Under his breath to the supermarket, the classroom,
The briskly unhooded
Bureaucratic typewriter. See how
Sol winks upon its clever keys, and Flora
In a northern winter, far underground,
Feels herself sore at nubs and nipples.

And that mob of ideas? Don't knock them. The sick pell-mell
Goes by the handsome Olympian name of Reason.

To a Teacher of French

Sir, you were a credit to whatever
Ungrateful slate-blue skies west of the Severn
Hounded you out to us. With white, cropped head,
Small and composed, and clean as a Descartes
From as it might be Dowlais, 'Fiery' Evans
We knew you as. You drilled and tightly lipped
Le futur parfait dans le passé like
The Welsh Guards in St James's, your pretence
Of smouldering rage an able sergeant-major's.

We jumped to it all right whenever each
Taut smiling question fixed us. Then it came:
Crash! The ferrule smashed down on the first
Desk of the file. You whispered: *Quelle bêtise!*
Ecoutez, s'il vous plait, de quelle bêtise
on est capable!
                    Yet you never spoke
To us of poetry; it was purely language,
The lovely logic of its tenses and
Its accidence that, mutilated, moved you
To rage or outrage that I think was not
At all times simulated. It would never
Do in our days, dominie, to lose
Or seem to lose your temper. And besides
Grammarians are a dying kind, the day
Of histrionic pedagogy's over.

You never taught me Ronsard, no one did,
But you gave me his language. He addressed
The man who taught him Greek as *Toi qui dores*
(His name was Jean Dorat) *la France de l'or.*
I couldn't turn a phrase like that on 'Evans';
And yet you gild or burnish something as,
At fifty in the humidity of Touraine,
Time and again I profit by your angers.

Widowers

'i segni dell' antica fiamma'

Atheist, Laodicean or
Whatever name our hand-to-mouth evasions
Earn for us, all of us have the thought
That states of soul in some uncertain sort
Survive us – sealed, it could be, in locations:
A yard, a coomb, an inn, a Cornish tor.

These leak their fragrances. To tap the fount
Of consolation calls on us for no
Dexterity at first; it isn't hard
To bruise a hip by falling in that yard
Or on that hillside. Hurt is all we know,
Stout alpenstock as we begin to mount

The purgatorial steeps, the terraces
Kicked back behind us. Then we sweat, we stink,
We fear that we forget. Our ancient haunts
Glow far above us, and the glimmer taunts
Our coming numbness. There she dwells, we think . . .
She does, although our need to think so passes.

Some Shires Revisited

1. *Norfolk*

The scroll is defaced; the worm
Is in the roof; and the flaking
Inscription may be cleared
Of ivy but, if it is read,
It must be on the firm
Presumption it is mistaken.

Reading from haunted air
Certain great (which is not to say, good)
Historical presences – Walpole,
Nelson, landmarks in Norfolk –
I had readers who thought that I could
Never in fact have been there.

2. *Devonshire*

'Into Spooner's, looking for remnants,'
Said Mrs John; and her face was wistful
As if the town she recalled, the tenements
Burnt in the blitz, the streets like tunnels
Turning and twisting at cliff-like corners
Under the web of the wires, were a haven
Unspeakably lovely and calm. The destroyers
Had threatened her future; the young rebuilders
Tore down that future perfect in the past
Of a new-planned Plymouth, 1951.

3. *Leicestershire*

Clinton-Baddeley, Richards,
Blunden . . . these I have blessed:
Three good men named, and as many
Of those who invited them there
Unnamed, their equals or betters,
Upholders of what they professed
To care for, the world of letters
In the not quite wholly benighted
Midlands of England. In these
Worthies I have delighted
With a droll rhyme or two;
Leicestershire, when it housed them,
Did better than it knew.

4. *Staffordshire*

for Charles Tomlinson

'As once on Thracian Hebrus side' (to use
Your own Etrurian idiom, jasper-ware)

'The tree-enchanter Orpheus fell
By Bacchanalians torn',

So I have seen you – gasping, bloodied – fall
Time and again over twenty-five years, and the Maenads

Quite honestly astonished: 'But we surely
(Serenely, suavely) always gave him his due?'

Your love of our country has not been returned, and won't be.

5. *Bedfordshire*

Crop-headed nonconformists,
  Cromwell's Ironsides, sprang
Out of this clay. But not all
  The sour battalions rang
With benedictions when
  The sage dictator willed
  A king was to be killed.

Redbrick, round-windowed chapels,
  Squat on these gravels, rose,
And yet not all their broadcloth,
  When the time came, chose
The Red Flag as the only
  Colours to march to. Some
  Never came back from the Somme.

Born one of them, I think
  How it might be to be French;
How Protestants might man
  Pétain's untenable trench
And, rendering unto Caesar
  What's due to Caesar, might
  Die fighting the wrong good fight.

Grudging Respect

As when a ruined face
Lifted among those crowding
For the young squire's largesse
Perceives him recognize
Her and she grabs, not for any
Languidly lofted penny
They scrabble for, but for his eyes
And pockets them, their clouding
That instant; and the abruptness
With which his obliging is checked,
His suddenly leaving the place...

Just so may a grudging respect
Be, from a despised one,
Not just better than none
At all, but sweeter than any.

A Spring Song

'stooped to truth and moralized his song'

Spring pricks a little. I get out the maps.
Time to demoralize my song, high time.
Vernal a little. *Primavera*. First
Green, first truth and last.
High time, high time.

A high old time we had of it last summer?
I overstate. But getting out the maps...
Look! Up the valley of the Brenne,
Louise de la Vallière...Syntax collapses.
High time for that, high time.

To Château-Renault, the tannery town whose marquis
Rooke and James Butler whipped in Vigo Bay
Or so the song says, an amoral song
Like Ronsard's where we go today
Perhaps, perhaps tomorrow.

Tomorrow and tomorrow and...Get well!
Philip's black-sailed familiar, avaunt
Or some word as ridiculous, the whole
Diction kit begins to fall apart.
High time it did, high time.

High time and a long time yet, my love!
Get out that blessed map.
Ageing, you take your glasses off to read it.
Stooping to truth, we potter to Montoire.
High time, my love. High time and a long time yet.

Townend, 1976

When does a town become a city? This
That ends where I begin it, at Townend
With Wright the Chemist (one of the few not changed),
Grows cityfied, though still my drab old friend.

Thanks therefore for the practical piety
Of E.G. Tasker, antiquarian;
His *Barnsley Streets*. Unshed, my tears hang heavy
Upon the high-gloss pages where I scan

What else, though, but remembered homely squalor?
Generations of it! Eldon Street
Smells of bad drains of forty years ago
Ah sweetly. But should penury smell sweet?

An end to it then. An end to that town. Townend.
A Tetley's house, the Wheatsheaf, holds its station
Since 1853, where Dodworth Road
Stars into five streets, 'major intersection'.

Portentous words! Hoist up to suit South Yorkshire's
Administrative centre, such perforce
This town must live with, must live up or down to:
'Intersection'; 'shopping precinct'; 'concourse'...

And not to be sneered nor sniffed at. This is not,
It never was, Blackheath or Tunbridge Wells;
No buildings 'listed', nor deserving it,
Press to be saved as civic ardour swells.

Of cities much is written. Even Scripture
Has much to say of them, though mostly under
The inauspicious name of 'Babylon'.
What a town is, one is left to wonder.

Is homely squalor, then, its sign and function?
Is it a swollen village? If it is,
Are swellings lanced? Have towns a size or shape
More than villages and less than cities?

I think of the Irish, or perhaps the Celtic
'Townland'. (Also, 'township' might provoke us.)
'Townland', so my Irish years persuade me,
Means never a star of roads, never a focus.

Never! By no means! There's a lead at last:
Focus, a hearth. The English circumstance
In town or village draws to a hearth, a fug:
Townend, the up-draught up five flues at once!

Whatever meets that need, it's certain 'concourse',
'Complex' nor 'intersection' ever could.
Upon their hunkers, 'carring' (cowering) down
By a spent flame, the colliers of my boyhood...

That was in the 'thirties, 'the Depression';
Outside whatever pub it is in Kingstone,
Unwanted in the open, nipping air,
All the one class, a hardship town, all one.

Something, I take it, not to be found in cities;
No, nor in villages, what with parson, squire,
Farmer and farm-hand. (Just as well: the once
And ever martyred stoke a sullen fire.)

Up above Glossop, weeping cloud at Woodhead;
Up again after, over the last high hogsback,
The clean black waters shine up steel, not silver,
The peat is black, the lowering skies are black.

Millicent Dillon, if you ever visit
This town as you say you will, this is the way:
Ashbourne to Buxton, Buxton to Glossop, over
To an ash-boled England and a Baltic day.

For this is under us now, as we come down:
The Silkstone seam, where woods compacted lay
Shade upon shade, multiplication of blackness
That seeps up through: '*black* Barnsley', we would say.

The sneer of it – black Barnsley, that my mother
Indignantly thought corrupted out of 'bleak',
'Bleak Barnsley'. Who else cared? Corruption in
All that we do, decay in all we speak.

Ireland, America, the Atlantic writ
Here runs no longer. Out of the sunset shires,
Ireland, and Wales, they called us; and we shut
Behind us the West that beckons, that aspires.

Westward, the moors: shield more than barrier, closing
Utopias off. We were not to be tricked:
Depravity stalked the streets with us. A city
Needs, on the contrary, a red-light district.

Barracks, industrial barracks: 'town'
In that late sense. Sensational the feat,
Making a city of the regimental
Lines, as you might say: Day Street, Peel Street, Pitt Street!

Well, it has started; air is let in, and light,
All to the good. And now what will befall?
Concourse and complex, underpass and precinct,
The scale not human but angelical:

Squalor on that scale; homeliness as 'home'
Might be for Rebel Angels, or their hordes,
Machinists of 'machines for living in';
No fug upon the windy drawing-boards!

Some things get better: not *in situ*, in
Stone (that gets worse), or steel; but in
Our knowing, though our architect were Wren,
We live in Babylon, we aspire in sin.

The end of a town – however mean, however
Much of a byword – marks the end of an age,
An age of worn humility. Hereafter,
The Prince of Darkness and his equipage!

THREE FOR WATER-MUSIC

The Fountain of Cyanë

1.

Her father's brother rapes her!
    In the bright
Ovidian colours all is for delight,
The inadmissible minglings are recounted
With such finesse: the beery ram that mounted
His niece and, hissing 'Belt up', had her, is
Hell's grizzly monarch gaunt in tapestries;
The thrashing pallid skivvy under him
A vegetation myth; the stinking slum
Is Enna's field where Phoebus ne'er invades
The tufted fences, nor offends the shades;
And her guffawing Ma assumes the land,
Coarsely divine, cacophonous, gin in hand.
Sky-blue, dark-blue, sea-green, cerulean dyes
Dye into fables what we hoped were lies
And feared were truths. A happy turn, a word,
Says they are both, and nothing untoward.
Coloured by rhetoric, to die of grief
Becomes as graceful as a falling leaf;
No chokings, retchings, not the same as dying
Starved and worn out because you can't stop crying.
Cyanë's fable, that one; how she wept
Herself away, shocked for her girl-friend raped –
'Her varied members to a fluid melt,
A pliant softness in her bones is felt...'
Sweet lapse, sweet lapse... 'till only now remains
Within the channel of her purple veins
A silver liquor...' Ah, the master's touch
So suave, mere word-play, that can do so much!
And now at last imperious, in bad taste:
'Nothing to fill love's grasp; her husband chaste
Bathes in that bosom he before embrac'd.'
The spring-fed pool that is Cyanë may
Be visited in Sicily today;
And what's to be made of that? Or how excuse
Our intent loitering outside Syracuse?

2.

Modesty, I kept saying,
Temperate, temperate...Yes,
The papyrus were swaying
Hardly at all, and late,
Late in the season the rings
Widened upon the reedy
Pool, and the beady-eyed frogs
Volleyed out after mayfly.

Fountain? No jet, no spume,
Spew nor spurt...Was this
Where Pluto's chariot hurtled
Up out of 'gloomy Dis'?
Male contumely for that
First most seminal rape,
Proserpine's, prescribes
Some more vertiginous landscape.

Late, late in that season...
Easy, easy the lap
And rustle of blue waters...
Wholly a female occasion
This, as Demeter launches
One fish in a silver arc
To signalize her daughter's
Re-entry to the dark.

3.

The balked, the aborted vision
Permits of the greater finesse;
The achieved one is fugitive, slighter,
One might almost say, 'loose'.

And yet the oceanic
Swells of an unencumbered
Metric jiggle the planes
Epiphanies must glow from.

So, though one might almost say 'loose',
One mustn't. They like the closed-off

Precincts all right, but never
When those exult in their closures.

The shrine is enclosed from the bare
Fields and, three miles away
Clearly in sight, the high-rise
Shimmering haze of the city.

But the fence is of wire; the warped
Palings give easy access;
No turnstile; and at the pool
Of Cyanë, nothing to pay;

No veil to be rent, no grille,
No holy of holies. The Greek
World, one is made to remember,
Was Christianized quite early.

Epiphanies all around us
Always perhaps. And some
Who missed the flash of a fin
Were keeping their eyes on rhyme-schemes.

4.

And so with stanzas... moving
From room to room is a habit adapted to winter,
Warm and warming, worship Sunday by Sunday,
And one is glad of it. But when
Now and again I turn the knob and enter
The special chill where my precarious Springs
Hang water-beaded in still air, I hear
A voice announce: 'And this is the
Conservatory!' Greenish misted panes
Of mystifying memory conserve
In an unnatural silence nymph and pool;
It is an outside room, at the end of a range of rooms
But still a room, accounted for or even
Entered upon the impatient plans in my
Infidel youth. At that time no
Nymph, and no pool: still, it appears,
Room left for them – and yet
Rooms should have an outside door, I think;
I wilt for lack of it, though my plants do not.

5.

Yet there was enough in this –
And it was nothing, nothing at all
'Happened' – enough in this
Non-happening to cap
What Scripture says of the Fall

Which, though it equally may
Not in that sense have happened, is
A postulate day by day
Called for, to explain
Our joys, our miseries.

A fish jumped, silver; small
Frogs took the mayfly; papyrus
In the Sicilian fall
Of the leaf was bowing. How
That weightless weighed with us!

Why, when an unheard air
Stirred in the fronds, did we assume
An occidental care
For proximate cause? Egyptian
Stems abased their plume.

So inattentive we are
We think ourselves unfallen. This
Pool, when Pluto's car
Whirled up, was wept by Cyanë
For her abducted mistress.

One could go round and round
This single and Sicilian less
Than happening, and ground
Therein what might suffuse
Our lives with happiness.

Wild Boar Clough

1.

A poet's lie!
      The boarhound and the boar
Do not pursue their pattern as before.
What English eyes since Dryden's thought to scan
Our spinneys for the Presbyterian,
The tusked, the native beast inflamed to find
And rend the spotted or the milk-white hind,
The true Church, or the half-true? Long ago
Where once were tusks, neat fangs began to grow;
Citizen of the World and Friend to Man,
The presbyter's humanitarian.
The poor pig learned to flute: the brute was moved
By plaudits of a conscience self-approved;
'Self in benevolence absorb'd and lost'
Absorbed a ruinous Redemption's cost.

This too a lie; a newer zealot's, worse
Than any poet's in or out of verse.
These were the hunting-calls, and this the hound,
Harried the last brave pig from English ground;
Now ermine, whited weasel, sinks his tooth
Deeper than wolf or boar into the Truth.
Extinct, the English boar; he leaves a lack.
Hearts of the disinherited grow black.

2.

When he grew up
in the England of silver
cigarette cases and
Baptist chapel on Sundays,

long white flannels were still
worn, and the Mission Fields
ripe for the scything Gospel
cost him a weekly penny.

The missionary box!
It rattled as he knocked it,

crouching near the wireless:
deuce, Fred Perry serving...

Doggedly he applies
himself to the exhumations:
these pre-war amateurs,
that missionary martyr.

As gone as Cincinnatus!
Still tongue-in-cheek revered, as
Republican virtue by
a silver-tongued florid Empire,

tired of that even, lately.

3.

To Loughwood Meeting House,
Redeemed since and re-faced,
Once persecuted Baptists
Came across sixty miles
Of Devon. Now we ask
Our own good wincing taste
To show the way to Heaven.

But if under clear-glassed windows,
The clear day looking in,
We should be always at worship
And trusting in His merits
Who saves us from the pathos
Of history, and our fears
Of natural disasters,

What antiquarian ferrets
We have been! As idle
An excrescence as Ionic
Pilasters would be, or
Surely the Puritan poet:
Burning, redundant candle,
Invisible at noon.

We are, in our way, at worship;
Though in the long-deflowered

Dissenting chapel that
England is, the slim
Flame of imagination,
Asymmetrical, wavers,
Starving for dim rose-windows.

4.

And so he raged exceedingly,
excessively indeed, he raged excessively
and is said to have been drunk, as certainly
in some sense and as usual he was;
lacking as usual, and in some
exorbitant measure, charity,
candour in an old sense. How
a black heart learns white-heartedness, you tell me!

Raged, and beshrewed his audience of one
without much or at all
intending it, having his eyes not on
her but on the thing to be hunted down;
or so he will excuse himself, without
much confidence. The rapist's plea:
not her but womankind. He has
the oddest wish for some way to disgrace himself.

How else can a pharisee clear the accounts, and live?

5.

Wild Boar Clough... known to his later boyhood
    As the last gruelling stage before,
Feet and collar-bones raw, the tarmacadam
    Past unbelievable spa-hotels
Burned to the train at Buxton. Julian Symons,
    His poems, *Confessions of X*, reviewed
In *Poetry London*, bought on Buxton Station...

A nut-brown maid whom he cannot remember
    Sold him herb beer, a farmhouse brew,
One day above Wild Boar Clough, whose peat-sieved brown
    Waters were flecked below them. Legs
Were strong then, heart was light, was white, his swart

Limbs where the old glad Adam in him,
Lissom and slim, exulted, carried him.

Somewhere that boy still swings to the trudging rhythm,
    In some brown pool that girl still reaches
A lazy arm. The harm that history does us
    Is grievous but not final. As
The wild boar still in our imaginations
    Snouts in the bracken, outward is
One steep direction gleefully always open.

So Lud's Church hides in Cheshire thereabouts
    Cleft in the moor. The slaughtered saints
Cut down of a Sunday morning by dragoons
    Grounded the English Covenant
In ling and peat-moss. Sound of singing drifts
    Tossed up like spume, persistently
Pulsing through history and out of it.

The Fountain of Arethusa

1.

A boy turned to a newt!
    A chuffy lad
Who dared be sly when Demeter ran mad
At loss, at rapine, or to find her rule
Of nature crossed to make a girl a pool.
A filmy scarf of water...and that first
Apparition liquefied, dispersed.
None of us but has indulged the same
Insanity, holding Sicily to blame
For tendering first the lovely benefit
Rushed at and clasped, and then retracting it.
But loss of love has nothing to do with place.
Time ticks, a flaw flies on the water's face
But that is not it either. Remonstrate
As Arethusa may, expatriate
From Elis, threading underseas, who found
Vent for Greek waters on Sicilian ground,

It cannot help. The loves that we have lost
Are not, like her, translated or transposed,
Somewhere intact. Who ever read, for these
Poor palliatives, the *Metamorphoses*?

2.

'Arethusa arose
    From her couch of snows
In the Akrokeraunian mountains...'
    More thrilling today
    My mother's way
With Shelley, than this fountain's
    Circus of grey
    Mullet, or sway
Of papyrus-fronds. Pulsations
    Still rill it through;
    What once she knew
Of crags, reverberations,
    Couches of snows,
    The nymph still knows,
Still pushing her liquid lever
    Up and out,
    As when it brought
Greeks once in a choleric fever
    To Syracuse.
    Mother, my Muse,
There are the springs that matter:
    Small thrills sustain
    The source, not vain
Glories, nor consonants' clatter
    Down a moraine
    In Shelley's brain
But smaller vaunts. One day
    In a parlour-game,
    Required to name
Mountains beginning with A,
    Proudly, aged ten,
    I pronounced it then;
The Akrokeraunian Mountains!
    Grown-ups demurred;
    But sand-grains stirred
Then, as now, in those fountains!

3.

To have failed to
measure up
not to myth, but to
the need for gratitude...

In a desert of
ingratitude, this was one
small triumph, one
spout of a filial spring.

4.

At Syracuse the blue pool,
Dragonflies, leaping silver.
But here, at Naxos...
Trouble.
        In the cafés
Of Taormina the black
American sailors, and the white
Sat at separate tables, and an old
Anglo-Sicilian made
Trouble; and 'Attaboy, Yank'
Was the best I could do for
Those beardless boys,
Not themselves enamoured
Of Europe, but enacting
Their hope against its hopelessness, like any
American *inamorato*, like the type
Of all of them, the pontifical Henry James.

They had made the Naxos passage, and their old
Destroyer lay for a day and two nights offshore
In a spill of dangerous late-October light
Over the shoulder of Etna, watery, weak
And inconstant as any American's sense of Europe.
And we had been to Naxos, had descended
The gradient of millennia, and met
Trouble: the male will splayed across its Honda
Wristily revving, and the motor-coaches,
Though out of season, nosing the Holiday Inn.

So when we made it at last
To the Cyclopean wall
And the sacred mound
Sheer from the shingle where the exhausted galleys
Lay beached once, blocked
Now from the sea by a tall and later wall,
Stillness there was, a profusion of late blossoms
In the leafy place, and we were grateful, lingered
For the trouble to settle, settle. But the god
Awaited in vain indignantly the lunge
Of a silver fin in our thinned-out devotions,
The blue burn of the dragonfly, living ingot,
Flaw in the too late amber of our season.

5.

The one in the poem is not
The one that you will visit.
Syracuse you may visit,
The poem also – one
Casts no light on the other.

Through the one there strays
One and one only walker.
The city has its claim
Upon this one who can
Meet it in curious ways:

By brilliant turn of phrase?
No. For it is the past
Is brilliant, Pasternak says;
The debt we owe it, only
More modest coin repays.

So in the padlocked, man-walled
Fountain of Arethusa
Papyrus wave, but of course
Cigarette-packets float
Above Ortygia.

Not a hard lesson to learn
That this is proper, since
History has to happen;
In this case at least it seems
A not unwarranted freedom.

And so in the verdant, man-made
Latomìa, a grotto
Loud with seepage houses
No lonely inscrutable Tristan
And Iseult, but a rope-walk!

Ropemakers gone from under
Mottled impendings, still
Their hempen gossamers ran
Taut and knee-high through the shafted
Light and the cavernous air.

Gratitude, Need, and Gladness –
These are the names of the walker,
These are the strands of the hemp:
Gladness at meeting the need
The gratitude imposes.

This is our walker's scope.
You think he makes too bold?
To make this visit, think
Of how to test a rope:
Swing on it, trust it to hold.

A gimcrack drum with spikes,
Knee-high, the T-shaped stretchers...
This is the phrase he will use:
Warm honesties of makeshift
Transvalue Syracuse.

The Battered Wife

She thinks she was hurt this summer
More than ever before,
Beyond what there is cure for.

He has failed her once too often:
Once, it turns out, more
Than she had bargained for

In a bargain that of course
Nobody ever struck!
Oh, she had trusted her luck

Not once too often, but
All along the line:
And even this last time,

This summer, when reduced
To surely the bone her hope

Was just to live it through, his
Incalculable enmity
Rose up and struck. That he

Could no more calculate
Nor understand it than
She can, absolves the man

For the first time no longer. He
Will come back, she knows. She dreads it yet
Hopes for it, his coming back. A planet

Or else a meteor curves at the extreme
Bend of its vector, vehicle of
Prodigy and plague, and hopeless love.

G.M.B.

(10.7.77)

Old oak, old timber, sunk and rooted
    In the organic cancer
Of Devon soil, the need she had
    You could not answer.

Old wash and wump, the narrow seas
    Mindlessly breaking
She scanned lifelong; and yet the tide
    There's no mistaking

She mistook. She never thought,
    It seems, that the soft thunder
She heard nearby, the pluck and slide,
    Might tow her under.

I have as much to do with the dead
    And dying, as with the living
Nowadays; and failing them is
    Past forgiving.

As soon be absolved for that, as if
    A tree, or a sea, should be shriven;
And yet the truth is, fail we must
    And be forgiven.

Short Run to Camborne

The hideousness of the inland spine of Cornwall!
Redeemed (for of course in the long run all,
All is redeemed), but Wesley's chapels and all
In the slipstream of our short run rock rock to their fall.

And we surge on for Camborne, cheapness cheapened
By our going by as, with wreaths to honour the end
Of one who endured this cheapness, with our reeking
Put-put exhaust we exhaust the peace we are seeking.

Cheapness of granite-chips on the oil-starred road above Looe;
Our wandering from the Wesleys and (it's true)
Dear-bought though they were, heaven-sent, their wanderings
    too...
Surge, surge we may but stray is all we do.

The spinelessness of the rock-ribbed once! The riven
Granite of Wesley's gospel that all are forgiven
Since all are redeemed...The loose shale slides and shelves
As we forgive each other and ourselves.

All are forgiven, or may be. But we owe
This much to our dead sister (at Polperro
Pixies and trivia...): humanly we know
Some things are unforgivable, even so.

Livingshayes

(A tradition of Silverton, Devon)

'Live-in-ease', and then to wash
    Their sins in Lily Lake
On Corpus Christi, for their own
    And their Redeemer's sake.

Easy living, with that clear
    And running stream below;
First contract the harm, and then
    Wash it white as snow.

Not altogether. Chris Cross first,
    'The top of a high hill.'
Living it up and easy needs
    Him hung and bleeding still.

The Admiral to his Lady

With you to Bideford,
Too old for stomaching
Rebuffs, not soon deterred
Nor often crossed of late,
I boomed along, not brooking
      The sky's mandate.

Habits of testy command
Forgot to say 'weather permitting'.
Though gales had rocked the land
And us, early and late,
There I was, squalls intermitting,
      Still hectoring fate.

Yet rained on, shoulders bowed,
Colour too high, too florid
In manner, voice too loud,
I felt like a youngster with you
That day, as wet winds flurried
      Torridge askew.

Wrecked body, barque of your wrecked
Hopes, or some of them – bitter
Reflections?...Harbours reflect
The changefulness of skies;
Bideford's waters glitter
      Like your hurt eyes.

Still, as the afterskirts
Of one black patch streel over
I brew up the next. It hurts
Each time a little less;
To cope with a demon lover
      Learn carelessness.

That rocking, jaunty way
You have, like Torridge's waters
Dancing into the bay...
You know what serves your turn;
You have, of all Eve's daughters,
      The least to learn!

Screech-owl

I had to assure myself:
What it seemed I heard...
Was it my own stale self
Exhaled, or was it a bird?

Therefore with pride and relief,
Half-awake, coughing in bed,
I assure myself that screech
Came from outside my head.

Not the disgusting pipe of
Mucus lees that are
Replenishing the soon
Choked chambers of catarrh,

Not snore I heard, nor wheeze,
But something out of phase
With all of me: an owl
Out over Livingshayes.

In fact the birdcalls I
Can name are precious few.
Nightingales sang to me
Once, and I never knew.

Woodpigeon, meadowlark
With coo and trill augment
A gamut that remains
Indubitably scant.

And if, now I remember,
I lifted my head out of books
Enough to know one other
Call out of England: rooks...,

Is it not crows I mean
Or, what I am told is rare,
The death-conveying raven's
Croak through leaden air?

Bowels, adenoids,
Bald logic, brazen tongue...
Where is the other song the
Blackcap and wren have sung?

Cuckoo, plover, and owl:
A perilously confined
Aviary of sound for
One bedridden, or blind.

Fare Thee Well

Bideford! Nothing will do
To make the place ring true
To its after-rain luminous presence
That day last summer, so
Precipitous, tempest-whipped
As that summer was to us two,
And as Bideford was also
That day we were there,

But embarkations: faces
Cheese-white in lamplight; lights
Dancing on blackness as
They rock away; oars are shipped,
'Ahoy!' and an answering growl,
And they climb aboard, and the wicker
Basket and bird-cage are
Hoist in; and the anchor is tripped.

Make what you will of the figure
Of outward, I cannot afford
To let you go, to unloose you
To that all-levelling
Hardship of ocean. See!
Some one has cast a hawser,
Some one has caught it. Wrapped
On a bollard, it checks, it is gripped.

Oh it is you I would check.
When it comes to the outward bound,
You are to be outstripped:
Farewell! I am far down the Sound,
Dwindled, my moorings slipped.
Somewhere by Barnstaple Bay
I have embraced you, I turn
Seaward. 'Farewell,' I say.

Because in the event
The hawser will not be bent
Nor gripped so handily, and
Goodbyes will be untoward
In some more sterilized place
Than Bideford, accept
This easy rehearsal: that when
The time comes, we be equipped.

Grace in the Fore Street

for Roy Gottfried

You saw the sunlight ripen upon the wall,
Inching daily as the year wore full.

Behind you as you worked at Shakespeare rose,
Slovenly shelved, the job-lot of my books

An image of my randomness. Across them
A bush in the yard on a fine cold morning throws

Calendared shadows wavering over Bishop
Wilson's Maxims, and Calvin excerpted in French:

One late lunge after piety; and one
Long ago at face-saving erudition.

Which motive, or what other one, procured
The Psalms of David in Arthur Golding's version

I wish I knew, and knew what price to put on
'The fear of the Lord is clean, and endureth for ever.'

I imagine you or another American friend
Explaining of me, when dead: 'Now in his day

As an Englishman...' But not my Englishness
Nor anything else about me ever ripened.

The English year revolves and brings to leaf
Great ancient oaks which then unleaf themselves;

In which there is no consolation nor,
The scale at best but saecular, grounds for hope.

A better hope let me from my unkempt
Bruised library bestow on you. It goes:

> 'Who can understand his faults?
> Cleanse me from my secret faults...'

Unearned composures have been known to enter
A place of unfirm purpose and fleet shadows.

Some Future Moon

after Pasternak

Before me a far-off time arises
Far in the future. You,
Whoever you are, are mine;
This is to say I know you.

The sodium street-lights beam
On to a stonescape as
Remote from the Plymouth I know
As mine from Frobisher's.

You are a girl or a boy;
All the same, one of the few.
Whoever you are, you are mine;
This is to say I claim you.

This which I need to tell you
Quietly is none
Other than what the Tamar
Shines to the Eddystone.

Listen! For the lisp of
The waters at Admiral's Hard
Decayed in my day already
Now can scarcely be heard.

They neither shine nor sound
Unless in a little tune
I name both them and you
And set you under the moon.

Watch with me how the moon
Sinks on Mount Edgecumbe. Think
How many lovers' joys
With that moon rose, and sink.

And yet think also how,
Whatever your war-machines
And your machine-made songs,
These are unchanging scenes:

Because I say so, Mount
Edgecumbe's shelving ground
Crowds to the dropping down
Of warships outward bound;

Because I say so, you
Unknown sit with me here,
Your eyes a-shine because
I will it so, my dear.

You have this world no man
Nor man's machine can take
Away from you because
I made it for your sake.

Ox-bow

The time is at an end.
The river swirled
Into an ox-bow bend, but now
It shudders and re-unites:
Adversary! Friend!

Adverse currents drove
This pair apart.
A twin tormented throe embraced,
Enisled between them, one
Quadrant of earth, one grove.

Now for each other they yearn
Across the eyot
That the peculiar flow of each
Carved out, determined. Now,
Now to each other they turn.

And it is past belief
That once they forked;
Or that, upstream and bypassed, trees
Mirrored in mid-reach still
Break into annual leaf.

A Late Anniversary

Constant the waterman
Skims the red water
Of sunset river,
Singing to Marian
The miller's daughter.

Wharf nor weir on this
Stretch of river, it pours
Mournful and nebulous, Time's
Unseizable accomplice.

Sing to her, waterman.
Woo her unfaltering,
Constant as best you can,
Self-same by altering.

Your traffic is yourself:
The sidelong pour off a shelf
Or the popple about a stone.
It is what she would wish,
You have to think.

No Epitaph

No moss nor mottle stains
My parents' unmarked grave;
My word on them remains
Stouter than stone, you told me.

'Martyred to words', you have thought,
Should be your epitaph;
At other times you fought
My self-reproaches down.

Though bitterly once or twice
You have reproached me with how
Everything ended in words,
We both know better now:

You understand, I shall not
If I survive you care
To raise a headstone for
You I have carved on air.

Utterings

(Bird)   To flex in the upper airs
To the unseen but known
Velocity of change
That both prevails and gives –
If anything that lives
That is able to know it, knows
Better to bend to the press
Of need, and so command it,
Him I envy, his
So much more strait duress.

(Salmon)   Pressures, pressures of water,
Of running water, because
As needs must downward driving,
Define imperatives.
If anything that lives
That is able to know it, knows
Better than I do the spine
Set taut against the grab
Of gravity, that thing knows
More happiness than mine.

(Man)   Making your own mistakes
And living the blame of them, making
The same ones time after time,
Which nobody forgives –
If anything that lives
That is able to know it, knows
A better happiness than
This – and he is Legion
That thinks he does – he is
Disranked from the branch of Man.

(Angel)   On us no pressures, none.
Adoration is
Not required, but what
Each one desirously gives.
If anything that lives
That is able to know it, knows
A better happiness, then
The frame of the world is askew;

I share the happiness
Of salmon, birds, and men.

(Sheepdog/   Knowing your own business,
Artist)   And such a delicate business;
            Uttering it with the promptness
            That such a knowledge gives –
            If anything that lives
            That is able to know it, knows
            A better happiness
            In his dog's life than this,
            He is welcome to it; most,
            I apprehend, know less.

Skelpick

sub galea pastor iunctis pice cantat avenis,
proque lupo pavidae bella verentur oves
                    (Ovid, Tristia*)*

Below us all day, a mile away, in a flashing
Bend of the river a manikin is for manly
Sport not sustenance casting after and gaffing
The innocent salmon while over us all the clouds
Choir the incessant the variously lovely
Descants of shadows up and across the valley.

This is their glen, the Mackays of Strathnaver who
Were Hanoverian in the '45, who
Furnished the thin red line at Balaclava,
Whose sole exploit in earlier centuries was,
On a tribal foray against the Morays of Dornoch,
The spoliation of Scotland's prime cathedral.

Our childish companion, thinking excrement
Though it be of sheep is hilarious, is shouting
With laughter at me as I kick away sheep-shit
From the green knoll our rented cottage stands on,
Grease on the toe of my boot, me silently cursing
The mindless machines that they are, cropping and cropping.

Yet this is the one who, heaving himself from the small
Citroën he has required should stop, Good Shepherd
Labouring stiff-legged, cradles a possibly crippled
And certainly dam-spurned lamb, and then transports what
If it survives, survives only for slaughter
To a more sheltered dimple in the bracken.

One is not – I hope one is not – escaping the blood
Of the lamb, the excrement, the unsteady gait
After the dug that is always withdrawn, or the holy
Gaffed and gasping fish, the stinking fishwife
Raped beside the Dornoch Firth, by calling
For air, for air, for a distance, calling on

Tristia, the threads of a destiny woven
From a black fleece when a poet was born in Sulmona;
Tristia, the pipe pitch-bonded played
From under a war-bonnet over the shuddering flock;
Tristia, the beldam black Chaldeans'
Disastrous flocking torrent through the birch-trees.

Strathnaver

Dear language, English, whose
'Loyal' means the thing
A cairn by the road records
In clearwater green Strathnaver.

It honours the 83rd
Sutherland Highlanders, of
A Presbyterian clan,
Mustered in 1800.

Their sons and daughters were
Prised out to populate,
Far from the lonely shieling,
Canada and New Zealand.

And under Ben Loyal by
The ruined Clearances village
Of Scrabster Sutherland can
Heal me with space and silence.

A temporary remission,
Sour in any case. Hour
On hour of loyal service
Thus to be rewarded!

Spare from your frenzied mutters
Of 'Fool, fool, fool!' the men
Of the earliest 83rd,
Their cornfields gone to sheepwalks.

Winter's Talents

for Peter Scupham and Robert Wells

Nebulous, freezingly moist,
The need for a feelingful voice
Moves athwart and away
And upon us again, as we move
Northwest. The silvery stripes
Of mist come in and recede.
Past Hereford, each tree,
Grass-stalk and hedge stands dressed in
The need, a fur of rime.

Dee-side and Mersey-side
Lie up ahead, blocked off
In freezing fog. To them
The voice must speak. The rime
Dies off in the chemical reek.
Whose swag, whose chiselled cadence
Crusts, or whose coral, in
Garston, Halewood, Speke?
The voice, though, needs must speak.

Nor will it be content
With the abrupt sweet carol
Peeled against April brick,
The lyric; no, nor the dry
Incontestably true
Chirrup of pathos. New
Poets move across England.

Islanded, I salute them:
Elaborate talents of winter.

Marooned as I am in my own
Undoubtedly misread season
(Smoky noons I remember
In Liverpool), I salute the
Articulators of winter
Wonderlands. Delamere Forest's
Ramifications extort
Arpeggio and cadenza,
Too ornate for the *scouse*.

The need for a feelingful voice
Thwarts me, moves away,
Moves back. The bands of clear,
Then claustral weather gather
And then disperse. Rehearse,
Voices not mine, in England's
Interminable winter:
Sycamore, Tarporley, all
Intricate, cavernous splendour!

To Londoners

I get, surprisingly, a sense of space:
As on the rush-hour underground, when in fact
Every one touches, still in his own place
Every one rises above the smirch of contact,
Resolute to assert his self-containment;
A charged field cordons every sovereign will.

The City empty on a July evening,
All the jam-packed commuters gone, and all
The Wren and Hawksmoor spires and steeples shining
In a honeyed light...But also mental spaces
As I see now, all energies withdrawn
To hold the frontiers each day menaces.

Trying to hold my own place just inside
The emptied space round Hawksmoor's drawing-board,
I shoulder, I am rancorous, I have tried
Too long, with too much vigour and the wrong
Sort of patience. On the District Line
Budge up a little, tell me I belong!

Gallant baritones whom nothing soured
Between the wars, still hooked on Rupert Brooke
Who adumbrated for the earlier war
A wide and windy Iliad in the embowered
Old garden of the Vicarage, Grantchester...
Is that the bugle-note you listen for?

Given a voice thus confident, thus confiding,
As intimate as a commuter's week
And yet as sweeping as imperial war
Or global peace, how spaciously I could
Bind in one *sostenuto* Temple Bar
With Turnham Green, St Paul's with Chorleywood!

But now or later you will have to say
I am one of yours. Do you not hear the cramp
Of overpopulation, of *mêlée*
In this too tamped-down, pounded-together ramp
Of phrases I manhandle towards what yawning
Yard of what temple, what too void arena?

A Liverpool Epistle

to J.A. Steers, Esq, author of 'The Coastline of England and Wales'

Alfred, this couple here –
My son, your daughter – are
Can we deny it? strangers
To both of us. Ageing, I
Find I take many a leaf
Out of the useful book
Of your behaviour. 'Prof.',
Your title for years, becomes

Me, or meets my need;
Mask for what heartaches, what
Uncertain, instantaneous
(Panicky sometimes)
Judgments how to behave in
This net we seem to have woven
Between us, or been caught in.

Under a rusty gown not
Actual but conjured
By our behaviour, what
In some diminished sense
Compromising situations we
Either escape, or handle! Still,
Today I was found at a loss,
Confronted with the local
University's stalwarts
Of a past age: Bernard Pares,
Oliver Elton, George
Sampson, Fitzmaurice-Kelly...
Not that they did not deserve
Attention, there in their daubed
Likenesses; but how?
What was required of 'the Prof.'?

In the event I managed
Well enough by my
Lenient expectations, but
I had such a sense of how
Tragical, one might say,
Our occupation is
Or may be. How
Beset it is, after all,
How very far from 'secluded',
This life of the scholar my son
And your daughter have followed us into!

It was explained to me,
For instance, there was one
Liverpool professor
Had had to be painted out
Of the group-portrait: Kuno
Meyer, Professor of German,

Whose notable devotion
To Ancient Irish took,
Come 1914, rather
A different colour. He
Declared himself for his Kaiser
Belligerently. And I
Must admit I am baffled:
Passion also has its
Claims upon us, surely;
Even the sort that is called
Smirkingly, 'patriotic'.

Kenneth Allott, a poet
I think you will not have read,
Gave us ('I give you', he wrote)
'The riotous gulls and the men
Crumpled, hat-clutching, in the wind's
Rages, and the shifting river',
Giving us Liverpool. Here
Anyone must be prompted
To solemn reflections in
A wind that must seem like the wind
Of history, blowing the chemical
Reek out of Runcorn over
The eerily unfrequented,
Once so populous, Mersey.

Cold hearth of empire, whose
Rasping cinders bring
Our erudite concerns
Home to us, with such
Asperity! This is
Liverpool, one enormous
Image of dereliction
Where yet our children warm themselves
And so warm us. We too
Are netted into it – you
Known as the protector
Of England's coastline, and
I, supposedly
Custodian of that other
Line around England: verse.

This turns, of course. Yes, one
Verse-line turns into the next
As Rodney Street into a slum, or
Philologists into Prussians;
Turnings in time as your
Headlands and bays are turnings
In space. A bittersweet pleasure
At best one takes in these
Revolutions, reversals,
Verses, whereas
The veerings of a coastline
(Seen from a lowflying aircraft,
A coastal road or, best,
A coasting ship) must be
Experienced, I think, as
A solemn sweetness always.

As prose at its saddest is less
Sorrowful than verse is
Necessarily, so
Geography, I have long
Thought, must be a sweeter
Study than history; sweeter
Because less cordial, less
Of heartbreak in it. More
Human warmth, it follows,
Is possible or common
In Liverpool than in
Some spick-and-span, intact,
Still affluent city. So
The warmth of our children's household
For the time being persuades me.

Well-found Poem

'Of tried goodness, merit, or value – 1887' (O.E.D.)

'We last of Yugo-Slav
Air Force. Please tell Alex.
we coming.' Signal received
21st April 1941 by
H.M.S. Chekla, towing,
somewhere south of Crete:

                        'the

port quarter fairlead was
used, because *Desmoulea*
would be sheering
violently to starboard, and
if the fairlead should collapse, the
wire would bring up against
the portside of the steering-engine house
against which it was hoped
to hold it by a heavy
shackle (around the wire)
on a chain, with a tackle rove
to bowse it against the house.'

These are zones of language, zones
of the affecting universe
of Pepys's English prose and Dryden's verse.

The use of the slip-hook made it
impossible to
'freshen the nip'
of the towing wire
through the fairlead, but

so they managed that ship

           *

At Ostend's
evacuation, 'one
lady who threatened to go
into labour unless she sailed
in a destroyer.' This
'pleasure she was accorded but

without result.'
                By which
he means presumably
labour was not averted;
the lady was delivered
safely of a nine-
or eight-and-a-half pound fruit
of pleasure once accorded:
sturdy destroyer, male.

                    *

'To re-establish tactics and
the skills of command...'

precision-guided missiles
favour it; so far from
'push-button warfare', the problem
is, with them,
no longer to
'hit early and keep on hitting'
but knowing what it is
you hit, and what happens to it;

as for instance Mr
Wilson, Commissioned Gunner,
'had his face blown away';
'unable to move him', nor
'had I the time',
'left him covered with a blanket.'

                    *

We last of Yugo-Slav
Air Force. Please tell
Alexandria,
Athens, Rome
in a violet light

we coming. Oberleutnant
Prell is coming, and
Commissioned Gunner Wilson
is coming, and

tactics and the skills
of command are coming and

these are zones of language and

we would not have it otherwise. The cities
form and re-form in the violet light, and

his face had been blown away and
we would not have it otherwise, destroyers

male, and tell Alex. We
coming, we always coming:

'...these brave men...'

Artifex in Extremis

In memoriam Howard Warshaw

Let him rehearse the gifts reserved for age
  Much as the poet Eliot did, but more
  Than thirty-five years after:...Rending rage
Discountenanced by his Church, the rent and sore
  Patient nods under gin or seconal
  Or his small fame, such drugs. His visitor,
The one and only in this hospital,
  Is nurse and woman. Time and time again
  She brings her numbing serum, whom to call
A button's by his bed. He calls her when,
  Ashamed, he feels his practised self-control
  Slipping a notch. Hotly he asks her then:
'Is there no choice? Am I to sell my soul
  Short, or fake it, for my nearest kin
  Forever, till I die?' Prompt on the whole
She brings her priceless needleful of guilt,
  Oblivion, and equality; his rôle
  Is possum, playing possum to the hilt.

The hilt, though, is a long way down and in;
  The whole blade is before it, going deep
  Bleeding and shearing. Though the mottled skin
Knits up and shines, the legless cries in his sleep
  For pain in the limb aborted. There was once,
  Torturing to remember, in that steep
Slope off to nowhere, stamping-ground and stance,
  Foothold, some hard earth under. He discerns
  Still many a cherished, hard-earned eminence
Loom from his past, on all of which by turns
  He took his stand. No need to specify.
  There is not one of them that now he spurns;
On all that ring of hills his drowsing eye
  Sees his young self still model rectitude
  Erect and certain. Clear against the sky
Above his drug-dimmed but still savage mood,
  Seen but by him, the things that he has held by
  Unchangeably enforce his solitude.

His arrogance is terrible to no one
  More than to him. It is incurable.
  The enormity of it ramrods bone on bone
When he stands up for anything at all,
  Rending both it and him. No palliation
  In trusting to posterity, at call
No longer for belated vindication;
  The future, if it comes (as he is not
  Sure that it will), will in his estimation
Be more obtuse, not less. His work is what
  Stands, but as if on Easter Island, rude
  And enigmatic effigies, a lot
Unsold at history's auction. When of crude
  Unlettered clergy Thomas Cranmer's prose
  Demands too much, what but desuetude
Attends one's best? This being what he knows,
  His own sick say-so and presumption can
  Alone sustain the artificer in the man.

Then why, he asks himself (his self-contempt
  Half self-pity), of late these reams on reams
  Addressed to a young kinsman? To attempt,
Having no heirs, to write one's will – it seems
  The enforced sell-out: exegetes pre-empt

Prophecies, polemics serve for dreams,
And pedagogue supplants protagonist,
    As rhetoric, action. Always in the event
    One must, despite the lacerating twist
Of disbelief, limp to a testament
    Too shrill for dignity. Of late he's missed
    That most – the dignity. A low sun lent
Once or twice, his monumental forms
    Upon the hill-tops just the effect he meant:
    Scrutable, yet unfathomable. Norms
Of expectation (anxious, confident,
    His kinsman's face . . .) obscure them; one performs
    Simply such things, intent, without intent.

For the most part now he drifts, his conduct as
    Considerate as has come to be expected,
    Querulous seldom. His *superbia* has
Been at such pains to ravage undetected
    (And swelled the more) that now he practises
    Unthinkingly the long ago perfected
Deceit of warming to the common touch,
    Much-loved, attentive. That too he has made
    A point of, staunchly – not to ask, for such
As he is, special licences. Betrayed
    By that pretence of unpretension, much
    As now he may regret the terms of trade
He fixed himself, he has to acquiesce
    When he perceives his own dear things are weighed
    And shelved at market-prices. To confess
The work that would, he thought, speak for itself
    Has not, comes hard. Benumbed, he stands himself,
    With all his other pieces, on the shelf.

'A good life,' he will tell me, 'though I wish . . .'
    And so on – much what anyone might say.
    Blind to his own case? Or this queerer fish
That terrifies me, reading him today
    Into myself tomorrow – which one thumbs
    The bedside button, and no woman comes?

The Bent

Thinking how it is
  too late to undertake
    one more dutiful office
against my bent ('the grain',
  I called it once), too late
    to make as much as can
be made of Paul Celan or
  Zukofsky's 'A', and
    recalling how I met
the latter, reluctantly though
  rewardingly in the event,
    and how he is dead, I am left
with the conjecture poets
  have treated me with as much
    compassionate gentleness as
we might ascribe to centaurs
  finding within their troop
    either a man or a horse.

When I consider these
  whose operations are
    not beyond me but
as it were beside me
  in an alternative cosmos
    I do not envy them.

Catullus on Friendship

'Cancel, Catullus, the expectancies of friendship
Cancel the kindnesses deemed to accrue there...'
           (tr. Peter Whigham)

It must make a great difference, having friends.
  Yeats had Pound and Pound had Yeats, and Frost
Had, briefly, Edward Thomas. It must make
  A world of difference, having trusted friends
And trustworthy – eh, my Lampadius?

It must make all the difference, having friends
    To be dealt with cleanly, honestly – must it not,
Busy Lampadius? Friends who are not too busy
    To recognize the claims one has on them,
The vise one has them in – that too of course.

A world, a world of difference, my
    Never quite trusted and yet far too trusted
Friend, Lampadius... One must rub along.
    Just so, just so; the debts of friendship must,
Given the state of the market, be adjusted.

Lampadius, you're a poet; a busy one,
    And not half bad. Whichever god you sing
Or speak to, it's a lonely business; if
    To no god but a friend, it's lonelier;
But loneliest when there's no one there but 'readers'.

What puzzles or intrigues me, then, is how
    Your busy-ness refuels. In our youth
Mere self-advancement is a sufficient target:
    The sort of fame that's 'being talked about'.
What kept you going when you'd tired of that?

A secret, and you'll keep it. I don't know
    Whether or not to envy you the possession
Of such pure fuel as it seems I never
    Had, or have lost. My name for it was 'friendship';
Which can't be right, I think when I think of you.

'Kindred souls' – a prettily old-fashioned
    Extravagant name for what we had and have,
A competition between siblings. Such
    Olympian squabbles as that phrase clears up,
Which exercised the ancestors so direly!

Cleared up, acknowledged, cleared away... And yet
    The gods help friendship, since the life-force holds
No stake in it. Lampadius, what I
    Mean to say is I can't sing or speak
When friends and kindred can be sold downriver.

346

Two from Ireland

1. *1969, Ireland of the Bombers*

Blackbird of Derrycairn,
Sing no more for me.
Wet fields of Dromahair
No more I'll see

Nor, Manorhamilton,
Break through a hazelwood
In tufted Leitrim ever.
That's gone for good.

Dublin, young manhood's ground,
Never more I'll roam;
Stiffly I call my strayed
Affections home.

Blackbird of Derrycairn,
Irish song, farewell.
Bombed innocents could not
Sing half so well.

Green Leinster, do not weep
For me, since we must part;
Dry eyes I pledge to thee,
And empty heart.

2. *1977, Near Mullingar*

for Augustine Martin

'Green Leinster, never weep
  For me, since we must part.
Dry eyes I pledge to thee,
  And empty heart.'

Travelling by train
  – For I am a travelling man –
Across fields that I laid
  Under this private ban,

I thought: a travelling man
   Will come and go, here now
And gone tomorrow, and
   He cannot keep a vow.

Forsworn, coming to Sligo
   To mend my battered past,
I thought: It must be true;
   The solder cannot last.

But, dear friends, I could weep.
   Is it the bombs have made
Old lesions knit, old chills
   Warm, and old ghosts be laid?

Atrociously, such changes!
   The winning gentleness
Gentler still, and even
   The poets not so reckless.

Twenty-five years at least
   Higher up the slope
That England plunges down:
   That much grounds for hope.

Easy pronouncements from
   The stranger, as he leaves!
The truth is, he was home
   – Or so he half-believes.

Penelope

   And so, the retraction.
Time for it: after much
Effusion, undertow.

   And all right, so;
The year wears, and the worn
Capacities, coarsening,

Honour the thing
Beyond them, the transaction
Clinched lately, clinched no more.

Charity for
A while; then, grace withdrawn;
The flow, and then the ebb.

What wove the web
Now frays it, with as much
Devotion in each breath.

Long-absent Death
Veers in the offing; nears
And goes off, to-and-fro.

And all right, so;
This being out of touch
Alone tests constancy.

It is to be
A prey to hopes and fears;
Fears mostly, as is right.

In landfall light
The faithless absentee,
Death, assays our loves.

Though nothing removes
The weight of it, when the year's
Circuit spells: 'dry',

Not asking why
But blessing it, is to see
At last impunity.

Devil on Ice

Called out on Christmas Eve for a working-party,
Barging and cursing, carting the wardroom's gin
To save us all from sin and shame, through snow,
The night unclear, the temperature sub-zero,
          Oh I was a bombardier
          For anyone's Angry Brigade
That Christmas more than thirty years ago!

Later, among us bawling beasts was born
The holy babe, and lordling Lucifer
With him alas, that blessed morn. And so
Easy it was, I recognize and know
          Myself the mutineer
          Whose own stale bawdry helped
Salute the happy morn, those years ago.

Red Army Faction could have had me then;
Not an intrepid operative, but glib,
A character-assassin primed to go,
Ripe for the irreplaceable though low
          Office of pamphleteer.
          Father of lies, I knew
My plausible sire, those Christmases ago.

For years now I have been amenable,
Equable, a friend of law and order,
Devil on ice. Comes Christmas Eve...and lo!
A babe we laud in baby-talk. His foe
          And ours, not quite his peer
          But his antagonist,
Hisses and walks on ice, as long ago.

Advent

Some I perceive, content
And stable in themselves
And in their place, on whom
One that I know casts doubt;
Knowing himself of those
No sooner settled in
Than itching to get out.

I hear and partly know
Of others, fearless and
Flinging out, whom one
I know tries to despise;
Knowing himself of those
No sooner loosed than they
Weeping sue for the leash.

Some I see live snug,
Embosomed. One I know
Maunders, is mutinous,
Is never loved enough;
Being of those who are
No sooner safely lodged
They chafe at cherishing.

Some I know who seem
Always in keeping, whom
One I know better blusters
He will not emulate;
Being of those who keep
At Advent, Whitsuntide,
And Harvest Home in Lent.

Some who are his kin
Have strewn the expectant floor
With rushes, long before
The striding shadow grows
And grows above them; he,
The deeper the hush settles,
Bustles about more business.

The eclipse draws near as he
Scuttles from patch to shrinking
Patch of the wintry light,
Chattering, gnashing, not
Oh not to be forced to his knees
By One who, turned to, brings
All quietness and ease.

Self-contradictions, I
Have heard, do not bewilder
That providential care.
Switch and reverse as he
Will, this one I know,
One whose need meets his
Prevents him everywhere.

Having No Ear

Having no ear, I hear
And do not hear the piano-tuner ping,
Ping, ping one string beneath me here, where I
Ping-ping one string of Caroline English to
Tell if Edward Taylor tells
The truth, or no.

Dear God, such gratitude
As I owe thee for giving, in default
Of a true ear or of true holiness,
This trained and special gift of knowing when
Religious poets speak themselves to God,
And when, to men.

The preternatural! I know it when
This perfect stranger – angel-artisan –
Knows how to edge our English Upright through
Approximations back to rectitude,
Wooing it back through quarter-tone
On quarter-tone, to true.

Mystical? I abjure the word, for if
Such faculty is known and recognized
As may tell sharp from flat, and both from true,
And I lack that capacity, why should I
Think Paradise by other light than day
Sparkled in Taylor's eye?

Siloam

for Clyde Binfield

'By cool Siloam's shady rill' (Heber)

Arkansaw's westernmost county
Is dry; we nip back over
The out-of-town stateline for
Liquor in Oklahoma.

In the next one, 'wet', a drive-in
Announces 'Kinky Ladies';
A shack says 'Modern Massage',
Not open yet for trading.

A titter: 'This is what
Free Churchmen mean by a *felt
Religion*? We are, are we not,
At the heart of the Bible Belt?

We are. This is Siloam
Springs. Once off the highway,
We walk in the 1930s,
Provincial yesterday:

The two or three blocks we walk
Of dark-brick downtown, sparsely
Frequented, could be almost
How I remember Barnsley,

Except for this river, whatever
River it is, scarved round
The whole small so-called 'city',
Flowing without a sound.

Green, deep-bushed green, the waters
And weir under the hill;
A little park by cool
Siloam's shady rill

Recalls in bronze the appalling
Highest the waters rose
Once, and the devastation –
By God's will, we suppose.

Imagine a deacon of
Drowned bottomlands, his brows
Sternly, despairingly knitted,
In the next county's whorehouse

Drowning himself! This country
Was lately and not completely
Humanized; here the dooms
Come suddenly and stately.

It is thus I perceive this lady,
Hatted and gloved, advancing,
Two grandchildren in tow,
Her eyes on us bright and dancing.

And this is on the bridge
Under the hanging wood,
Feeling precarious over
Siloam's fateful flood.

A Christian Hero

(J.H. Lefroy, Canada, 1843-44)

'Not the action of rowing:
Intentness, intelligent will
In the crewmen of the canoes,
Facing the way they go in...'

Who is this candid traveller, whose
Aquiline Christian mind pursues

354   POEMS OF THE 1970s

First, at *Portage deux Rivières*,
Distinctions sensuous yet severe?
Who was it first, between
Saskatchewan and Churchill
Rivers, where bare hills occur,
Asked himself what it could mean
For rock, mere unclothed rock, to stir
Such happiness? What questioner
Knew his idlest questions thus
The most momentous, least of use?

Whose the observances
The observations? Whose
Victorian rectitude
(He kept his sabbaths clear)
As soon would reason why about
The burden of a freighted mood
As what threw compass-readings out
Nearing the North? Who hunted down
Painfully the Magnetic Pole
Clocked through the months? The calendars
Of Keble's and of Humboldt's years,
Church's and Science's, confined
Doubly this least constricted mind.

Whose this enfranchised soul?
A much committed man's,
And straitly laced;
Would save the Cree for Christ.

An Anglican Lady

in memoriam Margaret Hine

Flattered at having no
less an authority than
Richard Hooker named
for my correction, I
had drawn, before I knew it, the
notepaper towards me for
the reference (Book Five:

sixty, three) when, live,
you sprang before me, Margaret.

                        I had chanced,
brought perhaps by sortilege or some
diviner leading, on
a sheet of your, the secretary's
notepaper. Oh my
poor Margaret, after how many
years, and since Hooker how
many centuries, does this
sad clod encounter, not in books but in
East Anglian blowing mornings, his
and Hooker's and your own, your decorous, God!

Mandelstam's Hope for the Best

1. *The Case Against*

'man must be the hardest thing on earth'

Stout and well-knit in fact,
But avian was the impression;
Skimming compacted bird-brain.
Everyone's ikon, martyred;
In life, not altogether
Lifelike, unless as a bird.

A bird that lives on bees!
No more classical emblem,
Gentile or Jew, will the age
That martyred him permit us
Than his own chirr of bees from
Stringent and high Taigetos;

Honeybees dried and strung,
Hard pellets, into a necklace
Of Russian words that he twines
And twines before us while
The deep blue Ovidian twilight
Purples internal exile.

Hard! As nails? No, harder;
Mailed with an unaltering
Assurance of redemption,
The Cross his *passe-partout*
To broad Parnassian fields
Under enamelled blue.

2. *Son of Isaac*

Ram caught in Stalin's thicket!
Rigged trials, typhus...Yahweh
Was Georgian, the 'I AM'
Expert in quickset mazes.

Though it is hard to say,
A Mandelstam's
Assurance of redemption
Huddles distress away.

The one-sided trade of man
With God has more of drama
Than his Parnassian
Enamel could gloss over.

His cupola, his cradle,
His ring (oh it is ringing
Home so bronze and true!)
All this settles nothing.

Much though it stirs us, still it
Forecloses on our hope
Too brutally. A harder
Trade earns wider scope

Than his so beautiful ring
Of memory, love and culture.
Wrestling with the angel
Pries the cupola open.

Jacob, the haunted child
Of him this surrogate
Saved by dying for,
Will not be reconciled.

3. *Hope Not Abandoned*

Hope so abstracted as
towards no temporal end
but 'a mode of address to facts,
to the world and to its persons',
however it be attested
by every grace of behaviour
sought for and found in language,
had better agree to be called
a living contradiction.

To avoid abuse of terms,
let poets say they are hopeless,
and this at whatever cost
in the self-approved dissenter's
brilliance of negation.
Better thus than to fox
ourselves by appropriating
a cardinal term to actions
by which, ourselves, we are baffled.

The alternative to the degrading
gibberish of the Gross
National Product is
known to, and hated by,
those who most gibber. It
is not the historical Church
but whatever asserts our ends
are, and therefore our hopes,
metaphysical, like our terrors.

4. *Sonnet*

As massive and dispensable as sculpture
Bees, dancing, point and utter their location.
Cotillions interspinning; monumental
Gossamer build-up of gnats' spiring wings
Punctuates space, commands it, by the river
Ephemerally, some evening. So a fly
Moves on the arm of Rodin's thinker with
No less weight than his effigy moves on earth.

Carve in that stone, Acmeist! Parian marble
You like to think so cold is all a-zing
With momentary fevers, and the scarp
Of language you would quarry, poet, whirls
Indeterminately shapely in
Helix on nebulous helix, not to be netted.

5. *Of his Armenia*

'Ararat has drunk the air' (Mandelstam)

Self-aggrandizing to say, and yet it is true:
When I went there in 1942,
Though I had read few of the books, and no one knew
All of the facts, the torn-apart suffering hung,
Suffusion or deposit of the years,
Glittering like mica or like tears
Around the Arctic toe-hold where we clung,
North of Murmansk, on to his mother-bear Russia.

Nothing was less like miasma. Mountainy air
It was, though there were no mountains. There was one
Mountain in our sense of it, hanging there,
Not to be dealt with by guides or expert advice,
No holiday chalets upon it nor excavators'
Trolley-lines disused among flowers at Delphi,
But there at our backs: a mountain that cast no shadow
Indeed, but excess of light – the Arctic ice.

Such he one time imagined, a serener
Than earth-bound mountain spilling the ice-flow Grace,
As pure and polar as music of Palestrina
He said, and pointed – where I cannot follow
Not now nor then, having too poor an ear.
Ox-like obtuse (though there are Armenian churches
Ox-like, he says), what can I do with a clue
Harder to grasp than what it sets out to construe:

The Eucharist? I had no way to know
The far other end of his lands, nor how he had
For those without an ear, without a head
For freezing heights, climbed an accessible mountain

As full of Grace, vineyarded, colour of ochre:
Ararat, earthenware mountain. It would be long
Before I could learn from him and in part for myself
The God-given mercy and warmth of terra-cotta.

Three Beyond

In memoriam Michael Ayrton, Claude Simpson, William Partridge

Judgment occurs, but is not
For the judged of much importance.
Who cares for the rank in which he
Utters his adorations?

Thinking of the blessèd
Company of the saints and
The army of martyrs, I find that
One friend of three absolves me.

Two artists and one scholar
I think of; and it is one
Of the artists, the less acknowledged,
Who comes through, solacing most.

One has to understand that
Over there, over the last
Hurdle, the race is over;
No one there is competing.

One has to understand that
The ranks, the armies are
Indeed there ranged in order,
But an order all will acknowledge.

Heavenly smiles from the two that,
Prayed to, gave limited comfort;
Delighted I should have reached to
Him of the highest standing.

A Garland for Ronsard

1.

Green eyes from under cornsheaf curls
    Dart out at him, belated
Masks of alarming Orpheus, gaping
    And uncoordinated.

In dreams, in dreams... It is not true
    They haunt the familiar Loir,
Capering their black classics of
    Provence and Navarre.

Why then should laurels above the acclaimed
    Brow and the haggard face
Attest a restive Athenian, half
    In love with incult Thrace?

2.

Dieu les tient agitez...

These – of whom only four or five are known
To have existed, mostly Greek – aspire
Not to the style of poet, but the stele
Erected in some secret glade nearby
Ancestral acres. Into these the god's
Sizzling probe pricks insecurity
At every turn. The common talk esteems them –
Not without some complacency – 'unsound',
Countryside crazies. It is thought they've much
Traffic with fairies, nymphs; with any not
Quite human *leman*, leaping the vales, woods, mountains.

3.

Antres, et vous fontaines...

Caverns, and you fountains
That off the beetling mountains
    Slide to this humbler place
    With stealing pace;

You also, forests; waves
whose gipsying current laves
These fields; woods, banks that bend
    Each side, attend:

When Heaven and my hour
Shall rule I be no more,
Reft from my happy stay
    In common day,

I make it your affair
No journeyman shall square
Marble to make ornate
    My entombed state.

Let my remains be hid
Under no marble lid,
But rather let the screen
    Be evergreen.

And earth-engendered from
Me may ivy come,
In which I may be wound
    Round and around.

The braided vine embellish
My sepulchre, and flourish
To cast on every side
    A speckled shade.

To that place shall repair
On my name-day each year
The droves of cattle and
    The drovers' band;

When, having made their fit
Oblation as is meet,
These words to the isle i' the river
    Shall they deliver:

'How widely are you known,
Who serve as tomb for one
Of whom the universe
    Intones the verse!

Whom Rancour, what is more,
In life consumed not, nor
Reduced to supplicate
    For grants the great;

Who'd not re-introduce
The aphrodisiac use
Of drams, nor yet have part
    In mages' art;

But rather to our own˙
Plains made the Sisters known,
Bending the grass to their
    Songs in the air.

For on his strings he knew
To winnow out such true
Accordance as adorns
    Us, and our lawns.

May the sweet manna rain
For ever on this terrain
That is his tomb, which let
    The May dews wet.

Grass crowns, and waters ring,
The site; the grasses spring
Green, and the fluctuant wave
    Brims round his grave.

To him we, mindful how
Glory redounds, will bow
As if to Pan each year
    Our foreheads here.'

Thus shall the rustic troop
Declare, while many a cup
Shall pour its votive flood,
    Milk and lamb's blood,

On me, who shall by then
Be gone to that domain
Where the blest spirits roam
    And make their home.

Not hailstorms nor the snow
Upon those quarters blow,
Nor ever thunder dare
    Break on them there;

But an immortal green
Adorns the constant scene,
And constant through all time
    Spring's at the prime.

Every solicitude
Kings care for, these elude:
They raze no world, the faster
    The world to master;

But live as brothers do,
And though they are dead pursue
The self-same trades they plied
    Before they died.

There I shall hear his lyre,
Alcaeus's, strung to ire;
And Sappho's chords, that fall
    Sweetest of all.

How much must those who long
Attend the diffusive song
Rejoice to be of those
    Who hear echoes

That the incumbent rocks
Rock back at, while what blocks
Old Tantalus fails for once
    His pain to advance!

Lyre! Sweet lyre! What more
Can heal our heartaches or
So far on us impose
    We hear repose?

4.

End to Torment

At Ste Madeleine de Croixval,
housebound with gout, four sonnets;
October –
        'dusty air...
September's yellow gold that mingled fair
With green and rose tint on each maple bough
Sulks into deeper browns'.
                He died in that
same year at the other priory, St Cosme.

Hélène, Cassandre, Yseult
Is-hilda, Undine, 'O
swallow, my sister' – look
out for whom you
fatuously endow, though
posterity fail not desert perhaps.

Frenetic and protean
(One noted: double chin!)
'perched like a bird at dusk',
huge eyes, thin shoulders; or
the strapping one perched, shoes off
at the foot of his bunk. They are
no good, you know, these girls.

What did he write?
'Myrrh and olibanum',
gum-resin from incisions
in South Arabia: *dendron*,
cecily, chervil – and
AMOR, the palindrome ROMA.
Backward or forward it read
the same: she-wolf.

'There is a mellow twilight 'neath the trees
Soft and hallowed as is a thought of thee...'
'Whisper in the murmurous twilight where
I met thee mid the roses of the past
Where you gave your first kiss in the last...'

And which of them all did he, oh well,
'love'?
      The Lady Loba.

        5.

Living without Marie
Makes him, since he has tried,
Know what it is to live
Without the one illusion
That he has lived inside.

France, Orphic Greece Renewed,
Himself the Orpheus – all
Farrago, all mistaken.
Yes, but to be by her
He staked it on, forsaken...

Of course not celibate
For all his tonsure. Still
Rossignols' orisons
Could hardly compensate
For never having sons.

Though how much that amounts to
How could he calculate?
One has not, or one has,
Sons; and no one can
Know both alternatives.

Forget the brigade of his fellows
And the adoring pupils.
What he lacks in the end
Is not the bedmate even,
But the sulky spitfire friend.

        6.

Génèvres hérissez, et vous, houx espineux...

Bush-bristling juniper and you the thorn –
Enjoying holly, one the desert's guest
And one the thicket's; ivy-cover drawn
Across waste caves; sand-spiring spouts and freshets;

Pigeons that sip at them; you mourning doves
In your unending widowhood; nightingales
Who day-long night-long in appealing jargon
Rehearse the unvaried versicles of your loves;

And you with the red throat, non-indigenous swallow –
If you should see *la Cara* in this Spring
Abroad for flowers, parting the young grasses,
　　Tell her from me I hope for nothing now
From her, no favours. Cut the suffering:
As well be dead as carry on like this.

'Pastor Errante'

for Robert Pinsky

'And you, Enscaldunac?' (Mary Austin, The Flock*)*

When you were explaining America, Robert, you did not
　　– Why should you? – explain
To your small daughter there had been a time when the *pastor*,
　　Meaning the shepherd in
Many tongues though not as it happens in Basque,
　　Roamed the Sierra Nevada.

It would, you must see, have made a difference: not
　　To have those alarmingly non-
Communicating Swedes or German-speaking
　　Bohemians on
The Willa Cather prairies for your girl
　　To grow wide-eyed at;

But instead in Inyo County Mary Austin's
　　Long-gone shepherds who might
As well have been Hebrew or Greek or Sicilian as
　　What they were largely – Basques,
Speaking their own impenetrable language
　　And yet familiar.

What we seem to be speaking of, if you agree with me, is
　　A sort of utterance
Made from out of earshot, the wonderful surely

Lexicons of gesture
Though of implements also – Californian shepherds
    Even had crooks!

Is it only to us, and not to our children, that
    A shepherd's crook, which I
Doubt I have ever seen, is more comforting than
    That appalling threshing-machine
You imagined in which, like Berryman waving, your hobo
    Pitched head-first?

Imagine an America that was what
 ˙   At one time I infer
It might have been: the West not lost, a true
    Pastoral, sheep-bells ringing.
Would it have made a difference? Would it not, and
    Why do you think so?

I do not expect an answer. The lord Hermes,
    Tutelary deity
Of shepherds, no doubt patronizes also
    Hermetic poetry, ours:
Wherein we ask unanswerable questions
    To what man's profit?

Errant through why not America? although Asia
    Is what Leopardi
Too plangently imagined, that much nearer
    The god's faint trace. And

        'Moon',
    He starts out, bald as that, *'what are you doing*
There in the sky? Unspeaking moon,
What are you about? You come
Up in the evening, and you go
Looking at deserts; then you stop, stand still.
What is this all about? Are you
Pleased to be pacing these eternal alleys?
Don't you get bored? Or is it
Still to your liking, looking down on these
Glens of ours? Ah well, your life is
Much like a shepherd's. Up he gets before
Dawn, and moves out

368   POEMS OF THE 1970s

His sheep to pasture, sees to
Folds, to water, fodder; then,
Tired out, snores through the evening:
Hopes for no more, ever. Tell
Me, you moon: what is it worth to
The shepherd, this life of his,
And what to you, your life? Tell me
The ends they move to: his brief, vagrant life
And yours, unending.'

       One perceives the question
  Looks for a no more
Reassuring answer than the worst we might
  Frame to alarm
Our daughters with, or else ourselves reflecting
  About our daughters. Where
Does it come in then, the incongruous sweetness?
  From an oaten reed and
Lyrical tortoise-shell? I wouldn't knock it,
  I tell myself
And tell you, Robert. Sicily, ancient Hebron,
  We cull their honeycombs.
Why should we not? And he goes on:

         'An old

White and unable man,
Half-dressed at best, and shoeless,
A heavy bundle toted on his shoulders,
By mountains, valleys and sharp boulders
In wind, in storm, and when it
Heats up and afterwards freezes,
Keeps going, keeps, keeps going
Through streaming and through standing
Waters he falls, he gets up, bit by bit
Quickens his going, he quickens it, torn and
Bloody; and at last he reaches
To where the road and where so much
Overstraining stretched him to: to the
Hair-raising gulch where he,
Oblivious, pitches in. Immaculate moon,
Immaculate, virginal, such
The life of the dying, the mortal, the set to deadward.'

Now why should we,
I ask you, derive any measure of consolation
From such a cry, or from
The way of life that past all responsible doubt it
Faithfully utters? I
Cannot explain why a pastoral life that I could not
Pursue should
Figure for me as, however uncouth, still
Human and proper, as
(To take a plain instance) the life of a rabble-rousing
Activist, though
He too has his classical prototype, the *rhetor*,
Emphatically is not.

'A man is born to
Painstaking, and his very
Birth is in hazard to death.
Trouble and worry are
The first things probe him. In his very
Setting out Mother and Father
Take on to console him
For having been born. And then
As he starts to grow up, the one
Takes over from the other
In heartening him, to come to
Terms with his human status.
This is the very best that parents
Can do for their children. But why
If that is the case donate them
To daylight in the first place? Why
Hold up at all in a life that
Crowds to such consolation?
If life is all misadventure,
Why does it keep going
Inside us? Untouchable moon,
This is the life of mortals, but
Mortal is what you are not;
And what I say perhaps
Very little concerns you.
To you, you solitary, you
Moon, eternal vagrant
Brooding upon yourself, perhaps this
Life on earth comes clear, and this

Undergoing of ours, this breathing out
Of sighs, all this
That is, and happens; also what
Happens in this
Dying, this ultimate
Changing of colour in the way we look,
This perishing off
The earth, this coming clean of
All settled habits and good neighbourhood.'

Skip a bit then, and:

'So it is that I
Cogitate, both on the grand
Immeasurable heavenly mansions and
On the uncountable kin. And then,
After so long on the stretch,
Coping with so many
Each and every first celestial motion
And each terrestrial, every one of them turning,
Turning only to return to
Where they started from, it is then I
Can find no use nor fruit of it. To you,
Undying bride, no doubt it is
Comprehensible. But this I
Both recognize and feel:
From the eternal turnings
Around, and my own unstable
Being, whatever may come of
Good or satisfying is
For some one else. For me, my life is evil.'

What sort of a frigid monster would one have to
    Be, to derive consolation
From such a confession? How to deflect, by any
    Muster of formulaic
Muting properties, crook and staff, the brute
    Drive, and the justified pain?

What should we be, will we be, have we been doing, persuading
    Our daughters they would be safe with
For instance a hulking great villain once, flagging us down,
    Sheepskin over his shoulder in

Arcady if you believe it, in rain, and not without menace
    Cadging a smoke?
The justified pain, the justified brute...So
    Telling our daughters
Of pastoral idylls, what we might mean is this:
    There are some failures in
Life, and I mean in a life-long effort, one would not
    Soon confess to, Robert; and
Knowledge, foreknowledge of them (they are not the shepherd's
    Ineluctable hardships, though
One found no way to elude them) – such foreknowledge
    Is, you would surely agree,
What none of us has the heart or the gall to transmit to
    Our gullible daughters. Isn't
That the best reason for rubbing their dear snub-noses
    Into a shepherd's mishaps?

Summer Lightning

for Seamus Heaney, in imitation of Ronsard

'L'argument du Comicque est de toutes saisons.'

Heaney, one can get word-perfect at
Any profession. Law needs working at
But can be mastered; practice of Physic makes
Practitioners perfect; grind is what it takes
To come by effective public speaking or
Become a consummate philosopher;
Even the best computer-wallahs know it's
Close study counts. It's not like that with poets...
    Perfect is what the Art has up to now
Not been, and won't be, here; God won't allow
That much credit to Humanity.
Unfinished as we know ourselves to be,
Earthy by definition, could we reach,
Ever, to perfect energy of speech?
    The gift of poetry is like the fire
Seen of a summer's night: flames that transpire
Like a foreboding over a river, over
A field, or again there, flickering, hover

To silhouette some plume on a far coppice
Become a sacred grove. This randomness
Makes people jumpy; seeing the weird flame,
Souls for a moment batter against their frame.
And in the end it gutters down, all this
Dumb foundry-blast of clarification is
Suddenly dull, and then it dies away.
Because it's not predictable day by day
But jumps from place to place, never at rest,
No country gets this migrant on request
Or is bequeathed her. Some emergent state
Is (so one hopes) her current favourite.
   And so no Hebrew, Greek nor Roman hand
Can handle all of poetry on demand.
Germany she has visited, she advances
Her claim to England's coasts, to Scotland's, France's,
Vaulting over, wheeling, taking great
Pleasure in picking some unlooked-for state
And some unlikely person. The bright flare
Illuminates some province here or there,
Then just as soon evaporates in air.
The Muse, in short, is international;
She is put up by, she puts up with, all;
Peculiar to no property, no one breed.
But whom she picks on, him she clips indeed.
   Take me now, Heaney – and let this suffice:
If I have made it, it was at a price
Such as I'm not sure others would have paid.
What I know is this art of mine has flayed
Me, and still does. I'm skinned! So, after one
Death let me have another one, to stun
Into insensibility. I've had much
Fun in this life; and yet the undulant touch
Of the Parnassian flood, Permessus, meant
I would be, as I have been, somnolent,
Unhandy, useless; worse, I must admit
I cannot give it up, I'm slave to it.
   I am opinionated and embittered,
Inconsiderate, gruff, low-spirited,
Pleased and displeased at once, huffy and raw;
And yet I fear God, fear the Crown, the Law,
Am spry enough by nature, cordial,
Content to have vexed nobody at all.

So there you have me, Heaney...I suppose
All of our lot have vices much like those.
    Now if Calliope, to make up for this,
Had made me better than the best there is,
Star pupil in her class, star of the show,
Then all these feelings that I undergo
I could put up with. But it isn't so;
Since I'm at best a halfway poet here,
I'd rather like some less godlike career.
    Two sorts of business flourish on that hill
Of the nine Lovelies. One's compatible
With those who like to say that they 'compose',
Who tot up and keep tallies, who dispose
These many verse-lines here; beneath them, those.
(Tell off fourteen, and bless me, you've a sonnet,
Its subject: Time, a poet's reflections on it.)
By 'versifiers' (which these are) is meant
That verse on verse is all that they invent,
All cold too, ice-cold. Brought to bed, these brought
Out some small slice of life – which they abort!
Such verse does best as drapery for a pound
Of sugar or rice, ground ginger, screwed around
Cinnamon, say. And such work, if at last
It sees the light of print, is quickly passed
Over with 'What a drag!' So from the start
It goes unread. The Apollonian dart,
Corrosive and austere, has made no sores
Upon these creatures. They are sophomores
In painting or creative writing; no one
Taught them to write, or to put pigment on,
So ink and paint are squandered; both are laid
On so thick, the daub disgusts the trade.
    The other track provides for those who seem
In their sense of themselves, in an extreme
Consumption of the fire. Whatever odd
Sense 'poet' has, they pass it on the nod;
Fed, for their part, on Terror, and the God.
    Of these no more than four or five are known
To have existed, mostly Greek. Their tone
Is matter-of-fact and prosy – that's a blind;
Silly old tales on the surface, but behind
A beautiful science. That's the trick of it:
To be, while easy, cryptic. They could profit

In this way by the confident obtuseness
Of their much pampered public, and its less
Than open mind; its eyebrow raised, its jeer
Reserved for arcane verities made clear.
  These first made current whole theodicies
And abstruse astrological expertise,
While camouflaging this, by an astute
Highly developed use of anecdote
From a purblind public. God won't let them be,
His sizzling probe pricks insecurity
Into them always. Men like these are found –
Not without some complacency – 'unsound',
Countryside crazies. It's believed they've much
Traffic with fairies (those!), and nymphs, and such.
  Cutting between these two tracks there's a third
Which, since it holds the middle, is preferred
As what God has supposedly designed
To satisfy the appetite in mankind
For culling an elect. This kind supports,
So runs the theory, the performing arts;
It's educational, irrigates the masses.
It spreads civility through evening-classes,
Where sinking selfhood in a common cause
Is a point much stressed. But then, our trip-wire wars
Or (worse) our big-time cosmos-splitters seem
Hardly at all to share a common theme
With Drayton's 'Agincourt'. Belligerent airs
Do wonders for morale, so long as there's
No chance we hear the enemy singing theirs.
So, if it comes to patrons, there's no doubt
Bellona and mad Captain Mars are out.
Which leaves us with the staged, or stagey; not
The happiest prospect . . .
                          Tragic plots are what,
So it was thought, some few great houses foster:
Plantagenet, Gore-Booth, Adams, Malatesta,
Atreus, Thebes. But ritual couplings, treasons,
Condign kills and shames are for all seasons
And all conditions. Thinking of your bog-queen,
Intact, tar-black when disinterred, I've seen
This calls for Comedy, never more demonic
Than when Divine, involved and unironic,
Painful and pitying. (This she also knew,

Your wife, who took the cannibal Ugolino
As type for poets: brain devouring brain,
One 'rabid egotistical daisy-chain'.)
Knowing what's out of joint is our dilemma
In Ireland, Denmark, England, the Maremma;
What is, what isn't. In your singing-school,
Dante's and yours, the dreadful is the rule.
    Dread; yes dread – the one name for the one
Game that we play here, surely. I think Sisson
Got it, don't you? Plain Dante, plain as a board,
And if flat, flat. The abhorrent, the abhorred,
Ask to be uttered plainly. Heaney, I
Appeal to you who are more in the public eye
Than us old codgers: isn't it the case
The Muse must look disaster in the face?
    Well, but – here comes the compliment, somewhat late
But sent with feeling – none should denigrate
Your early Georgics. None of us would steal
From your tin scoop plunged in a tub of meal
Its pre-Dantesque Homeric virtue. Those
English who prize your verse as rustic prose
Are not all wrong: Agricola is one
Hero persists. Farmer and farmer's son
Are two 'scape whipping. And the traveller,
Odysseus Weather-eye the navigator,
He's another. Both of them you've been,
And lover too; Apollo set the scene
And then these various provocations planned,
Providing that in ancient Ireland and
Historic England Heaney should rehearse
Cottage economies, curtness of good verse.

Death of a Voice

After Pasternak
and to him

1.

Here is its mark left, thumbnail of enigma.
– It is late, you will sleep, come dawn you will try to read it.
And meanwhile to awaken the loved one, and to touch her
As you may do is given to no other.

How you have touched her! Though your lips were bronze
They touched her, as tragedians touch the stalls.
A kiss there was like summer, hung and hung
And only after that, your sound of thunder.

It drank, as birds drink; took till the senses swooned.
Long, long the stars flowed in from throat to lung.
Nightingales too, their eyes start, as by spasms ·
Drop by drop they wring night's arches dry.

2.

Dawn will agitate the tapers,
Spark and propel house-martins to their mark.
Admonitory, in you dart:
Let life be always as bran-new as this.

Dawn, like a shot into the dark.
Bang, bang! – the wadding as it flies
Out of the rifle sees its spark go out.
Let life be always as bran-new as this.

Once more, outside – a puff of wind.
What night-long waited on us quivers.
With dawn came rain, and the rain shivers.
Let life be always as bran-new as this.

It is distinctly ludicrous!
Why should it bother with the man on guard?
It saw its own way in was barred.
Let life be always as bran-new as this.

Give us your orders, now, upon the drop
Of a handkerchief, the while you are still *seigneur*
While, for the while that we are at a loss,
The while, the while the spark's not blown upon!

3.

In the unparented, insomniac
Damp and universal vast
A volley of groans breaks loose from standing posts,
And still the nightwind, self-aborted, idles.

And hard behind, in an unseeing scurry
Some slant drops fall. About a stretch of fencing
Damp branches quarrel with the pallid wind
Sharply. I quail. You, bone of their contention!

Mandelstam's 'Octets'

66.

I love the way the weave, when two or three or
Four sometimes great gulps can't draw it tight,
Comes up, comes clear; when I achieve a more
Shuddering breath, and get it sounding right.
So much good that does me, yet I fetch
Much weight upon me, as the moment nears
When the arched breastbone, onerously a-stretch
Through my slurred mumblings, signals in your ears.

67.

I love the way the weave, when two or three or
Four sometimes great gulps can't draw it tight,
Comes up, comes clear; when I achieve a more
Shuddering breath, and get it sounding right.
Meanwhile, by the arch of spinnakers beguiled
To open-form regattas, Space is idling
And adumbrating, half-awake – a child
That's never learned what would be meant by cradling.

68.

When you have shoved aside the scribbled worksheet,
And what you hold in your intent mind is
Contentless, not to be glossed, just one complete
Arc on your inward dark, one sentence's
Periodic structure (eyes screwed shut
Upon itself, on the strength itself supplies) –
This had to do with the page that you will blot
As much as a cupola does, with vacant skies.

69.

Advise me, draftsman of the drifting sands,
Geometer of wilderness, are these
Intractable alignments countermands
More clinching than the wind's voluminous scurries?
– Nothing to me such tremulous demurrers,
Judaic qualms! His baby burble builds
Experience out of babble, burble slurs
Imbibing the experience, modelling it.

70.

Butterfly-girl of the Mussulman, all
In a cut-to-ribbons winding-sheet, who are
Livelong and deathlong, lifeling, deathling, tall
Insectile apparition, this same one
With the immense antennae and her chomping
Head hooded in a burnous, she has strayed
Out, at large. O, the flag of a winding-sheet, please
Furl it, and fold your wings – I am afraid!

71.

Well, but the saw-edged maple-leaf can suffer
To have its claws drawn for it, in some fine
Perfected corner; butterfly-markings offer
Themselves that way, motifs for a mural design.
I have it now, of a sudden:
                              mosques there are
That live and persist along with us. In our throes
We are perhaps ourselves Hagia Sophia,
That looks with our eyes out through innumerous windows.

72.

Schubert from water, from birdsong's gamut Mozart;
Goethe, a trill down much-bewildered byways!
Hamlet's balked gait, itself his pensive part –
All took the crowd's pulse, banked on the crowded phrase.
Maybe, before we lipped them, lispings moved;
Where woods were not, already foliage flittered;
And those we propose experience to, have proved
In advance of experience fitted for it, and featured.

73.

Those plaguy, needling games of ours, where stooks
Of jackstraws figure, phials whence we drink
Illusions of causality! These hooks
With which we touch on Quantities, we think,
Are deathly playthings; one small figure catches
On to another as the hook is cast
Over, and snags. The child, though, sleeps. The vast
Universe sleeps, where cradled Eternity watches.

74.

I come in out of Space, and with a rake
In Quantity's garden that can do with tending
Grub up self-knowing Causes and the fake
Invariant there. My one book you, the Unending,
Wrote for me and I read it alone, in seclusion;
It is your leafless, your wayward Guide to Wild Herbs,
It is your book of difficult sums for solving,
Telling of massive roots, the squares, the cubes.

75.

To get past harping on the laws of Nature
The blue-hard eye has pierced to the Law behind:
Lodged in the earth's crust, zany is God's own creature
And upthrust, grubbed from the breast, his groan is mined.
The aborted foetus, deaf, something can bend it;
Like a forge-ahead road it is bowed back, hooped to a horn
– The plenty of bent-in Space, to apprehend it
Takes up the pledge of the petal's, the cupola's form;

76.

And of the sixth sense, the infinitesimal suffix;
Or else the minute sincipital eye of the lizard;
Cloisters of cochlea, cockles, the snail-shell helix;
And the cilia's small-talk, hairline flicker and hazard.
The unattainable, how near it comes!
No disuniting it, no scrutinies –
As with a message pressed into your hand, that is
To have an answer by return, at once!

Note: Of Mandelstam's 'Octets' or 'eight-liners', composed as a whole in Moscow in 1933 (though incorporating some writing from as late as July 1935), Clarence Brown has said: 'these poems are in no sense an isolated statement or a momentary excursus into metaphysics. They are central to an understanding of Mandelstam...' The text I have worked from is that established by Professor Brown in 'Mandelstam's Notes Towards a Supreme Fiction', in *Delos* (Austin, Texas, 1968), Vol. I, no. 1; the order of the poems in the sequence, and accordingly the numbers given to them, are those of Professor Brown – they have been printed in another order. In the case of poems so cryptic as these, translation cannot help but be at the same time interpretation; and I am greatly indebted to Clarence Brown's commentary (loc. cit.), though I have dared to differ from him somewhat, and the difference is registered in my versions. Though it must by no means be supposed that Henry Gifford approves of this enterprise, I am pleased to acknowledge that he assisted me crucially at several points.

TO SCORCH OR FREEZE

The Thirty-ninth Psalm, Adapted

I said to myself: 'That's enough.
Your life-style is no model.
Keep quiet about it, and while
you're about it, be less overt.'

I held my tongue, I said nothing;
no, not comfortable words.
'Writing-block', it's called;
very discomfiting.

Not that I had no feelings.
I was in a fever.
And while I seethed,
abruptly I found myself speaking:

'Lord, let me know my end,
and how long I have to live;
let me be sure
how long I have to live.

One-finger you poured me;
what does it matter to you
to know my age last birthday?
Nobody's life has purpose.

Something is casting a shadow
on everything we do;
and in that shadow nothing,
nothing at all, comes true.

(We make a million, maybe;
and who, not nobody but
who, gets to enjoy it?)

Now, what's left to be hoped for?
Hope has to be fixed on you.
Excuse me my comforting words
in a tabloid column for crazies.

I held my tongue, and also
I discontinued my journals.
(They accumulated; who
in any event would read them?)

Now give me a chance. I am
burned up enough at your pleasure.
It is all very well, we deserve it.
But shelved, not even with mothballs?

Hear my prayer, O Lord,
and please to consider my calling:
it commits me to squawking
and running off at the mouth.'

Benedictus

Importunately
inopportune,

blessed is he that cometh in
the name of the

splendour between
ice and pearl cover in
the clockless distance,

flying the polar route as
we did in those days
                    (We have been
                              modern
                                    so long!)

Poet Redeemed & Dead

Feeling good, green light, the earthly paradise,
where is it, poet? Not
in this or that inn, on this or that fell, supplying
this or that cheese, but in
old age, innoxious,
knowing its guilts and not
forgiving itself but assured,
you knew how, of pardon.

Attar of Roses

The mind (the soul) is not
a ghost in the box of the body or brain, although it
excusably seems so. For instance at times
recalling our priests who instructed us in
The Resurrection of the Body

– at Judgement Day, the cadavers out of their coffins,
boxes emerging from boxes! What nonsense,
he blindingly observed –

who was himself, it may be said, a little
fleshy, more than a little coarse,
and maladroit with it, not to say uncivil.

What female parishioner wants him resurrected,
if so in what shape, and for what fanciful purpose?
But all the same, do we live in a nest of boxes,
the nubs of ourselves, so tiny, secreted in
the innermost, most reclusive, most
cramped of the boxes? If not

we have to believe in, we already believe in,
the resurrection of the body

which is not a box, but a main
sweet-smelling part of what the box encloses.

Sing Unto The Lord a New Song

Cheerfulness in lordly
leisure; and
holiness in thunder and high wind.

The lordly thunder
cleaves out flakes of fire.

The lightning uncovers the woods,
making the roe-deer calve
untimely in the bracken.

It is the holiness thunders.

Do not ask for the storm to ease.
Spirits rise, the longer it goes on.
Imagine Him yawning, hear Him
crack His joints as He stretches,
magisterial!

Praise the Lord upon the harp,
sing to him on the damnable steel guitar!

'So make them melt as the dishousèd snail'

'or as the embryo, whose vital band
breaks ere it holds'.
                        As we grow old, the basics
(as you might say) emerge
with an uncanny force:
we and our siblings each day more alike.

'The ungodly are froward
                even from their mothers wombe;
as soon as they be borne they go astray;
born and perverted in one day,
lie, flatter, and betray.'

It seems there are such doomed creatures;
morally
spina bifida. But

as we grow old the features of one
or the other parent show up in the mirror
frightening and affecting, and we can

under the heavenly justice

be equalled with slug or snail but
hardly with the aborted
almost-brother who would have
been so like us. The psalmist goes too far:

Best not be born, he means.

Better be born a snail,
or lying and betraying,
so you be born.

God Saves The King

To the chief Chanters
upon the dumb Dove in far places:
    either your brows are knitted,
    or you whinny and smirk, such teasers,
    you take such pains.

Far the places
and you are in their hands
who feast on squabs.

But care for that other way
of being debonair:

the sauntering monarch's, David's,
whose vigorous warmth did variously impart
to wives and concubines, to chariot-wheels,
to realms and officers,

religious faith; that is,
light spareness, unconcern.

Meteorologist, September

We shall break out
into the mention of God's great goodness,
and the abruptness of it.

The year goes round,
yes, but with what ructions!
The violence of the turns!
Why else are Revolutions always bloody
except that seasonal change is the type of them,
calamitous though foreseen?

At the autumnal equinox
gales.
      Though the belief is
'unsupported by observation',
rationality and
superstition alike require it:
God does not make His changes
without some pother.

His steady counsels change the face
of the declining year.

He flings gross icy gobbets from His hand –
fire and hail, snow and vapours,
wind and storm, subduing the land.

By Him the rain
supples the clods of indurated acres.

His whirled-down snows are laid
like bleaching wool beside the streams
to clad the tender blade.

Breath steams on the sharpened air.
And who so hardy as to bear
the quickness of His frost?

He blows a cold too strong for strongest things.

His power declare,
you empty air,
and snow out of nowhere, suddenly.

Vengeance Is Mine, Saith The Lord

You that would bite the whole pie and
mell with the pack, yet pout yourself ill-used,

you have committed crimes
against the innocent for
no profit but self-promotion.
Mouse has a broken back by
the coarsest cheese in the larder.

The creaking scissors and the penman's knife,
derailed from their proper business, will do justice
in a *collage* of your cruelties.
                              'The children
wore their cagoules, but these were mortar-bombs.'

In the casinos most were vacuous, some
were fleshy and flaming, some profuse, some grasping,
far from Beirut.
                  Though I
address the mute, He hears, will testify.

Standings

'One Law for the Lion and Ox is Oppression.'

For Woman & Man, for White & Black, for Bent &
Straight, for Sick & Sane
one Law is Oppression?

Across the Albion of William Blake,
a tesselation of ghettos,
the traveller beds down at night in
a Fabian or Lesbian canton, in
a Rastafarian or Israelite republic,
crossing from jurisdiction
to jurisdiction, never
tyrannised, never chastened.

Divers waights and divers measures are
abomination to the Lord.

There is not the psychiatrist's truth,
and then the poet's;
the white man's truth, then the black's.

The Lord admits diversity of gifts,
but not disparity.
We need to know where we stand.

Happy the man or the brute
who stands corrected,
stands like that, helped like that to stand,
enabled to,

hungry for judgement always.

Church Militant

In the day of the mustering of thine army,
thy people shall be willing:

the young men come to thee as dew,
the dew of thy youth comes unto thee.

From everlasting to
God knows... But this is history,
vouched for over and over:

as dew from the sources of the morning
sparkles upon the grasses,
the Commander recruits His youth
repeatedly, the converts crowd
the rail and His army masses.

Always they all passed muster;
always they were triumphant.
Always, you would have it,
they were insincere or deluded.

Curtains!

The Lord is King, be the people
never so impatient; He
sitteth between the Cherubim,
let the earth stir as it will.

> 'And what if I
> fall down and die?
> Can the sun go down at noon?
> His years are one perpetual day,
> and shall His children die so soon?'

Soon is not soon. This earth grows old,
Auriga and the Bear shall be folded away
like the costumes for Act One.
The star-scene shifts at His command.
The Twins, the Southern Cross, the Scales
flap on their hangers, ungainly.

'Stars, far things...'
But in the reach of His arm.

For He is One, still One;
the clock-hand wavers, uncertain.
Whatever the next production, you
are there when the curtain rises.

Auriga and the Bear,
The Twins, the Southern Cross
show that He is there
for ever, as they are not.

'And Our Eternal Home'

> Time like an ever-rolling stream
> bears not its sons away,
> but its own segments, years and days.

> They fly forgotten, not as dream,
> as thought:

'We have spent our years
as it were a thought',

few and short, or long and many
according as we think of them.
Keeping a tally is
little to the purpose.

'So teach us to number our days...'
Certainly number amazes.
Numberlessness however
astonishes mathematicians
more than the innumerate; they
live with it every day.

Suppose we counted our birthdays
by the difficult measure, *stasis?*

Fill us with gladness betimes
(betimes!) and we shall be glad
all our days,
seeing the calendar is
an illusion – and blissful at that,
if you can face it squarely.

Zion

Mired in it! Stuck in the various
rust-coloured, dove-coloured, yellowish
or speckled muds of history, you mistook
clarity, the dayspring from on high,
for a satisfaction of art, or the condition
of addressing the untutored.
                                    (As you never
did, they were otherwise tutored.)

Once, stuck in the mud by the Capitol,
you thought of the ninth buried city,
Richmond, Montgomery, what you had built them for,

of Troy, and of Rome, of Richmond, of Rome, not Zion;

of Troy, of Troynovant, of London,
the West Country, sometimes Geneva,
never of Zion;

of New Caledonia, New
Amsterdam, New Zealand,
Rome (Georgia), other Romes
and Athenses of the North,

New Delhi, Athens, Syracuse, not Zion.

Tutored in computer-processing,
still they may learn of Zion.

Trained in marketing techniques they
may discern in that murk the clarity
of a city not built on seven hills,

not guarding a river-crossing
nor plugging a gap in the mountains.

Unskilled in Islamic culture, they
may still make a Mecca of Zion.

Having heard or not heard of Lindisfarne, Iona,
are not the lot of us pilgrims?

The variegation of muds,
the iridescences,
constitute for some
in youth a passion,
in age a distraction from boredom

which, if designedly aimless
for long enough, merits the name of
Zion or some say Eden.

Felicity's Fourth Order

Men of business, of pleasure,
too often men of learning,
must not be left at leisure.

Their satisfaction is
forgetting themselves in work.
Nothing else is diverting.

Concupiscence, though of knowledge,
is a debauch, and only
an art against thinking of ends.

Vacancy however, if
careful of its ends but
aimless, may earn the Fourth Order:

'Being gathered into their chambers,
and guarded by angels in profound quiet,
they understand the rest that they enjoy.'

Put Not Your Trust in Princes

Let them give up the ghost, then there is nothing but dust
left of their presumptions we were fools enough to trust.

Pin no more hopes on them, nor the promissory collective;
the light at that end of the tunnel is glass, the credit
    delusive.

In the presence of the authorities we spent our days
turning our caps in our hands, and the manful,
    inveigling phrase.

We combed our sparse hair in the mornings (silvered,
    we observed).
We regarded our consort sleeping, whom we had
    shabbily served.

They are lost among the histories, names of world-mastering
    heroes:
this, the peace-fixer; that, the cuckolded smith of Infernos.

Having the sceptre no more, no more the ambiguous terms
of an unbelieved spokesman parade them; their press-men
    too feed worms.

Their Rectitude Their Beauty

'The angels rejoice in
the excellencies of God;
the inferior creatures in
His goodness; sinners only
in His forgiveness.'

His polar oppositions;
the habitable zones,
His clemencies; and
His smiling divagations,
uncovenanted mercies,

who turned the hard rock into a standing water
and the flint-stone into a springing well.

The voice of joy and health is in the dwellings of the
    righteous;
my eyes are running with rheum
from looking for that health

in one who has stuck by
His testimonies;
who has delighted in
His regimen; who has run
the circuit of His requirements;
whose songs in the caravanserai
have been about His statutes,

not to deserve nor observe them
(having done neither) but
for the angelic reason:

their rectitude,
their beauty.

Except The Lord Build The House

A song of the degrees,
of the gradations,
the steps to the temple...

There is no need to insist;
it is enough to name them.

For Zion is a city
uniform in itself,
compact together.

Why are you so strenuous, my soul?
Vain to get up early,
to sit up late,
to bolt your bread in a hurry.

Short be your sleep and coarse your fare
in vain. The Lord shall turn
the key in the captivity of Zion,
and all go like a dream.

The grass grows over the ruins of Eblis,
nobody's hayfield;
you are loitering there, or studying
hard (you are a hard
loiterer) but no one
going by in the road calls out
'Good morning' or 'Good luck'.

No use of early rising:
as useless is thy watching.
No traveller bestows
a word of blessing on the grass,
nor minds it as he goes.

Climb the stair
manfully, and sing
a short song on each step of the stair.

It is not an arduous duty.
Eblis was hard, not Zion.

Inditing A Good Matter

I find nothing to say,
I am heavy as lead.
I take small satisfaction
in anything I have said.

Evangelists want your assent,
be it cringing, or idle, or eager.
God shrugs. We taste dismay,
as sharp as vinegar.

He shrugs. How can He care
what *billets-doux* we send Him,
how much we applaud? Such coxcombs
inclined to commend Him!

My heart had been inditing
a good matter. My tongue
was the pen of a ready writer
who had been writing too long.

Whoever supposes his business
is to commend and bless
is due for this comeuppance:
feeling it less and less.

But I find something to say.
I pump it out, heavy as lead:
'Buoy me up out of the shadow
of your ramparts overhead.'

Like one of those vanished performers
on an afternoon-matinée console,
I arise:
        'Admit to your rock
this ready, this shriven, soul.'

The Creature David

The disposings of the heart in man,
and the answer of the tongue...
Not the domain of any
main poet's song;

not the halcyon, the mid-ocean range
where Ceteosaurus spouts, and Christopher Smart
numbers the streaks of the mollusc, where
the Spaniard is challenged for the Main
comradely, and Drake takes on the world,
a hirsute pirate. None of this
is documented history, it is not
fastidious, but dreadnought David's song.

Speech murmurs, and is always ·
forked, but this is song.
Nothing in this is talked.

There goe the shippes; there is
that Leviathan, whom Thou hast made
to play therein

upon the harp.

Saw I Never The Righteous Forsaken

I have been young, and now am old:

but I never saw Mr Worth
denied all reputation,
nor Mrs Worth and the children
go begging in the long run.

Reputations have
what seems when you get to my age
a shortish innings at best.
Remember the champion jockeys?
How many? From how far back?

'He shall bring forth thy
righteousness as the light,
thy judgement as the noonday.'

Banking on posterity
is an unwise investment.
Cold comfort, the little Worths!
Perpetual false dawn!

But merit is ascertainable as daylight;
unarguable justice follows
as certainly as noon ensues from dawn.

The Elect

Battle of Britain Sunday, RAF Gatow, Berlin

In their conventicles
stone-built or notional
they have withdrawn
from the life of the nation, or
have been excluded from it.

Strident, unaccommodating,
inelegant, sometimes smug,
they have despaired, and exchange
their Hosannas with each other.

An enclosed subculture,
they speak of such a one
no one has heard of, as
a guide to their devotions.

They comprehended, as
no others did, the fate
of the burned-up, scorched and screaming
sergeant-pilots:

as

gold in the furnace has He
tried them, and received them
as a burnt offering.

Luftwaffe pilots, also?
Don't fuss me. Yes, of course.

They shall shine and run to and fro
like sparks among the stubble,

for though in the sight of men and in
the sight of the unwise they seem to die,

they are in peace and

shall judge the nations.

'The just die young, and are happy.'

What sort of a nation is this,
bows its sleek head to these
outrageous obsequies,

born of a happiness in
the ghetto of the elect?

The Zodiac

It won't stand up to the light;
disgraceful, though

They fought from heaven, the stars in their courses fought
against Sisera, sang
Deborah, and Barak the son of Abinoam sang,
but Deborah in those days, saying:

Star-crossed, ill-starred, oh ill-starred Sisera!

Infirmity no doubt
of our nature, that we guess at
this nonsensical band in
the heavens dispensing justice.

But that much should be allowed us.
Misfortune undoubtedly strikes
unequally, and to the worst
worldling one would not deny
the chance of blaming, rather
than God, a star-struck Nature.

In this way the sad Lorine
Niedecker, to explain
the ill luck of her father and mother,
remarked not once but often
Mars rising in Pisces, if
that is possible;
                              she,
raised and persisting in
a watery, piscatorial
district of Wisconsin,

assured the elemental
energies must have some
relation to the cosmos:
a God-enforced decorum.

'Just You Wait!'

To justify God's ways to man
like Eliphaz the Temanite
is a presumptuous folly;
it cannot be done.

Until the hurt comes I shall glorify
God on account of the ostrich,
hippopotamus, elephant,
crocodile, and whale.

(Zoological marvels:
King Edward the Seventh's racehorse,
his vertebrae fused together
from carrying a weight of jockeys.)

Who is confident though Jordan
rushes against his mouth,
who also lieth under the shady tree
in the covert of the reede, and fennes?

This is a riddle-me-ree.
'Hippopotamus' is the answer.
Until the hurt comes, and after,
play piously riddle-me-ree.

It comes, it is on its way, that hurting business;
it shall not be my affair until it comes.

Bowing The Head

Importunate for attention,
hanging around
the ante-rooms of Eternity,
the position of prayer, it must be
allowed, lacks dignity.

How much more, if it is not
hanging around so much as
hawking our goods, and the claim
we have by them, each howling
the loved one's, the needed one's, Name.

It is the position of love,
and which of us has not known it?
Lothario cannot gainsay it:
virility is the more
abject, the more we display it.

So, how to be manly in prayer?
'Hawking about for attention...'
It is a pungent phrase.
Getting down on your knees,
remember it all your days.

Widower

That sneaky Thomas Cranmer!
Turns out he had two
illicit marriages. One
cost him his fellowship at Cambridge.

Whence Matrimony, his
doing
in 1549:
'a remedy against
fornication'. (Other things also.)

Which makes ungrateful
sense for those
whose penis is a sacred member.

Poor Thomas Cranmer, his
doings in the dark!

'As Isaac and Rebecca gave
      A pattern chaste and kind,

To make domestic burthens light
        By taking mutual share,
        When we asunder part,
        It gives us inward pain.'

It is for you like tonsured
Ronsard, less
the bedmate you miss than the faithful,
the sometimes spitfire friend,

whatever the small hours' stress.

Master & Man

(Proverbs 19.22)

Chaste and kind...'a pattern'
(Isaac and Rebecca)
'chaste and kind'. Such words!
What we have done to you
both long ago and lately....

For 'chaste', read 'pure'; for 'kind'
('The desire of a man is his kindness')
read, 'What is desired in a man
is loyalty.' Biddable man!

My lord, my liege lord, my dear
lord, what I desire is
my own and not your kindness.

A poor man is better than a liar,
dear my lord, suppose the
desire of a man is his kindness;

extended also
to the unthankful,
whose kindness is as a morning cloud
and as the early dew it goeth away,

milord.

Levity

What is man that you should weigh
the gravamen of his 'grievous unto me'?

The weight of his sins he must
profess intolerable;
'imponderable' comes nearer.

For he knows them light as a feather;
changeable, like history or the weather.

'Laïs, boy-prostitute, wife'
(he addresses them), 'were we not
all on the side of Life?'

The beam kicks: lift-off Man,
no counterweight in the pan,

no peise, no pondering, no
poise, no *avoirdupois*,

no slug of compassionate lead
to weigh him saved or convicted,

soars into and over the sunrise.
The angels are all eyes.

Oh slender, eternally youthful
balloonist, what you have missed!

For there He is, steadily weighing
your airy, your weightiest, saying.

Witness

Bearing and giving are different, it appears.

In the latter case (constrained)
one supposes, or may suppose,
a judge and a jury. In the case of

bearing

witness, there is a load
that has to be discharged
in physical fact, the weight
on the grieving shoulders
thankfully hefted off,
a sack into the shadows of God's barton.

No judge, no jury, but one,
that one incalculable, His
authority established by no statute.

'Come, O my guilty brethren, come,
Groaning beneath your load of sin.'

We bear like a weight in the gut
witness, a load that
must be evacuated
in the hedge-bottom or elsewhere.

Our Lady

The sea is all that they say: it wreaks death one way only;
it neither begins nor ends, nor ever suspends its motions;
indifferent as to racial stock and
era, it drowns
or does not drown, impartially, godlike in this,
not to be walked on.
                        One who
walked on the sea, though briefly,
walked also alone under olives also briefly,
seldom alone and always.
                        This his mother,
crude-painted odalisque, holds in her left hand
a seaport sacked, in her right hand a votive ship
tiny among trumperies, cheap mirrors.

She the recalcitrant sailor's
one and one only reached-after landfall, but under
an interdict he hymns, he worships instead,
and plumes with his perjured feathers
of spume and inconsequent waterspout, the faithless
indifferent non-god, Ocean.

The Ironist

'Sacred? or sacrosanct?
or sanctimonious, even?
Suppose you chose these topics
(which, you will say, chose you),
hoping to escape
the debilitating scope
of your kind in your time and place:

irony.'

It is Lord Haw-haw speaking;
it is Mephistopheles speaking,
the syphilitic; it is
Germany speaking.

A masterly ironist
of history knows
his subject inside out;
his dry wit drying out
a sop of sentiment from
the cerements of the West.

Lover of the mephitic,
of fog and stink,
his natural haunt the road by the chemicals plant,

his elegant strong suit
is tacit and total carnage:
the Devil's work, whose mark
(frivolity and distraction)
is on this page also

as on the best we can do.

'Thou Art Near At Hand, O Lord'

Or: *They are come near me that*
persecute me of malice.

How near was near? Were their camels
cropping his starveling pastures?

Or were they behind the skyline,
though they might be his 'nearest and dearest'?
Were they never in fact (though in truth)
shouldering for house-room?

It is thus with words on the page:
'Mephistopheles' and 'mephitic'
are more nearly juxtaposed
than two that are side by side.

Moreover, space is encoded
to signify lapses of time.
(One verse-line under another;
this one *after* that one.)

The nearness of God is known as
an aching absence:
the room the reception-desk
cannot locate nor account for,

in a fictitious or
analogous space that does not
answer to or observe
the parameters of Newton,

any more than a page of verse does.

The Nosegay

The roses of irony blossom
floridly on the trellis
of inexperience crossed with
a need for the fell and certain.

Seeing that irony is
the adolescent's defence,
'An end to irony!' means
death to most of our lyrics.

The objection to the God
of Islam and of Judah,
'He lacks a sense of humour',
means, He is not ironical,
He is not a lyrical God.

He does not come and go;
He is not glimpsed in gaps of
time. Alas, it is clear that
He claims to be omnipresent,
and had better be thus acknowledged.

He has His sense of fun
surely; He has even
(as we see it, who wait on deathbeds)
a mordant wit.

It is the bite of the wit
mauls our sense of humour.

Lyrists may proclaim their
intermittent visions;
ironists, their protective
clothing; but the surgeon

of Islam and of Judah
makes His incisions
justly, and He is not
deprecating about it.

Stepping along the Turl,
selecting a buttonhole
half mauve, half mustard-yellow,
what God and what men you malign!

Gripping Serial

Man fought against beasts, and won;
Man fought against priests, and won;
Man fought against kings, and won;
Now he fights the Collective.

This drivel is still believed.

Man fought against beasts;
Man fought against Man, and still does;

And there's the end of the series.

I Have Said, Ye Are Gods

And so you might have been:
a groaning light, a light that risked eclipse
and underwent it. Oh
luminaries, oh
sun and moon and stars of a low-browed heaven,

Enlighteners,

Captain Cook was the best of you,
bashing his bowsprit through
the gap between ice-floe and
a bruised cloud-ceiling, past
Bering's best, and may even have died for his friends.

But in twenty centuries,
not under the cove and whelm
of the *tsunami*, nor
splintered upon the wakes
of any nation's navy, breaks
the light that saves.

He maketh men to be
of one mind in an house,

and ye princes shall fall as one of the common sort.

David Dancing

Infrequently, dreams are heavenly.
How if the caustic 'Thou
dreamer!' excoriate those
hagridden by what, in a sleep
we learn to dread, comes often?

For dreams, most dreams, are hell.
Sundry authorities
exhort us to 'come to terms',
get used to our hells, distrust
the dull or brilliant daylight.

Neither to move nor console,
David dances before
the Ark. And the Ark is not
the dance, but what the dance
honours and accedes to.

Neither to move nor console
he dances, not in a dream
but exceptionally wakeful
in a recurrent morning.

Dancing Measures

Noah drunken, taking
his daughters in bed; a common,
seldom avowed occurrence.

How then for the dance, that is always
a self-abuser, glassed
in the pond of its own procedures?

The wrath of God! Yet Dance's
habitual incest seems
not to call down thunders.

Wrong! The penalty is
imposed in intimate places:
a rhythm imposed by no
more than proclivity, yet
prohibitively binding.

Measures, the prison of measures:
rumtitum, tumtitum, rum.
You know of a worse crucifixion?

What drunken stupor or
generative torpor sets
fingers or feet to tapping like Astaire?

Sometimes the drink implants it;
sometimes, God-induced, it
shakes free and runs loose, if the dancer's
executive will dispose it, to high meadows.

Being Angry With God

'Anger, yes. But God is God',
the impious Pakistani
explained to V.S. Naipaul.
'God is not like people.'

Profound: God is not like people.

Shallow: He ought to be.

Indifference, if you can
manage it (youth can),
disposes of God well enough.

Imran runs up to bowl. The Rajput palaces
live not as art but as the youth
Imran, accelerating, is on the verge of losing.

Even with people, what did
anger ever dispose of?
It ties you in, like love.

Thanks to an undevout Muslim,
we recognize anger with God is
one more way to own Him.

The ex-Christian exclaims:
'But my angers amount to something!'
It is not at all clear that they do,

as Imran Khan
turns and begins his run:
poetry in motion.

The motion is unforgiving;
so is the poetry; so
(unless it is tempered) the Judgement.

The Comforter

St. Patrick bound unto himself
the Trinity, but showed his practical sainthood
by playing down the third
member of the triad. No
anxious souls would be won by
that vaporous Holy Ghost.

'The whirling wind's tempestuous shocks'
registers Patrick's obeisance, but
no one is taken in, no one prays to the wind.

And indeed He is the strangest
of the Three Persons,
the most estranged.

For the Holy Ghost is nakedly a ghost.
Father and Son may be masks
compassionately adapted
to our capacities, but
Person is not *persona* and
the Ghost is a ghost, no fiction.

Integration, fulfilment
have nothing to do with this Person;
cure, or harmony – nothing
like that is intended.

Invasion is His note:
disintegration.
A wind from the outside corners
of the human map;
disorienting;

His strangeness for the comfort
of those not at home in the grid.

Cannibals*

As if to take in ocean
through a needle's eye,
a sundial divines
not why light moves, but when;

when, and how. He moves
now. And perhaps He loves us.
He moves in any case.
We trace, not chart, His passage,

like Uruguayan, defiled
prop-forwards and blind-side flankers,
iced up in the Andes,
cannibals, knowing Him near.

*My horne shalt thou exalt
like the horne of an unicorne.*

Presence, the nearness, is
the needle's eye;
not to make any more
proof of it, the trial.

Pray to the Holy Spirit, Let
not the most polluted
translation impede the witness:
ram's horn of unvarying plenty!

* 'The Old Christians', a Rugby football team from Montevideo, was
isolated in a wrecked aircraft from October to December 1972.

Woe Unto Thee!

Compunction at presumption
is a sentiment
conspicuous by its absence
from the college of prophets.

David the King, Isaiah,
Micah – what
regal or less than regal
prerogative gave them the right
to be so unforgiving?

Choked with the god, or blinded
by arrogance,
they were – by what right? – lifted
above being fair-minded.

Had they not thought of circumstance
extenuating?

'He that is free of sin, let him
cast the first stone.' Had they,
the fulminating,
nothing to atone for?

Baldly declarative,
their comminations live
on in the Scriptures like
an unacknowledged toothache,
bruising and assertive.

The nerve sings, and so long as
it sings, presumption calls for
no halter of compunction.

Kingship

It would have been because
they smelled so bad,
that the scriptural nomads and
city-dwellers made
so much of oils, of resinous
exudations
of Gilead; and we,
if our stick of deodorant is
jammed, what indignity!
The feel of that, and the fear

unfelt by the cheerful, the fearless
non-conforming whom
we hate accordingly with
olfactory revulsion.

The sweat of honest labour is
too honest for our noses.
And of dishonest?

Joy unto thee, if thou canst
muster a patience beyond
'The time will come.' It will not.
Idyllic earth where the hay smells of the dream
in Samuel Palmer's Shoreham
will not, it is certain, surface
in history, though a few
institutions hint of it: for instance

'the Lord's anointed',

sweating beneath his robes,
holding the orb and sceptre,
who would have been happier in
the malodorousness of Goodwood;

and over him Another
enthroned in majesty
'no sweat'.

Ordinary God

'Do you believe in a God
who can change the course of events
on earth?'
                               'No, just
the ordinary one.'
                                       A laugh,
but not so stupid: events
He does not, it seems, determine
for the most part. Whether He could
is not to the point; it is not
stupid to believe in
a God who mostly abjures.

The ordinary kind
of God is what one believes in
so implicitly that
it is only with blushes or
bravado one can declare,
'I believe'; caught as one is
in the ambush of personal history, so
harried, so distraught.

The ordinary kind
of undeceived believer
expects no prompt reward
from an ultimately faithful
but meanwhile preoccupied landlord.

Nashville Mornings

Saint Cecilia:
        between
man as vehicle traversed
by constant, by unchanging
biological forces; and
his actions as reactions
solely to speedy changes –
where is the third term? Is it
what in the ghetto of letters
we least can stomach: Noise,
the appalling Rock and Country?
The damnable steel guitar?

                Cruising Canadian
                coaches pause
                by the patios of the stars,

                expensive silences, Olympus,
                Arcturus, a loft above tundra
                built by and out of
                clang, twang, nasalsong
                and corybantes? There is precedent:

                at Stonehenge, ululations,
                the nuptial hymn a disco.

                Dawdling the Franklin road
                Ontario plates;
                gardeners, sprinklers,
                          Elvis
                his platinum-plated Rolls
                garaged in splendour. Old
                Etonian freshman gawped
                along with the rest. There is
                spring on the world, and all the
                time in the yawning

                road for pleasurable
                memories, anticipations
                of strum and drum. The form is
                a rhythmical suck. The air-brakes

ease from the sidewalk gently:
Homes of the Stars!

'thought I would like to
if it's all
right. On my way to Chicago.
You knew me when I was two.'
Youth on the road.

Graze the glass bowl, however
musically, the fish
in the fishbowl flick their tails
once, and are gone.

Flaw and withdraw, the
exquisite
accomplishments of flautists,
is that an achievement?

If we inhabit a gap
between the departure of gods and
their necessary return,

their absence is a salience
no doubt, as with
Chinese ceramics also,
a scrape on the ineffable. It
makes sense. Makes enough?

'What I had known, no one had known.
What I had seen, no one had seen.'
A man in love with silence, in
terror of silence, and in love with that:
tundra, snow-oceans. Rasp or whisper,
the wind outside.
'A silence fell between them.'

Celia, her music
confined in its operations
to a metaphysical annex,
irks on Nashville mornings.

Brilliance

Some virtue in
            the ultimate
lack of emphasis: 'Gods
            or it may be one God moves
about us in bright air.'

Not for you. You were brilliant. You always meant to be that.
You were, and still are at times.

Brilliance, still you want it
impenitently. Truth, oh as for....

You were not in love with the world
or never for long, and only with bits of it:
the usual bits. Trees in a forest? Not often.

Better in a vicarage garden
in the fens, a shelf of cedar
above two deck-chairs, untenanted then and for ever
at four o'clock of a summer afternoon.

But that was not brilliant enough, or not for long.

            Diamonds, and still the blonde deserves
                them
            a whole tiara, festoons on the sky at
                night

            or on the white page, black facets;
            impenitence, a diamond in itself,
            unbreakable, breaking others.

The sinne of Judah is written
with a pen of yron,
and with the point of a diamond it is graven
on the tables of their hearts.

Constant, but only in
the impenitent pursuit
of self-destruction – has
that little earned the garlands
of cadence and clear colour?

The alcoholic's delusion
that he controls his habit,
the warrior, his –
is this to be esteemed and
heroically lamented

      in Dylan Thomas, in
      a broken Coriolanus?

If to be free of delusion
is the worst delusion of all,
are we to save our applause
for those whose delusions are noblest;
for instance, loving the world?

Granted, the noble is
unarguable, known as
soon as apprehended;
still, Delusion limes his
limp nets also for eagles.

Brilliance is known in
what the tired wing, though
it never so crookedly towers,
wins at last into: air
diamond-clear, unemphatic.

Brilliance, then, is noble;
not in the subject but
in what the subject attains to:
a metaphysical, not
in the first place human, property.

'Can you tell the down from the up?'
The unthinkable answer: No.
God moves about us, and
brilliance is His preferred
supernal way of moving.

If I Take The Wings Of The Morning

taking off at dawn
to circle *ultima thule*,

threading the splendours between
ice and pearl cloud cover,

God is not only also
there, but signally there,

who made the heavens skilfully,
who made the great lights
with a strong hand and a strained-out arm,

who brought forth clouds from the end of the world
and sent forth lightnings with rain
and out of His treasuries high winds.

When those who keep us in prison
ask of us mirth in our hang-ups
with 'Sing us a song of Zion',
what can we sing or say
under the mourning willows
of a common suffering in
the river-meadows of Babel?

It is our lingo utters us, not we.
Our native tongue, our endowment,
determines what we can say.
And who endowed us?

Speak if you cannot sing.
Utter with appropriate shudders
the extremities of God's arctic
where all the rivers are frozen,

and how He tempers our exile
with an undeserved planting of willows.

North & South

for Emily Grosholz, who asked about metre.

Emily, you were sick
Of Arctic computations.
And you would go to Zen,
New Mexico, the Aegean,
Anywhere, to escape them.

The unfortunate Isaac Newton!
Philosopher of science,
You lived with his likes all day.
But herding them north of the Alps,
Weren't you carried away?

And poetry now, as for
Many another, must
Reconstitute, restore?
Well, sweet mole, you go
About it the right way:

Enjoying the lovely fibs,
But nosing the veins of the clay
Deep under the uttered fictions
Chambered and tunneled for: breath
Under the modelling thumb.

Breath, the sculpting of that!
Not synaesthesia, not
Spectacular mental pictures,
Not fables, not generous maxims –
Is this what you'd be at?

Well, and you are right;
Underground, groping and dumb,
Where there are no more rules
That schools can teach, but only
A trembling rule of thumb.

Emily...Persephone!
You see breath wreathe on the cold
Air of an arctic morning
Or fogging a southern glass;
In any and every landscape.

Its shape when it utters 'Eve'
Is as long as the edge of a roof
Or a day that seems never to end
On a Mediterranean island.
And yet, dear friend, we mine it.

If we would learn to scan,
We have to be exact;
Indeed, Newtonian.
The syllable's breath at the mercy
Of Apollonian measure...

Prosody has been thought
Also a science, and
A baffling one; for what
Kind habitat is built on
The count and crimp of breath?

Emily, I can only
Enter a plea for the north,
The sternness of long evenings:
Sun and moon together
In skies over the Orkneys.

They, to Me

'Life is over and you are its
    Memorialist. Such peace,
You ought to think, and be pleased.

You are not supposed to make
    More history. It is what
We have insupportably much of. Now lie still.

The frame, or the several frames
    Are sprained already. Let
"Already" be your quietus.

It would be nice to say:
    "Go on being yourself" But
Your selves were so mutably many.

Must sons and grandsons be
    For ever disconcerted
By a new or revised programme?

The self as elder statesman
    Is an acceptable posture.
But please, no further sorties!

The lack of any but wary
    Approbation is
Itself a kind of distinction.

You were always in the running;
    Earnest and talented fellows
Cannot say that, so be thankful.

How many, not less haughty
    Than you, have been loved? It is true.
But the shame of your need to be loved!

How many of us do you
    In fact recall? Not many;
Obliviousness your helpmeet.

In short you have made your bed
    And now you must loll on it. Patience:
A skill you have not acquired.'

Thus they, to me... Ah, they!
    In dimity gowns;
Pendulous breasts in bikinis;

Skinny in a black
    Bathing-suit, who now
Heaves herself round on two sticks;

Skeletal in a nightgown: 'Can't
        Be first and last, Don, can't
Be first and last...';

And her, incontinent
        In a fragrance of eau-de-cologne:
Mother at sea in Frinton.

By the Road to Upper Midhope

Tares make the corn to grow,
Tares make the corn to grow.
The sweetest hours that e'er I spent
Were spent beside the thistle-row.

Poppies make the corn to grow,
Winds have bared the barleymow.
The sweetest hours that e'er I spent
Were not where Boreas winters O.

Ill fares the winter wheat,
Ill fares the winter wheat,
The sweetest hours that e'er I spent
Were sportive in the summer's heat.

Tares make the corn to thrive,
Choked the more, the more alive.
The sportive hours that I have spent
Made corn and tares alike revive.

Poppies make the corn to grow,
Winds strip the barleymow.
The sweetest hours that e'er I spent
Were spent amang the lassies O.

Dule of a Dewsbury Matron

Why should we   defer   our joys?
While we may   the fruits   of love
Let us, lad   o let us   prove!
    Whistle and I'll come to thee, my lad.

Let us beware   the shepherd's warning:
Saturday night   brings Sunday morning.
    Whistle and I'll come to thee, my lad.

Cannot we   delude   the eyes
Of a few poor   household spies?
Here's my cabinet of joys.
    O whistle and I'll come to thee, my lad.

To be taken   to be seen
These have crimes   accounted been.
Pakistani brown ye be
    But whistle and I'll come to thee.

Cedarscented is this closet
I ope to thee, this cabinet
Of all the joys   that you'll disprize.
    O whistle and I'll come to thee.

Black Hoyden

Mary Jane, she's after me,
Mary Jane, black hoyden.
'Touch of the tar, lad', says my Dad,
'Kitts Nevis or Tahiti'.

Mary Jane has been betrayed.
Don't meddle with Black Hoyden.
'Black eyes like that,' my father said,
'Would scythe a feller's garden.'

Black Hoyden's coming down the hill,
The sleet beginning to fall.
It wavers through the wintry air,
She wavers not at all.

Black Hoyden homing from the mill,
Black Hoyden, Black Hoyden.
Black honour coming tall and still,
A knife in her shawl.

Who is that knife for, Mary Jane?
But I know well, and I know why.
Black eyes lovingly have flashed,
This flash will leave a stain.

Harridan, black hoyden!

The Right Lads

To re-insert it in
The Yorkshire Post . . .
The venerable decorum
Of doughty drinking:
>   *For a'that and a'that,*
>   A staggering toast.

Shall we commend it to
The bullies of Leeds United?
Dear to the dumb, unlettered
And unemployable,
>   A precedent shall be cited:
>   *A man's a man for a'that.*

Is there for honest poverty
Wha hangs the head an a'that?
Hang loose, hang nail, hang dog!
Oh you are made of use,
>   Acting the part assigned:
>   Capitalism's refuse!

Grazia Deledda, young

*

How funny, she beat him, she
Beat him all through the week
And he knows we know it, and we
Giggle and don't know why
We choke when we learned to speak.

Our fists are balled against
Our treacherous mouths, our small
Handkerchieves screwed up tight.
Why are sadnesses funny,
Sad people such a fright?

Life is suffering, says
Mama, and Mama is right.
Mama, how does it happen
That laughing has to come when
Weeping might?

A crippled boy would be
A leggy girl's first lover.
What a disgrace she is!
She whistles, snorts, bows over
In agony, not to laugh.

Others have told, with almost
A giggle, stories of trees
That bleed, and girls that are birds
With tongues and without them,
Struggling short of words.

*

Don Sebastiano,
You speak of the not-quite-language
Of donkey, stone and cuckoo.
Stone? we say. But yes, you
Say, stone utters too.

A roll of thunder. Mountains
Lounge like big girls around
The dreadful horizon. Their
Languid and spiky eyes
Mutter over the playground.

Don Sebastiano,
How can I tell you? The hem
Hangs down in front and is
Rucked up behind, and because
They will notice, I hate them.

The unkind, stifled laughter
At cycle-rack and sickbay
And First Communion, is
This what explodes in the peacock,
The ass, the jeering jay?

Does all of the Creation
Deride us? Is it this that
The stone, the cuckoo, the stone-chat
Really intend? There are
So many questions I'd ask you!

A harder one, that I
Know your answer to
(You'll point to the Madonna):
Is girlhood a condition,
However we act, of dishonour?

Don Sebastiano,
Gravely you point your finger
Up to the heavenly blue.
That means you judge the gym-slips'
Horrible surmise true?

No, it is sadder than that:
Girl-geese, the hilly-billy
Goat, the demented ass...
Sometimes it seems the entire
Creation cries 'Alas!'

At last I am growing up:
Even our stories giggle,
Our sayings bray their dismay.
We are all of us aching to utter
More than we can say.

Hermes and Mr Shaw

The narrow backyard garden
    Of Mr. and Mrs. Shaw
Ran between us and, in its cutting, the railway;
    Ran right to left across the end of our,
Our and our neighbours', slightly more ample gardens.

Quite young, a childless couple,
    Mr. and Mrs. Shaw kept
Themselves to themselves; and so it was no light matter,
    When a ball had sailed over the fence, to
Go round and ask to retrieve it.

A minor clerk or else an artisan (I
    Never knew, I imagine), Mr. Shaw
Kept mostly a kitchen-garden, though
    Next to his house a patch of lawn
Was where a mis-hit cricket-ball mostly pitched.

The grass there was of a deep, an Irish green,
    And not cropped close. I think it was grown from seed
Not sods. I have the impression lawns
    Grown from seed were thought to be second-rate
As most things were about Mr. and Mrs. Shaw.

Once, vividly, I saw from my upstairs bedroom
    A flock of white doves dense on that patch of grass
And in the midst of them, accusingly
    And neatly side by side, a pair of my
Canvas shoes, in the dream called quaintly 'plimsolls'.

And dreams – is it not so? – dreams are insistently verbal;
   Vocabulary is the key to them.
Not that I can, or care to, unlock this one:
   What did it guiltily mean, for things of mine
To show up there? Why shoes? Why a snow of doves?

Unlocking dreams is some one else's business.
   What comforts me is that in that
Year, as the *kristallnacht* splintered
   In Germany, or soon would, as Stalin moved
Elated to his Great Terror, dramas were

Enacted in my obscure pacific boyhood.
   For was it not that, my dream undeniably proved?
Mr. and Mrs. Shaw are almost certainly dead.
   Their thin grass, they should know, once took the tread
Of what? Winged sandals? Settle for that: winged sandals.

Articulacy. Hints from the Koran

First lesson: Don't
get ahead of yourself, don't gabble.
For a pell-mell of syllables, is
that what it means to assemble,
as when He assembled our bones
like the articulated members of a saying?

Be sonorous.
                    Like a goose?
When the Writ is goose-like
(which will not be often), honk,
honk like a goose. And when
the text, as you may call it,
is plummy, gorge it with plums,
savour the vowels, give them,
each as it comes, full presence.

Next, imagine yourself
the privileged herald to
your chosen, not
chance-met companions;
with whom there is much that can be
taken for granted, since
they know all that you tell them,
though in an inferior fashion.

When the Writ runs into
consonantal crackle,
cacophonies, crackle with it.
This is the most of music:
thorn-hedges set round orchards.

Next you imagine yourself
the angel Gabriel who
divulges to the privileged
intermediary
what he shall relay.

And this is perilous, as
assuming the Angel is
always perilous. Now you
address a generality
of strangers, and there is
temptation, since you fear them,
to bully, or inveigle.

When Holy Writ quotes writ,
acknowledge the quotation-marks
by a doubled pause and poise,
keeping the voice lifted.

When the sense rides over
the end of a verse, accord it
enough and no more than enough
check, to gather its haunches
before the brush- or water-
obstacle that you,
no steeplechase-rider, will not
accelerate to get over.

Last (this not often attained)
you imagine yourself the Speaker
of what He divulged through angels.
So holy the act of reciting.

These are not prescriptions
on how to wow an audience,
but to diaphragm and pharynx
and parts more inward, how to
give body to the unbodied.

Man imagines his bones shall
not be reassembled.
He wants to be open-ended
as far as he can see:
one discrete happening after
another, all exclamation,
the palm of his hand unaware what his fingers are up to.

But the first, the second, the third
knuckles of every finger
are articulated more
closely than the best
reciter or singer can manage.

The act of reciting, however,
generates faith, done rightly.

Reminded of Bougainville

for Howard Erskine-Hill

'The rest is not our business'. Come the end or
a good deal sooner rest is
our only business. Up to
and battering that
a swarming
intelligence names the names, the
localities. Who is to say when
shearing the boom and in a way we

least expected H.M.S. Coventry shall
recuperate the Malvinas,
les Malouines, into renewed
restiveness and the wasps
of doubt, of self-doubt, of
resolution, of
intelligences swarm?

'a culture of regressive repetitions...'
Brave men and a gallant ship, her
namesake also sank
in World War Two
by bomber aircraft.
Carried aboard were
large mediaeval nails
from the bombed cathedral, formed in
the shape of a cross. She entered
the 1st of May the total exclusion zone;
3rd of May her Lynx
helicopter scored
direct hits, totally
with its Sea Skua missiles
destroyed one target.

Sheffield was sunk the 4th of May;
Glasgow out of action
by the 11th. In the last
week of *Coventry*'s life, the
24th was a good day: three
aircraft down, and later another six.
The 25th, with *Broadsword,* in exposed
water, shortly after
six in the evening 'sprang
very brave and determined
at us from behind
the land' four aircraft, one
persistently with four
bombs, three in the portside,
exploded. Immediate flooding
and fire, very thick black
suffocating smoke. 'Get the ship...'

'Aye aye sir', though
no power, the ship on fire
listing to port some fifty degrees, in fifteen
minutes on her side, in thirty
her keel horizontal a few
feet above sea level. Later
she sank. Many brave deeds...

'In the Cathedral Three Great Nails once held
Hearts of Oak until in war they were felled.'
Nineteen dead.

The verse-line is commodious, has to be.
A sea-borne landing launched without
command of the air, a foredoomed operation
or not, as now appears. What is the rôle
of the term 'professional' in the expression:
'professional and brave men'? When did we last
hear: 'the profession of arms'? A stout, outmoded
or not, it appears, conception. Bloody business
is some men's business decently, as when
Bougainville made the Falklands briefly French
so now, and we may rest in that. It is
always our business, always.

A Measured Tread

for Kenneth Millar dead

Walking about the emptied house I
jangle softly at each heavyish step,
an old plough-horse, some parts of his harness upon him,
who strays, tired out but happy with that, through musky
honey-shot glooms of a barn where, though he
strays only idly towards it, sweet hay will be found in a crib.

Hello, Ken...I imagine, as everyone has,
the impossible: my living and my dead
looking in on the mote-shot Elysium they have emptied,
hearing the *ictus*, the chink of pocketed coins,
the household meter that my father once,
he from among the dead, both was himself and moved to.

I tread at my disoriented will
with a chime or a ding that, now I have emptied my pockets,
I if no other still hear and will attend to.
The hay in the bin will not be so sweet, after all?
No matter for that, it is sweet as I stumble towards it.
Such pacings of things seems all there is, sometimes, of wisdom.

Northern Metres

for Tony Harrison in Florida

Your grandad worked the signals
At Haworth, mine at Horton:
Old railwaymen.

Self-satisfied a little,
Their and our preference for
The overtly neat and tidy.

We have to be so overt!
The signals clack down smartly
Yes or No; no fudging

Unless it were... why yes,
As between fragrant cedar
And stinking, lasting cypress.

Done with a lovely touch, your
Emblem of that: the chairs
Standing opposed on your porch.

One cedarwood, one cypress,
I see them and yes, I smell them;
Together, but distinct.

No Old World sentinel
Of graveyards, but the bald
Cypress of the swamplands,

Of alligator-haunted
Original stews: a symbol
Of rationality taunted.

Symbols make at best
A puttering sort of logic.
Aerosol does the trick:

Obscenities spray-painted
On parents' headstones have
Made a morass of Beeston.

Pitiful understanding
Will not disperse that stench,
Nor tidy metres quench it.

Yorkshire's man-made swamps!
Cedar, a cedarn fragrance,
How plant it, how impart it?

Church of Ireland

for Barbara Hayley

Status indeed and protocol I pay
Too little regard to, since they rib our doings
To some ascertainable order. There's a mouthful!

Mouthful of rocks, of crags... which is as if
Equivalent to, or asked for by, small Sligo's
Dense knobbed hills. But it's not right, this language.

And yet it seems right, seems enforced by some
Home-made decorum, say, or protocol;
Except that home-made language never works.

What a rash thrust at being explicit leads to
Often is as little short of ugly
As the inside of the Yeatses' church, Drumcliffe;

Where things may happen that are beautiful,
But are so not by any or much decorum
But by their unavoidable and proper

Mismatches, incongruities: the bulky
Battered officiant, man of God, our Canon,
Out of his vestments such a good sort always

Holy behind his unreserve. One sees
The point of that in his less than elegant church,
Thirst though one may for an order more in keeping.

Knobbed hills, Ben Bulben, and the skinny Shee,
Phantasmagoria that englobed a poet
Once, and touchingly...and yet not there

The measured, the less abrupt, less adventitious
Fall of phrase I need when I think of us
Rain-dashed, in Sligo, walking to church together.

The Scythian Charioteers

'Black quadrigas reared
In veering triumphs'
(Mandelstam)

When it was found a fault
In Moscow that it lacked
Leningrad's Attic salt,

The charge was brought not in
The era of Peter the Great's
Contempt for Balt and Finn,

When every sucked-out mile
Of drained ground groaned to bear
Stoa and peristyle;

But rather when already
The sand was once again
Blood-slick, the ground unsteady,

Did the untimely Pindars
Of Russia acclaim the Olympic
Contests of brazen cars.

Not when each city-scape
Of Northern Europe cherished
Olive, acanthus, grape,

Did these wheel out the *quadriga*,
The jet-black four-in-hand
Dressed in the colours of Riga.

Now when it is known the modern
City of Athens is
Vociferous, vehicle-ridden,

When jerry-built prose and verse
Everywhere lethally topple,
The loftier the worse,

Now (and best so) they find
Occasion to exalt our
Lost Athens of the mind.

Mother

Taxis were beyond us
As ever beyond most
In Barnsley. So to attend us
Disembarkers, no
Limousines come and go,
No hackneys cruise and coast.

Well, from the station yard
In the now more affluent town
A mile's walk is no hard
Imposition on
A fat and prodigal son
As the summer day goes down.

How unlikely, though,
That there, unchanged, should stand
From twenty years ago
A structure that seemed meant
To be impermanent:
A shed with the blurred legend:

'TAXIS'. Thus it stood,
Locked and unattended,
When in fierce rain I would
Have found a car for her
Who with the hairdresser
Was having her wild hair tended.

Afoot I must pursue
In default of taxis,
Unpenanced pilgrim, two
Cousins whose stylish aunt
Shopped at the elegant
'Butterfields and Massies.'

No such pretensions were
Left to her that day
When I pursued for her
A non-available car.
There are who die, like her,
Puzzled, their wits astray.

At the Café Parnasse

for Turner Cassity

Sealed into the cocoon
Of light and water, face
And racked reflection, voice
And the nymph Echo answering, the grub
Narcissus throbs at high noon. Slapping
Languidly, the rocked
Wave on the bridge-piers means a speedboat passes
A half of a mile and all of a minute away,
Tensed for the seaway. Ah Narcissus, ah
Dreamboat of self! In Amsterdam the brick,
So I am told, abides no pulse but yours!

Perfection of the noon...
The waterfront *Café*
Parnasse safe harbours him, the smoke
Circling straight upward from his cigarette

(Always the same brand, with that special tang,
The Unfulfillable). He sits
Hour after hour, small glass or coffee-cup
Cold at his elbow; sees, as night comes on,
The knots of sailors speaking foreign tongues
Stream past him pell-mell, though as yet but idly,
Towards excess; then calls for the waiter; leaves.

Ensues his worst hour:
What if the grub he is
Should flap wet wings, and tower? What
If – the construction is unknown to him
Except in acquired and treasured English – this
Unfulfillable were
Fulfillable, in a high gale or a whorehouse?
A slowed-down speedboat! – ears that should
Hear their own memories of a pulse late heard
Repeated with some difference. Ah, free verse...
A scion of Narcissus, that one was!

And so he shrugs it off;
Prepares a frugal meal;
Recalls how there are carapaces more
Armoured than his – the dense, secure delusions
Of liberty, husks of so tough a rind
(The liberated seamen!) no one can
Tell if inside is a being alive or dead;
So falls asleep; and so sleeps through, against
The hour when he will take his seat again
At the *Café Parnasse*, the small waves slapping the brick,
His own blue smoke aspiring and dispersing.

Though dry, not dry

for Doreen

Dry season. Block. So, rain...
Why am I too proud
To pray for rain? Am I
The Muses' Lucifer
That I will not confess
A need so commonplace?

Truth is, I no longer care.
Rain would clear the air,
But foetid air suits well
My dozing in this chair.
Sloth; why is it always
Spoken of so ill?

It does no harm; it spares
The inattentive world
One more triumphant play
Out of my one strong suit,
Sardonic paradox:
This age's mask for Love.

A dancer's or an actor's
Mask, it is not dishonest;
Donning it, I do not
Betray myself to the age.
Deciding punctuation
Even, I mount the stage,

But it is an honest stage,
Mirror of men and manners;
This man, his manners. Why
Then, should the nice distinction
Of colon from semi-colon
That once absorbed, now bore me?

How merciful is our God,
My love, that it should be
Not Love but only love
In this abstracted mode
I cannot stir the will
To ask that I be stirred to!

To a Bad Poet

To break the pentameter, Pound's first heave
Sufficed where we were concerned. It was you
Who launched her again,
A foul old bottom, lurching,
Oars like trunks.

Was this, we said,
What once held spices,
Found the Americas
In ragged seas?
This tub?

(1951-75)

On a Proposed Celebration of Ezra Pound

for Clive Wilmer

He who proposes
Assembling those
Whose ear for verse is
Worse than for prose,

To celebrate
One whose least airs
Moved at a rate
To out-pace theirs,

Does him and us
Nothing but harm:
The infamous
Wish to disarm

Does no-one good.
When all is said,
He that could
Judge us, is dead.

Revenge for Love

Neither dead nor alive, neither asleep nor awake,
In a dreadful calm I drowse the night hours through;
No pride to nurse, no pains I need to take,
Not wanting you, and not not wanting you.

'Revenge for, or betrayal of
Love by change and death...'
'Revenge' is better, my
Love, 'revenge' is better:
I am certainly somebody's debtor
For you, and the debt it seems
Is paid this way. Not what
Any one had in mind;
Still, nobody is betrayed.

You and I, we have made
Very little of love, as it was
Sold by the big-band sound
That led me when I found
You in the 1940s.
Whose was the band? I remember
The startled glance we exchanged
When it turned out for our eldest
His discs were collector's items:

Glenn Miller! There was no price
We wouldn't have paid
In San Francisco for one
Of his to give our boy;
Paying over the odds
Already for whatever
Damage we did our children
By being so ready to move
On, and always on.

Neither dead nor alive, neither asleep nor awake,
These are the thoughts that float
Into and out of my mind, where once they might
Have taken me by the throat.

Vengeance is mine, saith the Lord. And surely it is
A gentle revenge to take:
Nothing to fear, merely a lapsing away
Neither asleep nor awake.

A Garland for Ivor Gurney

1.

'God be praised that made
Gloucestershire...' The fool!
Gloucester or Avon – what
Administrative fiction
Shall God be praised for? Oh
For Crabbe and some sane depiction!

Gurney, whose burning need
And uninstructed eye
Were partisan for Gloucester,
Yet at St. Albans too
Endowed mere masonry
With meanings out of true.

Of clouds and tower, he cried,
Of tower and cloud!... and pointed
To Tewkesbury. The use of
Dilapidated altars?
Unhinged the text, disjointed.
'Lo Gloucestershire,' he falters.

2.

Poor thing, perfection; he
Came to it though, at last.
Mother-of-pearl!

His lot were done for: not
On account of the War, which he
Knew made a poet of Ledwidge;

But because he would not,
Nor any of them, settle
For less than ecstasy.

Jacked up to that, its rough
And windy contours, nothing
But neurasthenia could

Cut him down to what
The Ancients settled for:
Krater and *patera*.

Ecstatic enough, the cup
Of red clay that
Sparkled with argent water,

We are happy to think. But he,
Unreconciled to that,
Committed himself to madness.

3.

Whether Howells was
To die or not develop,
Beethoven wouldn't tell.
Bach was there but does not
Care for Gurney; Schumann
Also but Gurney's love
For him is less.
Oh, out of balance, oh
Too highly strung, poor Gurney,
What's to be done with you?
A ticket to the asylum?

Only a sufficient
Black surge of pain, he says,
Upon the fair thing standing;
Red block of power, St Albans,
Or Tewkesbury by Severn;
Mask above meadows in
Light that promised rain.

A promising composer
Stares at the stony mask
And cannot pierce it. What
Service is there like
The making of a great
Thing in stone? he asks;
And aches with promise of
Mask after mask, and veil
On drifting veil of rain,

And service not rewarded.

Wombwell On Strike

Horace of course is not
a temporizer, but
his sudden and smooth transitions
      (as, into a railway tunnel,
        then out, to different landscape)

it must be admitted elide,
and necessarily, what
happens up there on the hill
      or hill-ridge that the tunnel
        of syntax so featly slides under.

I have been reminded of this
when, gratefully leaving my native
haunts, the push-and-pull diesel
      clatters into a tunnel
        under a wooded escarpment:

Wentworth Woodhouse, mounded
or else in high shaws drifted
over the miners' tramways.
      Horace's streaming style
      exhorts me never to pause;

'Press on,' he says, and indeed his
suavities never entirely
exclude the note of alarm:
        'Leave the unlikely meaning
        to eddy, or you are in trouble.'

Wombwell – 'womb well': it is
foolish and barbarous wordplay,
though happily I was
        born of this tormented
        womb, the taut West Riding.

Yours was solid advice,
Horace, and centuries have
endorsed it; but over this tunnel
        large policemen grapple
        the large men my sons have become.

After the Match

Hardly a one but here he is improved,
Long-legged, shell-chested, stepping to the bath.
The too long hair, the fatuous moustaches,
The fussy or the battered, beery face,
Do not, we see, do justice to the man

Who, naked, is quite free from all deception,
More simply strong and weak than in the scrum.
We felt them ardent then, but in a crowd,
Disguised in shirts and numbers; and the rank
Smell of them good, but not so spirited.

We now, however, having seen them naked,
Briskly and neatly towelling and stooping,
Seeing them flesh, see spirits in them walking,
The bridegrooms of some far-fetched metaphor,
Sophia or Idea, going crowned.

Mustered into the Avant-Garde

I am supposed to apologize
To you, old mumbler?
And to you, haughty reclusive
Master of the opal? And
To you, the not quite faithless
Friend and driving rival?
For being clear, if you please,
For making it seem as easy
As I can manage! Well
(At a summer-school in the Quantocks)
No, I will *not* be sorry!

A bugle-call to the Vanguard:
His Majesty's Light Horse?
You, with your plod-a-clollop!
(What have you got in those panniers?
What leaden inedible forage?)
You, phantom-like over the flanking
Hills where the enemy isn't?
And you, who appear in mid-column
Suddenly, here, and disorder
The main line of march with your sidelong
Bewhiskered and smiling troopers?

Such weight as they carry! Yes, even
Captain Phantom, back from
Another invisible skirmish
He isn't allowed to report on,
Look how he droops in the saddle!
See how the twitching and turning
To note who's in front and behind
Attenuates Colonel Driver!
And then of course poor old General
Mumble, encumbered with all our
Humanity, no less!

You know what does for them, don't you?
You know what that weight is, they carry?
Responsibility, trooper!
These are the antennae.
The whole damned army depends on

Them to know where it's going.
William Pitt and the Duke of
Wellington depended
For their intelligence on
A coterie at Racedown:
Coleridge and Southey! Wordsworth!

Sculptures in Hungary

A Hun turned sculptor spoke
Of the styles of Etruria. Under a basin-cropped

Black cap of hair, his drooping thick moustache
Was style of the First World War, style of Attila.

His toad-hipped plenteous nude
Pannonia bears

The name of a Roman province, but the art
His barber practised was

For art's sake also: more than a Magyar manhood
Spoke from the hairfringed lip wide in its welcome.

The closed still forms wear from his classic chisel
A smile like an enigmatic property,

But his hid nothing: human, it deserved
Better than I could rise to, when he spoke

Of the unfinished as a form of art,
Fragments entire. Not womanhood but through

Each woman's nub of breast and belly, stone
Spoke from a polished torso in the corner.

Pannonia! her bastion heaped the west
Outside the plateglass of a warm hotel

Against the luminous evening over Buda,
Still in bright cold gradations, grey and rose.

The frogged hussar
Curvetted there on terraces

And men alive in Germany have watched
Where plateglass glares from Pest

The Russian gunflash. When De Gaulle
Advanced upon Algeria

In armoured cars, the colonists
Howled, choking through the teargas, 'Budapest!'

He spoke through smiles. His hands braced up the air
Poising ideal objects. The matrix

Adheres a little, Istrian nor Carraran
Not of locale nor race but meaning, 'broken'.

Sounds of a Devon Village

1.

Many compacted summers
Unpack for the ear
Viridities to come, as under
The watershed that wedges Culm from Exe
Long squeals of birdsong aggravate the eaves.

2.

The long-haired husbandman forks hay;
Across an autumnal half-mile, solid-state
Blasts out his country, his some-other-country
Music, who will tend his little children
Devotedly tomorrow. The high branches
Crack on the hill-ridge, region of lichen and ivy.

High noise, no thud, but clash, moan, breaking clatter.
The wood's in trouble. Far below,
A jar of altercation in the lane
Signals his twin daughters are at hand
With pert expostulations home from school.

3.

Companionably creaking, elm and oak,
Baucis and Philemon, bowed and feathered
In conjugal felicity in the hedgerow,
Hard-pressed, hard-earned, and blest at last by the gods.

The elms are shattered. It is not his fault,
Nor fault of a grinding gear-box, if Philemon
Be disjoint from Baucis in this end
Though they befriended gods. Dutch elm disease
By night and day travels in eerie silence.

4.

Clatter of hooves, of iron-shod wheels over cobbles . . .
The ancients were not prone to understatement.
Stolidity has classic precedent
And so has noise. A Cynic schoolmaster
May think noise fevers, but his neighbours sweat
Most, and prickle, when a silence comes.

5.

The church-bells clamour, the full-uddered heifer
Entreats the shuddering air, but is unheard
Above the inflexible thud. The human voice,
Strained to a scream to penetrate, is toneless
As if, what it is not, impassible.
'Your lunch,' she screams, 'your LUNCH!' and points to it.
He waves and nods, to show he's understood.
The binder-reaper curtains him with sound.

6.

'Sylvan', from *silva*: a thesaurus of
Words and phrases is an unlikely meaning
Silva had, once. The greenest, most
Sylvan man is epicure of din,
Sorter of noises. (*Florilegium*:
A cultured nature, sedulously thinned.)

Woods: and to clear them, was that not his vocation;
Then to restore as windbreak, and plantation?

On Generous Lines

Hanoverian silverware, this jug
Though small amply dispenses cream
Out of the skin-tight flask of its silver belly;

Tunbelly never clumsy but as crescent
As there in Beverley
The Gothic font's Augustan cover, carved

In, would it be true to say, a settled age
That in a portly contour
Could safely read fecundity, not cancer?

Their resolutions – into hooking curves
Of a handle's poised relation, or to a darting
And avian grace the pouring lip – evince

A victory hypochondriac like ours,
Achieved against all odds
By battening on them, clamping down, provoking.

And would it be true to say:
'Be generous. Take risks. Give hostages'?
It would be true; incautious curves enforce it.

Equestrian Sestina

Horse, our poor creature, we treat as if elemental,
Stupidly. This is unfeeling. True, he is fabulous;
Goes, though, not like the wind, whatever his mettle;
Nor, much as he ripples in motion, is he conditioned
By a sky-god's whims, like a river. Not there did the Norman
Culture, that made him its talisman, ground its attachment.

Rather, he was their technology; unsentimental
Reasons made barons and bishops, bloodthirsty and emulous,
Curry, caparison into the finest fettle
Him their scout-car, halftrack, their efficient
Weapon-carrier. Dearer to them than Woman
The destrier trampling the Legate's obstructive parchment.

Why then so often, seeking a type for the gentle
And powerful, such as we once were, needing a stimulus
Even to think of that humanness lost, do we settle
On him, on the horse? Why are our horses commissioned
To stand in for what we think best in ourselves, for a yeoman
Sturdiness, or knighthood blurred in a lozengy hatchment?

Is it their having, except for holiday rental
Like jeeps or a sand-yacht, vanished, that now they compel us
Only as fluid, their hoofbeats soft as a petal
Floating to earth on a moonlit hill? A deficient
Sense for the civic has exiled even the Roman
Charger, all laurel and bronze, to eerie detachment.

This has us craning, to trace on a pock-marked lintel
The arms of Sir Hugo, the psychopath. Miscreant, infamous
Cavalier, his horsemanship counts for little
To earn him remission; yet that, no more, was sufficient.
Time, the sad torrent, has washed off his vices, and no man
Builds jetty or pier in that current, or measures its catchment.

There has to be reason why beings not elemental,
Divine, nor supernatural, soothe us as fabulous
Creatures moving among us. A horse of mettle
Or merest Dobbin ought to find us conditioned
To a sorry awe. Call it the flower of Norman
Or Saracen chivalry, this was a noble attachment.

Homage to George Whitefield

(1714-1770)

Born at 'The Bell' in Gloucester,
where you can go to this day
to sink a pint, and see
a piratical black beard
and fingers combing it and
a burly frame, all at sea.

Earth bound George Whitefield, not
a man to panic
at metaphysical terrors, having
a relish for them,
wanting his God to be
not oceanic but
earth-bound like him to the earth he knew,
shards and mosaic in it.

That Roman viniculture
in the Severn valley was
venal? He stands corrected,
considering: Well, perhaps.

He traversed the Atlantic.
This weeping day's corsair
is a second-order artist,
and womanish in his cups;

whereas this one was a hero,
dreadful and dreaded. Search
the Methodist roster now
in vain for such a pirate:
Bluebeard evangelist!

Two Widows in Tashkent

In, of all places, Tashkent
They were reading Keats; and were wrong
As the wives and widows of
Poets are always wrong:
'Each word is a self-confession.'
True; but not to the point.

To the point is how
It (his poem) measures
Up to, takes note of, departs from
Ovid or Dante. Ladies,
This is where he departs from
You, and you cannot abide it.

Helena Morley

*

In winter in Diamantina
(Which is in Brazil)
Does the wind blow keener,
December try you sorely,
Helena Morley?

In winter, in
Diamantina
(Which is in Brazil)
The month is June, and nothing
Stiffens the air or the will.

In high pure air in
Diamond-land
You have heard it said: 'A hundred
Minds the winter enamours
For one kind child that is summer's'.

This will vex you surely,
Helena Morley, Helena Morley,
Whose English cousins know
So lovingly ice and snow.

Disown them, Helena Morley.

*

Be sorry for those English
Cousins of Helena's dreams:

Their Daddies built the railways,
Their Daddies built the ships,
Their Daddies made their daughters
Their Ladyships.

Their gossamer wings whirr fast
At onset of winter weather.
Now they are summer's children,
Through the Green Park together
Crying, through or without
Tears: 'Here we are, we are dying.'

Pity those foreign cousins
Whom Helena could not know,
Accorded such esteem
So long ago.

*

'Every one in the end
In good time or in high time
Is summer's friend',

You might have said, discovered
Late in life in your mansion
By the lagoon in Rio.

Instead you said, severely
Darning linen: 'Hours
To spare are spent on chores.'

Spend, or save...The words hang
Brightly in the air
If all time is to spare,

Waiting for Resurrection.

Sorting the Personae

Once the broom has started,
A cleansing of every corner
Of what has become a wide
Working-area is
A labour of anxious love.

None but old brooms here.
It cannot be called a rhythm,
The way I wield them, though
A certain jerky pattern
Does emerge from the proddings.

What odd inconvenient spaces
Some of the students prefer!
Consider the draughty landing,
Grand enough in its day,
Paul shares with grimy *putti*;

Or notice how Thomas and Trevor
Compete for the awkward angle,
Lit it is true by a bleak
Skylight, still an embrasure,
Burne-Jones glass in the casements;

Or Fiona and Frances,
One so disorderly, one
A furious miniaturist,
Side by side in the ballroom,
Easels together always.

Would it be better for them,
As the regretful committee
Is confident, were they allotted
Space in some custom-made
Airy and clean Polytechnic?

Or are they too old to change?
I am only the cleaning-lady,
But some of what Paul does, for instance
(And he has been at it for years)
Strikes me as *very* old-fashioned.

That dark little niche which no one
Since old Mr Housman died has
Been attracted to, still
Cannot be overlooked, must
Be given a lick and a promise.

Sometimes they dedicate,
Though never the way you'd expect,
Their unfinished works to each other.
Who'd thought that wild-bearded Trevor
Cherished a crush on Frances?

A lot of the time they quarrel.
They stamp around, waving their arms.
Bad days those are, when not
A stroke of even indifferent
Work gets done in this school.

They live and work in muck.
Yet 'clean' I have heard them give
As the highest praise to each other.
I am only the cleaning-lady
But anxious for them, and loving.

'1945'

A string of the scarlet rubies of Ceylon
Cheated the Customs in a re-sealed tin
Of boiled coagulate sweets...to which I turned
My officer's blind eye. The carillon
Was all 'St. Budeaux' as I brought them in
By rail, the ship-boys, Devonport's draft returned!

Though not in fact: the halt at Keyham slept
In mild mid-morning and its signal-box
Absently clapped down its signal as
We, crawling from Southampton, smoothly crept
Home from Kowloon, from Trinco, from the shocks
And blithely endured alarms of the Moluccas.

My scapegrace sea-pups, what are the memories stir
In us, grown fat? A too white monument
Tall on the Hoe, ships' plaques, a name like 'Howe',
The shot-torn ensign of the 'Exeter' –
These are not what we want, nor what was meant;
Instead, the bells – in whose ears, then and now?

No one had said whom I reported to.
I skipped the train before the Dockyard, tore
In a lucky taxi up the marble-streeted
And marble-hearted town that Hardy knew,
In a bawdry of bells, the mess-deck's innocent roar
'Get up them stairs!' pealing for her I greeted.

Where's that West Country where each belfry peals,
Where no one's given cottonwool for bread,
Flowing with scriptural honey, milk, and wine;
Where the artificer guides the easy wheels
And no cranked labour blacks the overhead?
In women's arms, oh you who crossed the line!

Sheer hulk, Tom Bowling, I observe you climb
Staggeringly the Forder Valley tamed
Into industrial suburb. Novorossisk
Road, a sardonic legacy of wartime
Naively or duplicitously named,
Sees your arms flail at fame, betrayal, risk.

Somewhere a gross or ghostly woman plucks
At washed-out cottons, pats her hair behind
Absentmindedly, and measures on
Her bony breast something a battered box
Unopened in years has suddenly brought to mind:
A string of the pale small rubies of Ceylon.

GOODBYE TO THE USA

Sunday Morning

for Doreen

No point in looking. The
    Comanche were
A terror on this trail, the
Cimarron Cut-off. Now
The farmers' station-waggons
Feed at the gospel trough;
And while they worshipped, none
But you and I were astir.

Big mostly Baptist churches
    Crowned every hill.
Nothing to hear; if they
Sang, as no doubt they did,
Around us and above the
Noise of our engine, only
The gimlet larksong pierced
By snatches, fierce and shrill.

Eclogues of pick-up trucks!
    Georgics of
Jouncing springs, and the
Bucolic beer-can! Such
Good time we made, oh such
Good time, reeling off mile
On undistinguished mile that
Landscape of peace and love.

Not picturesque, although
    One hour ahead
Eastward the Cimarron,
Originating Lord,
Would round on us again
In pinkish buttes and vast
Eroded washes, where he
Coiled in a narrow bed.

Upstream New Mexico
    Makes much of his
Choked canyon, and the town
That on the Santa Fe
Trail was the famous last
Staging-post but one:
Cimarron, much reached for.
But here, few memories...

Such as they have, they would
    Sooner forget.
The past of this spread of land
Does no one credit: twice
Or many times evicted,
Cherokee, Choctaw, Chickasaw
Here were dispossessed
Once more, more brutally yet.

'Landscape of peace and love';
    And as construed
In the Chickasaw tongue? Who wonders?
Under whose past is there not
Greed, and injustice? We took
Nevertheless the blessing
Of the unjust at worship.
For once, then, gratitude!

For once, for once, the heart
    Can overprice its
Overt occasion. Over
The black-top streeling miles
Of the panhandle of
Oklahoma the heart hawks,
Remembering, baffled but
Convinced of benefits.

The University of the South

for Andrew Lytle, aged 80

That shrewd character Will Percy in
Lanterns on the Levee (that's pronounced
    'Levvy') lost his level
    Head over you, Sewanee.

Lammas House and Apthorp House and such
Or such a college housing a famous bell
    Were mellowed brick, but this
    Is the midwest, pretty well;

Aligned with Indianapolis although
Old, the old South. No matter for that, he peoples
    With clerics, with cavorting
    Dryads, your leafy mountain.

Grecian as saccharine as early Forster,
As Gothic too, in shattered Picardy
    Serving with Pershing he
    Preserved your episcopal stone.

An idiom we can hardly now remember,
Fatherly and white-supremacist,
    Sealed you, Sewanee, in
    Defaced, untenable amber.

So love is no preservative; Will Percy's
Enraptured idyll of you came apart.
    What youth now takes your bosky
    Artifice to heart?

Some, there's no doubt. Milan and Chattanooga
Are all one world, we have to think. The ghoulish
    Noble ambition after
    The shapely is universal.

Ghouls haunt the tombs of Will Alexander Percy
And Quintus Horatius Flaccus, sieving their dust
    For stanza-forms or the musty
    Adumbrations of myth.

And with them or not with them, seldom under
Your wintriest boughs, Sewanee, stalks the one
    Whose sharper hunger prowls
    That bone-yard, the Argonne.

His need of shapes more skeletal impels
Over the shattered carrion fields the last
    Exemplary monster. Now
    The veridical idyll emerges.

Savannah

for Alex Heard, administrator

Executive speed is poetry! Whereas,
Benevolently dallying, earnest Berkeley,
    Having his city planned,
    Abandoned it for Rhode Island,

Oglethorpe, philanthropist, had landed
A hundred and twenty souls to set in brick
    A philosophical blue-print
    Intended for Bermuda:

A pretty, rational city. And at Christmas
Incongruous with cane-brakes, we are grave:
    This was a place some thousands
    Died to take, or save.

None so murderous as geometers.
Quadrant, ellipse, short avenues beget
    Under their shade-trees furies:
    Claymore and bayonet.

And grave as we are, we are glad. The abrasive weather
Scouring the Factors' Walk, chill off the river,
    Gives us to think, engraves
    That solemn thought: the civic.

Proper but leaden piety of those
Amending generations! Thank the founder
    For black-white hurly-burly,
    Those streets your mother walked.

It is his act of mind we walk about in.
It is as one frequents a poem, gladly:
    The reek of the initial
    Implosion guarantees stillness.

Oglethorpe: magnanimous decision;
Then implementation, fast! His actions reek
    Of nothing now but sweetness,
    In Christ the Founder's week.

To an American Classicist

Shallow or deep, snows on Soracte won't,
    if they ever did, deliver
an agreeable end for the means you expend on them;
nor Greek boys, dancing, dance themselves into a frieze.

Kentucky Bourbon, glossed as Caecuban vintage,
    won't elevate, beyond
the gratification of a squalid hour, the squeamish
mistaken resolve never to sound like Whitman.

Because in all this you call on the ancient Roman's
    precedent, do not
misconstrue him: a carnal indulgence is
one thing, and self-refrigeration another.

Mull the wine all you like, it will not warm you.
    You know what will: your native
firewater, moonshine. Moonshine on Soracte
weave you a withering chaplet, leaves of grass!

H.D.

This lady was danger, this
lady was no lady;
authentic American poison.

The lady suffered, but
how many suffered for Lady!

Pussycat, lynx, and horse;
all the petnames were wrong.
'Lady', a name for bitches.

Ransacked Europe and
never noticed it, Europe.
Hysterical catamount.

This catamount, this
lioness of the mountains
of Pennsylvania, her
venom from mountain stills;
from the Moravian
hymns that appalled John Wesley.

Bestrid poor British
Havelock Ellis
like a colossus.

The Trip to Huntsville

To be constant through a lifetime
does every one some harm
more than conceivably in
a stiffening self-esteem.

A curious freedom that
feels like incarceration
is to recognize, at sixty,
one has become an *exemplum*.

It is long past midnight now.
Birds begin to squeal their
too little experienced chirpings
the other side of my drawn
curtains in Tennessee.

Chirp, chirp, my little tyros. A
        bird's life is a short one.
Practise your amorous changes.

Chirp, loyal turtles, and
        cheep, libidinous sparrows,
each according to nature and
        I too have no choice in the matter.

Eos and Hesperus have
waxed and waned unnoticed.
No thanks to me, on no
grounds of my beseeching
whether for eyes, for ears
to hear, or a nose for the new,
the sun all the same has risen;

ball of fire, no less.
Charioteer would be more.

Challenger is the latest
space vehicle, named not christened
in Huntsville, Alabama,
the Werner von Braun motel
in and against the sunrise.

The great sun rises;
flashes; it
cuts no ice
with or within me, approaching
in terror the cigar-shaped
bounties of Peenemunde.

Was at the receiving end
of those, my bride was, in
a long-ago war in London.

Pulaski, Tennessee
I pass by, where
Nathan Bedford Forrest,
a Christian gentleman,
created the Ku Klux Klan.

Defeated but unvanquished
after a hundred years,
a Christian gentleman
blasts off against Mugabe.
He wanted Ian Smith
to go down fighting.

Avenues of perception
are choked with those to action,
my Christian gentleman says,
and with some show of reason:
numbness is no sort of
response to shining-eyed
grandsons already recruited,

seeing a loud moon-buggy
and a tinted visor are
the gods they carry from Huntsville.

Constancy? To be sure.
See, the exemplary sunset!

Shadows begin to lengthen;
small boys start to be fractious.
Equinoctial storms had
in autumn flurried the Gulf of
Corinth, so we drove to
Olympia's weeping twilight.

Night comes down on the Cumberland
River some hours after
night comes down on the Thames.

Night comes, however; night
        has fallen on Corinth also.

Alzheimer's Disease

for Kenneth Millar (Ross Macdonald)

It is said that he laughs at himself,
Betrayed into such grotesque
Non-sequiturs. I am told he
Powerfully still plies his
Breast-stroke across the pool
That was the arena or focus
Of his most disturbing fictions.

Focus, a pool; a fluid,
A watery hearth he found
For any of us, this
Californian-born and
Canadian-raised, this unfathered
Quester after arenas
Familial and stable.

The chlorinated hearth
He swims and swims has not
Held his mind together;
Keeping his head above
Private waters he
Absently-mindedly earned
A world-wide reputation.

Non-sequitur! No wonder
If, now his mind is gone,
He chuckles at the bizarre
Concatenation of
Circumstances that a private
Eye can disentangle
Retrospectively always.

Wonderful all the same, or
Wondrous, there in the thresh
Of the directionless lengths
Of days, how the artist snorted
And seal-like turned himself round
To plunge upon the next
Pitiless, pitiful fable.

Ken, you were a powerful
Swimmer always, tireless.
Not you tired, but your brain.
When you wrote *The Galton Case*,
I fiddled with *Pan Tadèusz*.
(Sons sought fathers in both.)
Those days won't come again.

Recollections of George Oppen
in a letter to an English friend

'This lime-tree bower my prison'
(Coleridge)

That lime-tree – no, what is it? mulberry? –
bower at combe's bottom, your Brook Cottage
where the light sleeps so evenly in silence
one would not say even in summer's heat
it pulses... there you entertained
George Oppen, along with Mary who survives him;
of whom, and just there, you and I have talked
not without malice while George Oppen lived.

That we should do that, should make mock of his
style of public reading (which he hated),
his unpretentious chuntering monotone
that could not mark when a poem began or ended,
would have dismayed them both. Such vipers, such
English ingrate stingers as they had
taken to their bosoms! How could they
understand how that milk-candid, flowing
bosom it was, that armed and drew the stings?
Too good to be true, such nice Americans – we
had to pink them, that way to pinch ourselves!

Hearing in due course of his mindlessness
(Alzheimer's, terminal) that Mary could
towards the end not cope with, were we not
happy to have them down on our grubbing level?
And on that level, ours, Poetic Justice
I swear made her appearance in a toga.
Alzheimer's, yes – the diagnosis was

all very well, but surely George's dealings
with language had for years anticipated,
almost provoked, the visitation? Such
pains as he had been at – in verse, in prose,
in conversation – to subvert, discount,
derange articulation. Destiny
strikes, and for months before he dies
he's inarticulate. A hideous justice.

I've not the energy nor the confidence
for playing God like this with George's shade,
his fragrant shade my prison. For indeed,
often as I have settled George's hash
to my own satisfaction, proved him wrong
– my spare and handsome gaoler with the cropped
moustache, so Jewish when one thought of it
yet on a first impression soldierly,
frontiersman even – still he shoots the bolt;
won't go away, nor let me be, reproachful
as always the dead are, however in life indulgent.

'Friends, whom I never more may meet again,
On springy heath, along the hill-top edge,
Wander in gladness, and wind down, perchance
To that still roaring dell, of which I told;
The roaring dell...' Dells round Brook Cottage must,
and that whole dell itself, defile or vale,
roar when the wind is up, undoubtedly.
Did it, when George was with you? Hard to think so
of him whose scenes for preference were
wind-scoured indeed but wide and open, hills
in and about the city of San Francisco,
or else the flowing and unsteady bosom
of off-shore Maine. That semblance, the frontiersman,
was not unearned by such a small-boat sailor,
no messer-about. Pathfinder, though? Trailblazer?
Never for me, threading the roaring dells
and snapping branches of morose
inspirations, aspirations, habits
held up to the weak light, scowled at. Not a bit
of help to me was George, or George's writing;
though he achieved his startling poignancies,
I distrusted them, distrust them still.

But hope, such hope he had, such politics
always of hope! Hope is a strenuous business;
I hope the roar of it enlivens your
west-country dell, as a whisper of it mine.

West Virginia's Auburn

'Sweet Auburn, loveliest village of the plain'
(Goldsmith)

Ejected Indians haunt the lawns
    Where Alabama's youth
Loud on the Auburn campus yawns
    At Goldsmith's mournful truth.

New Hampshire's lakeside Auburn keeps
    A little faith with him
But is, agreeably though it sleeps,
    Too vigorous, too trim.

But West Virginia, rural slum,
    The idyll! Only there
In our excursions did there come
    Such silence on the air

As, we were surprised to learn,
    We had looked for more and more:
Placidities we could not earn
    And were not fitted for.

Silence of hopes foreclosed, foregone –
    That, we'd already found
In derelict installations on
    Lost capital, lost ground,

First in Maine, then in New York,
    Whose indigent Auburns drift
Under grime-blackened dates that talk
    Of once effectual thrift.

No thrift nor thriving ever was
    Invested in this green
Corner of West Virginia's
    Dilapidated scene.

It would be wrong to think it prinked
    Ever as right or pretty;
It has at best the indistinct
    Unpruned amenity

That topers in a village inn
    Might unconcernedly share,
Who found no project to engage in
    Worth their hope or care.

The poet who in Meath or West
    Virginia hails this breed
As his own congeners, justly blest –
    He rusticates indeed!

Yet across oceans, once again
    Old adages still mutter
Adagios of the plangent strain
    We are ashamed to utter.

Keen-eyed, the idyll has no salve
    To ease the throb in the verse:
'You can't go home again. You have
    Gone further, and fared worse.'

Through Bifocals

This you have heard before;
Have heard to the point where it serves
Only to numb, of the insult
Historical markers invite
With such inconsequence: Battle
Of Murfreesboro, of Franklin...

Two hours ago a boom
And a brief billow of pink
Dust was how a small
Recalcitrant bluff was cleared for
'A Planned Community in
The Williamsburg Manner.'

Earth-movers on that hillside
Lie still now, and a jiggle
Of off-and-on orange flashes
Seemed, when I looked over there
Through reading-glasses, a pulse
Of pain in the pink earth's wound.

My trustier bifocals
See lights atop the blazon,
Red on yellow, of
'Country Store' in this
Uncomplaining tract of
Tennessee disembowelled.

Among the supposedly fine
Arts, one at least has weaseled
Out of the tatterdemalion
Rearguard, and puts its trust in
The double focus: 'plan'
Enforced; then (optional) 'manner'.

Architects! Co-workers
With Louis Sullivan once, you
Wink at as foolishly 'dire'
My warning to your consumers:
The wider the range of manners,
The more inhumane the enforcement.